YOUR MOST COMPREHENSIVE AND REVEALING INDIVIDUAL FORECAST

PISCES
1994
SUPER HOROSCOPE

February 19–March 20

DIAMOND BOOKS, NEW YORK

CONTENTS

NOTE TO THE CUSP-BORN

First find the year of your birth, and then find the sign under which you were born according to your day of birth. Thus, you can determine if you are a true Pisces (or Aquarius or Aries), according to the variations of the dates of the Zodiac. (See also page 7.)

Are you *really* a Pisces? If your birthday falls during the third week of February, at the beginning of Pisces, will you still retain the traits of Aquarius, the sign of the Zodiac before Pisces? And what if you were born late in March—are you more Aries than Pisces? Many people born at the edge, or cusp of a sign have difficulty determining exactly what sign they are. If you are one of these people, here's how you can figure it out, once and for all.

Consult the following table. It will tell you the precise days on which the Sun entered and left your sign for the year of your birth. If you were born either at the beginning or the end of Pisces, yours is a lifetime reflecting a process of subtle transformation. Your life on Earth will symbolize a significant change in consciousness, for you are either about to enter a whole new way of living or are leaving one behind.

If you were born at the end of February you are newly hatched into the sign of the Fishes. You may want to read the horoscope book for Aquarius as well as Pisces, for Aquarius holds the key to your secret wishes, your private uncertainties and guilts—some of them, anyway—and the mystical means to your cosmic unfoldment.

Though you don't often know quite where to begin, you would like to find a place in life where you can be simply happy, surrounded by friends you love and who love you—for your true identity puzzles you and you long for simplicity.

When you are undisciplined and guilt-ridden, you can pursue pleasure or vice in an effort at self-destruction. When you accept your role in the world and the people around you, the freedom you are always seeking suddenly comes to you, and then you wake up to know what it means to be free.

If you were born the third week of March, you are a symbol of winter's end, and faith must be your keyword. You may want to read the horoscope book for Aries as well as Pisces, for through Aries you begin to make all your dreams happen. Your urges come alive and you wake up to the world around you as your materialism is sparked.

You may get depressed and discouraged, defeated and saddened, by the tribulations of this life on Earth, but of all the Zodiac signs you symbolize the time when faith is the ultimate savior of all people. Forgiveness and compassion characterize your spirit and you blend a gentle poetry with verve and dynamism. You can waver between self-doubt and selfishness, but at best you are the symbol of the turning of the tide and spiritual regeneration.

DATES SUN ENTERS PISCES
(LEAVES AQUARIUS)

February 19 every year from 1900 to 2000, except for the following:

February 18:				February 20:
1900	1954	1973	1989	1917
21	57	74	90	
25	58	77	91	
29	61	78	93	
33	62	81	94	
37	65	82	95	
41	66	85	97	
45	69	86	98	
49	70	87	99	
53				

DATES SUN LEAVES PISCES
(ENTERS ARIES)

March 20 every year from 1900 to 2000, except for the following:

March 21:				
1901	1911	1923	1938	1955
02	13	26	39	59
03	14	27	42	63
05	15	30	43	67
06	18	31	46	71
07	19	34	47	75
09	22	35	51	79
10				

HISTORY AND USES
OF ASTROLOGY

Does astrology have a place in the fast-moving, ultra-scientific world we live in today? Can it be justified in a sophisticated society whose outriders are already preparing to step off the moon into the deep space of the planets themselves? Or is it just a hangover of ancient superstition, a psychological dummy for neurotics and dreamers of every historical age?

These are the kind of questions that any inquiring person can be expected to ask when they approach a subject like astrology which goes beyond, but never excludes, the materialistic side of life.

The simple, single answer is that astrology works. It works for tens of millions of people in the western world alone. In the United States there are 10 million followers and in Europe, an estimated 25 million. America has more than 4000 practicing astrologers, Europe nearly three times as many. Even down-under Australia has its hundreds of thousands of adherents. The importance of such vast numbers of people from diverse backgrounds and cultures is recognized by the world's biggest newspapers and magazines who probably devote more of their space to this subject in a year than to any other. In the eastern countries, astrology has enormous followings, again, because it has been proved to work. In countries like India, brides and grooms for centuries have been chosen on the basis of astrological compatibility. The low divorce rate there, despite today's heavy westernizing influence, is attributed largely to this practice.

In the western world, astrology today is more vital than ever before; more practicable because it needs a sophisticated society like ours to understand and develop its contribution to the full; more valid because science itself is confirming the precepts of astrological knowledge with every new exciting step. The ordinary person who daily applies astrology intelligently does not have to wonder whether it is true nor believe in it blindly. He can see it working for himself. And, if he can use it—and this book is designed to help the reader to do just that—he can make living a far richer experience, and become a more developed personality and a better person.

Astrology is the science of relationships. It is not just a study of planetary influences on man and his environment. It is the study of man himself.

We are at the center of our personal universe, of all our relationships. And our happiness or sadness depends on how we act, how we relate to the people and things that surround us. The emotions that we generate have a distinct affect—for better or worse—on the world around us. Our friends and our enemies will confirm this. Just look in the mirror the next time you are angry. In other words, each of us is a kind of sun or planet or star and our influence on our personal universe, whether loving, helpful or destructive, varies with our changing moods, expressed through our individual character.

And to an extent that includes the entire galaxy, this is true of the planetary bodies. Their radiations affect each other, including the earth and all the things on it. And in comparatively recent years, giant constellations called "quasars" have been discovered. These exist far beyond the night stars that we can observe, and science says these quasars are emitting radiating influences more powerful and different than ever recorded on earth. Their effect on man from an astrological point of view is under deep study. Compared with these inter-stellar forces, our personal "radiations" are negligible on the planetary scale. But ours are just as potent in the way they affect our moods, and our ability to control them. To this extent they determine much of the happiness and satisfaction in our lives. For instance, if we were bound and gagged and had to hold some strong emotion within us without being able to move, we would soon start to feel very uncomfortable. We are obviously pretty powerful radiators inside, in our own way. But usually, we are able to throw off our emotion in some sort of action—we have a good cry, walk it off, or tell someone our troubles—before it can build up too far and make us physically ill. Astrology helps us to understand the universal forces working on us, and through this understanding, we can become more properly adjusted to our surroundings and find ourselves coping where others may flounder.

Closely related to our emotions is the "other side" of our personal universe, our physical welfare. Our body, of course, is largely influenced by things around us over which we have very little control. The phone rings, we hear it. The train runs late. We snag our stocking or cut our face shaving. Our body is under a constant bombardment of events that influence our lives to varying degrees.

The question that arises from all this is, what makes each of us act so that we have to involve other people and keep the ball of activity and evolution rolling? This is the question that both science and astrology are involved with. The scientists have attacked it from different angles: anthropology, the study of human evolution as body, mind and response to environment; anatomy, the study of bodily structure; psychology, the science of the human mind; and so on. These studies have produced very impressive classifications and valuable information, but because the approach to the problem is fragmented, so is the result. They remain "branches" of science. Science generally studies effects. It keeps turning up wonderful answers but no lasting solutions. Astrology, on the other hand approaches the question from the broader viewpoint. Astrology began its inquiry with the totality of human experience and saw it as an effect. It then looked to find the cause, or at least the prime movers, and during thousands of years of observation of man and his *universal* environment, came up with the extraordinary principle of planetary influence—or astrology, which, from the Greek, means the science of the stars.

Modern science, as we shall see, has confirmed much of astrology's foundations—most of it unintentionally, some of it reluctantly, but still, indisputably.

It is not difficult to imagine that there must be a connection between outer space and the earth. Even today, scientists are not too sure how our earth was created, but it is generally agreed that it is only a tiny part of the universe. And as a part of the universe, people on earth see and feel the influence of heavenly bodies in almost every aspect of our existence. There is no doubt that the sun has the greatest influence on life on this planet. Without it there would be no life, for without it there would be no warmth, no division into day and night, no cycles of time or season at all. This is clear and easy to see. The influence of the moon, on the other hand, is more subtle, though no less definite.

There are many ways in which the influence of the moon manifests itself here on earth, both on human and animal life. It is a well-known fact, for instance, that the large movements of water on our planet—that is the ebb and flow of the tides—are caused by the moon's gravitational pull. Since this is so, it follows that these water movements do not occur only in the oceans, but that all bodies of water are affected, even down to the tiniest puddle.

The human body, too, which consists of about 70 percent water, falls within the scope of this lunar influence. For example the menstrual cycle of most women corresponds to the lunar month; the period of pregnancy in humans is 273 days, or equal to nine lunar months. Similarly, many illnesses reach a crisis at the change of the moon, and statistics in many countries have shown that the crime rate is highest at the time of the full moon. Even human sexual desire has been associated with the phases of the moon. But, it is in the movement of the tides that we get the clearest demonstration of planetary influence, and the irresistible correspondence between the so-called metaphysical and the physical.

Tide tables are prepared years in advance by calculating the future positions of the moon. Science has known for a long time that the moon is the main cause of tidal action. But only in the last few years has it begun to realize the possible extent of this influence on mankind. To begin with, the ocean tides do not rise and fall as we might imagine from our personal observations of them. The moon as it orbits around the earth, sets up a circular wave of attraction which pulls the oceans of the world after it, broadly in an east to west direction. This influence is like a phantom wave crest, a loop of power stretching from pole to pole which passes over and around the earth like an invisible shadow. It travels with equal effect across the land masses and, as scientists were recently amazed to observe, caused oysters placed in the dark in the middle of the United States where there is no sea, to open their shells to receive the non-existent tide. If the land-locked oysters react to this invisible signal, what effect does it have on us who not so long ago in evolutionary time, came out of the sea and still have its salt in our blood and sweat?

Less well known is the fact that the moon is also the primary force behind the circulation of blood in human beings and animals, and the movement of sap in trees and plants. Agriculturists have established that the moon has a distinct influence on crops, which explains why for centuries people have planted according to moon cycles. The habits of many animals, too, are directed by the movement of the moon. Migratory birds, for instance, depart only at or near the time of the full moon. Just as certain fish, eels in particular, move only in accordance with certain phases of the moon.

Know Thyself—Why?

In today's fast-changing world, everyone still longs to know what the future holds. It is the one thing that everyone has in common: rich and poor, famous and infamous, all are deeply concerned about tomorrow.

But the key to the future, as every historian knows, lies in the past. This is as true of individual people as it is of nations. You cannot understand your future without first understanding your past, which is simply another way of saying that you must first of all know yourself.

The motto "know thyself" seems obvious enough nowadays, but it was originally put forward as the foundation of wisdom by the ancient Greek philosophers. It was then adopted by the "mystery religions" of the ancient Middle East, Greece and Rome, and is still used in all genuine schools of mind training or mystical discipline, both in those of the East, based on yoga, and those of the West. So it is universally accepted now, and has been through the ages.

But how do you go about discovering what sort of person you are? The first step is usually classification into some sort of system of types. Astrology did this long before the birth of Christ. Psychology has also done it. So has modern medicine, in its way.

One system classifies men according to the source of the impulses they respond to most readily: the muscles, leading to direct bodily action; the digestive organs, resulting in emotion, or the brain and nerves. Another such system says that character is determined by the endocrine glands, and gives us labels like "pituitary," "thyroid" and "hyperthyroid" types. These different systems are neither contradictory nor mutually exclusive. In fact, they are very often different ways of saying the same thing.

Very popular and useful classifications were devised by Dr. C. G. Jung, the eminent disciple of Freud. Jung observed among the different faculties of the mind, four which have a predominant influence on character. These four faculties exist in all of us without exception, but not in perfect balance. So when we say, for instance, that a man is a "thinking type," it means that in any situation he tries to be rational. It follows that emotion, which some say is the opposite of thinking, will be his weakest function. This type can be sensible and reasonable, or calculating and unsympathetic. The emotional type, on the other hand, can often be recognized by exaggerated language—everything is either marvelous or terrible—and in extreme cases they even invent dramas and quarrels out of nothing just to make life more interesting.

The other two faculties are intuition and physical sensation. The sensation type does not only care for food and drink, nice clothes and furniture; he is also interested in all forms of physical experience. Many scientists are sensation types as are athletes and nature-lovers. Like sensation, intuition is a form of perception and we all possess it. But it works through that part of the mind which is not under conscious control—consequently it sees meanings and connections which are not obvious to thought or emotion. Inventors and original thinkers are always intuitive, but so, too, are superstitious people who see meanings where none exist.

Thus, sensation tells us what is going on in the world, feeling (that is, emotion) tells us how important it is to ourselves, thinking enables us to interpret it and work out what we should do about it, and intuition tells us what it means to ourselves and others. All four faculties are essential, and all are present in every one of us. But some people are guided chiefly by one, others by another.

Besides these four types, Jung observed a division into extrovert and introvert, which cuts across them. By and large, the introvert is one who finds truth inside himself rather than outside. He is not, therefore, ideally suited to a religion or a political party which tells him what to believe. Original thinkers are almost necessarily introverts. The extrovert, on the other hand, finds truth coming to him from outside. He believes in experts and authorities, and wants to think that nature and the laws of nature really exists, that they are what they appear to be and not just generalities made by men.

A disadvantage of all these systems of classification, is that one cannot tell very easily where to place oneself. Some people are reluctant to admit that they act to please their emotions. So they deceive themselves for years by trying to belong to whichever type they think is the "best." Of course, there is no best; each has its faults and each has its good points.

The advantage of the signs of the Zodiac is that they simplify classification. Not only that, but your date of birth is personal—it is unarguably yours. What better way to know yourself than by going back as far as possible to the very moment of your birth? And this is precisely what your horoscope is all about.

What Is a Horoscope?

If you had been able to take a picture of the heavens at the moment of your birth, that photograph would be your horoscope. Lacking such a snapshot, it is still possible to recreate the picture—and this is at the basis of the astrologer's art. In other words, your horoscope is a representation of the skies with the planets in the exact positions they occupied at the time you were born.

This information, of course, is not enough for the astrologer. He has to have a background of significance to put the photograph on. You will get the idea if you imagine two balls—one inside the other. The inner one is transparent. In the center of both is the astrologer, able to look up, down and around in all directions. The outer sphere is the Zodiac which is divided into twelve approximately equal segments, like the segments of an orange. The inner ball is our photograph. It is transparent except for the images of the planets. Looking out from the center, the astrologer sees the planets in various segments of the Zodiac. These twelve segments are known as the signs or houses.

The position of the planets when each of us is born is always different. So the photograph is always different. But the Zodiac and its signs are fixed.

Now, where in all this are you, the subject of the horoscope?

Your character is largely determined by the sign the sun is in. So that is where the astrologer looks first in your horoscope.

There are twelve signs in the Zodiac and the sun spends approximately one month in each. As the sun's motion is almost perfectly regular, the astrologers have been able to fix the dates governing each sign. There are not many people who do not know which sign of the Zodiac they were born under or who have not been amazed at some time or other at the accuracy of the description of their own character. Here are the twelve signs, the ancient zodiacal symbol, and their dates for the year 1994.*

ARIES	Ram	March 20–April 20
TAURUS	Bull	April 20–May 21
GEMINI	Twins	May 21–June 21
CANCER	Crab	June 21–July 22
LEO	Lion	July 22–August 23
VIRGO	Virgin	August 23–September 23
LIBRA	Scales	September 23–October 23
SCORPIO	Scorpion	October 23–November 22
SAGITTARIUS	Archer	November 22–December 21
CAPRICORN	Sea-Goat	December 21–January 20
AQUARIUS	Water-Bearer	January 20–February 18
PISCES	Fish	February 18–March 20

The time of birth—apart from the date—is important in advanced astrology because the planets travel at such great speed that the patterns they form change from minute to minute. For this reason, each person's horoscope is his and his alone. Further on we will see that the practicing astrologer has ways of determining and reading these minute time changes which dictate the finer character differences in us all.

However, it is still possible to draw significant conclusions and make meaningful predictions based simply on the sign of the Zodiac a person is born under. In a horoscope, the signs do not necessarily correspond with the divisions of the houses. It could be that a house begins halfway across a sign. It is the interpretation of such combinations of different influences that distinguishes the professional astrologer from the student and the follower.

However, to gain a workable understanding of astrology, it is not necessary to go into great detail. In fact, the beginner is likely to find himself confused if he attempts to absorb too much too quickly. It should be remembered that this is a science and to become proficient at it, and especially to grasp the tremendous scope of possibilities in man and his affairs and direct them into a worthwhile reading, takes a great deal of study and experience.

*These dates are fluid and change with the motion of the Earth from year to year.

If you do intend to pursue it seriously you will have to learn to figure the exact moment of birth against the degrees of longitude and latitude of the planets at that precise time. This involves adapting local time to Greenwich Mean Time (G.M.T.), reference to tables of houses to establish the Ascendant, as well as making calculations from Ephemeris—the tables of the planets' positions.

After reading this introduction, try drawing up a rough horoscope to get the "feel" of reading some elementary characteristics and natal influences.

Draw a circle with twelve equal segments. Write in counterclockwise the names of the signs—Aries, Taurus, Gemini etc.—one for each segment. Look up an ephemeris for the year of the person's birth and note down the sign each planet was in on the birthday. Do not worry about the number of degrees (although if a planet is on the edge of a sign its position obviously should be considered). Write the name of the planet in the segment/sign on your chart. Write the number 1 in the sign where the sun is. This is the first house. Number the rest of the houses, counterclockwise till you finish at 12. Now you can investigate the probable basic expectation of experience of the person concerned. This is done first of all by seeing what planet or planets is/are in what sign and house. (See also page 72.)

The 12 houses control these functions:

1st.	Individuality, body appearance, general outlook on life	(Personality house)
2nd.	Finance, business	(Money house)
3rd.	Relatives, education, correspondence	(Relatives house)
4th.	Family, neighbors	(Home house)
5th.	Pleasure, children, attempts, entertainment	(Pleasure house)
6th.	Health, employees	(Health house)
7th.	Marriage, partnerships	(Marriage house)
8th.	Death, secret deals, difficulties	(Death house)
9th.	Travel, intellectual affairs	(Travel house)
10th.	Ambition, social standing	(Business and Honor house)
11th.	Friendship, social life, luck	(Friends house)
12th.	Troubles, illness, loss	(Trouble house)

The characteristics of the planets modify the influence of the Sun according to their natures and strengths.

Sun: Source of life. Basic temperament according to sun sign. The will.
Moon: Superficial nature. Moods. Changeable. Adaptive. Mother.
Mercury: Communication. Intellect. Reasoning power. Curiosity. Short travels.
Venus: Love. Delight. Art. Beautiful possessions.
Mars: Energy. Initiative. War. Anger. Destruction. Impulse.
Jupiter: Good. Generous. Expansive. Opportunities. Protection.
Saturn: Jupiter's opposite. Contraction. Servant. Delay. Hardwork. Cold. Privation. Research. Lasting rewards after long struggle.
Uranus: Fashion. Electricity. Revolution. Sudden changes. Modern science.
Neptune: Sensationalism. Mass emotion. Devastation. Delusion.
Pluto: Creates and destroys. Lust for power. Strong obsessions.

Superimpose the characteristics of the planets on the functions of the house in which they appear. Express the result through the character of the birth (sun) sign, and you will get the basic idea of how astrology works.

Of course, many other considerations have been taken into account in producing the carefully worked out predictions in this book: The aspects of the planets to each other; their strength according to position and sign; whether they are in a house of exaltation or decline; whether they are natural enemies or not; whether a planet occupies his own sign; the position of a planet in relation to its own house or sign; whether the planet is male, female or neuter; whether the sign is a fire, earth, water or air sign. These are only a few of the colors on the astrologer's pallet which he must mix with the inspiration of the artist and the accuracy of the mathematician.

The Problem of Love

Love, of course, is never a problem. The problem lies in recognizing the difference between infatuation, emotion, sex and, sometimes, the downright deceit of the other person. Mankind, with its record of broken marriages, despair and disillusionment, is obviously not very good at making these distinctions.

Can astrology help?

Yes. In the same way that advance knowledge can usually help in any human situation. And there is probably no situation as human, as poignant, as pathetic and universal, as the failure of man's love.

Love, of course, is not just between man and woman. It involves love of children, parents, home and so on. But the big problems usually involve the choice of partner.

Astrology has established degrees of compatibility that exist between people born under the various signs of the Zodiac. Because people are individuals, there are numerous variations and modifications and the astrologer, when approached on mate and marriage matters makes allowances for them. But the fact remains that some groups of people are suited for each other and some are not and astrology has expressed this in terms of characteristics which all can study and use as a personal guide.

No matter how much enjoyment and pleasure we find in the different aspects of each other's character, if it is not an overall compatibility, the chances of our finding fulfillment or enduring happiness in each other are pretty hopeless. And astrology can help us to find someone compatible.

History of Astrology

The origins of astrology have been lost far back in history, but we do know that reference is made to it as far back as the first written records of the human race. It is not hard to see why. Even in primitive times, people must have looked for an explanation for the various happenings in their lives. They must have wanted to know why people were different from one to another. And in their search they turned to the regular movements of the sun, moon and stars to see if they could provide an answer.

It is interesting to note that as soon as man learned to use his tools in any type of design, or his mind in any kind of calculation, he turned his attention to the heavens. Ancient cave dwellings reveal dim crescents and circles representative of the sun and moon, rulers of day and night. Mesopotamia and the civilization of Chaldea, in itself the foundation of those of Babylonia and Assyria, show a complete picture of astronomical observation and well-developed astrological interpretation.

Humanity has a natural instinct for order. The study of anthropology reveals that primitive people—even as far back as prehistoric times—were striving to achieve a certain order in their lives. They tried to organize the apparent chaos of the universe. They had the desire to attach meaning to things. This demand for order has persisted throughout the history of man. So that observing the regularity of the heavenly bodies made it logical that primitive peoples should turn heavenwards in their search for an understanding of the world in which they found themselves so random and alone.

And they did find a significance in the movements of the stars. Shepherds tending their flocks, for instance, observed that when the cluster of stars now known as the constellation Aries was in sight, it was the time of fertility and they associated it with the Ram. And they noticed that the growth of plants and plant life corresponded with different phases of the moon, so that certain times were favorable for the planting of crops, and other times were not. In this way, there grew up a tradition of seasons and causes connected with the passage of the sun through the twelve signs of the Zodiac.

Astrology was valued so highly that the king was kept informed of the daily and monthly changes in the heavenly bodies, and the results of astrological studies regarding events of the future. Head astrologers were clearly men of great rank and position, and the office was said to be a hereditary one.

Omens were taken, not only from eclipses and conjunctions of the moon or sun with one of the planets, but also from storms and earthquakes. In the eastern civilizations, particularly, the reverence inspired by astrology appears to have remained unbroken since the very earliest days. In ancient China, astrology, astronomy and religion went hand in hand. The astrologer, who was also an astronomer, was part of the official government service and had his own corner in the Imperial Palace. The duties of the Imperial astrologer, whose office was one of the most important in the land, were clearly defined, as this extract from early records shows:

"This exalted gentleman must concern himself with the stars in the heavens, keeping a record of the changes and movements of the Planets, the Sun and the Moon, in order to examine the movements of the terrestial world with the object of prognosticating good and bad fortune. He divides the territories of the nine regions of the empire in accordance with their dependence on particular celestial bodies. All the fiefs and principalities are connected with the stars and from this their prosperity or misfortune should be ascertained. He makes prognostications according to the twelve years of the Jupiter cycle of good and evil of the terrestial world. From the colors of the five kinds of clouds, he determines the coming of floods or droughts, abundance or famine. From the twelve winds, he draws conclusions about the state of harmony of heaven and earth, and takes note of good and bad signs that result from their accord or disaccord. In general, he concerns himself with five kinds of phenomena so as to warn the Emperor to come to the aid of the government and to allow for variations in the ceremonies according to their circumstances."

The Chinese were also keen observers of the fixed stars, giving them such unusual names as Ghost Vehicle, Sun of Imperial Concubine, Imperial Prince, Pivot of Heaven, Twinkling Brilliance or Weaving Girl. But, great astrologers though they may have been, the Chinese lacked one aspect of mathematics that the Greeks applied to astrology—deductive geometry. Deductive geometry was the basis of much classical astrology in and after the time of the Greeks, and this explains the different methods of prognostication used in the East and West.

Down through the ages the astrologer's art has depended, not so much on the uncovering of new facts, though this is important, as on the interpretation of the facts already known. This is the essence of his skill. Obviously one cannot always tell how people will react (and this underlines the very important difference between astrology and predestination which will be discussed later on) but one can be prepared, be forewarned, to know what to expect.

But why should the signs of the zodiac have any effect at all on the formation of human character? It is easy to see why people thought they did, and even now we constantly use astrological expressions in our everyday speech. The thoughts of "lucky star," "ill-fated," "star-crossed," "mooning around," are interwoven into the very structure of our language.

In the same way that the earth has been created by influences from outside, there remains an indisputable togetherness in the working of the universe. The world, after all, is a coherent structure, for if it were not, it would be quite without order and we would never know what to expect. A dog could turn into an apple, or an elephant sprout wings and fly at any moment without so much as a by your leave. But nature, as we know, functions according to laws, not whims, and the laws of nature are certainly not subject to capricious exceptions.

This means that no part of the universe is ever arbitrarily cut off from any other part. Everything is therefore to some extent linked with everything else. The moon draws an imperceptible tide on every puddle; tiny and trivial events can be effected by outside forces (such as the fall of a feather by the faintest puff of wind). And so it is fair to think that the local events at any moment reflect to a very small extent the evolution of the world as a whole.

From this principle follows the possibility of divination, and also knowledge of events at a distance, provided one's mind were always as perfectly undisturbed, as ideally smooth, as a mirror or unruffled lake. Provided, in other words, that one did not confuse the picture with hopes, guesses, and expectations. When people try to foretell the future by cards or crystal ball gazing they find it much easier to confuse the picture with expectations than to reflect it clearly.

But the present does contain a good deal of the future to which it leads—not all, but a good deal. The diver halfway between bridge and water is going to make a splash; the train whizzing towards the station will pass through it unless interfered with; the burglar breaking a pane of glass has exposed himself to the possibility of a prison sentence. Yet this is not a doctrine of determinism, as was emphasized earlier. Clearly, there are forces already at work in the present, and any one of them could alter the situation in some way. Equally, a change of decision could alter the whole situation as well. So the future depends, not on an irresistible force, but on a small act of free will.

An individual's age, physique, and position on the earth's surface are remote consequences of his birth. Birth counts as the original cause for all that happens subsequently. The horoscope, in this case, means "this person represents the further evolution of the state of the universe pictured in this chart." Such a chart can apply equally to man or woman, dog, ship or even limited company.

If the evolution of an idea, or of a person, is to be understood as a totality, it must continue to evolve from its own beginnings, which is to say, in the terms in which it began. The brown-eyed person will be faithful to brown eyes all his life; the traitor is being faithful to some complex of ideas which has long been evolving in him; and the person born at sunset will always express, as he evolves, the psychological implications or analogies of the moment when the sun sinks out of sight.

This is the doctrine that an idea must continue to evolve in terms of its origin. It is a completely non-materialist doctrine, though it never fails to apply to material objects. And it implies, too, that the individual will continue to evolve in terms of his moment of origin, and therefore possibly of the sign of the Zodiac rising on the eastern horizon at his birth. It also implies that the signs of the Zodiac themselves will evolve in the collective mind of the human race in the same terms that they were first devised and not in the terms in which modern astrologers consciously think they ought to work.

For the human race, like every other kind of animal, has a collective mind, as Professor Jung discovered in his investigation of dreams. If no such collective mind existed, no infant could ever learn anything, for communication would be impossible. Furthermore, it is absurd to suggest that the conscious mind could be older than the "unconscious," for an infant's nervous system functions correctly before it has discovered the difference between "myself" and "something else" or discovered what eyes and hands are for. Indeed, the involuntary muscles function correctly even before birth, and will never be under conscious control. They are part of what we call the "unconscious" which is not really "unconscious" at all. To the contrary, it is totally aware of itself and everything else; it is merely that part of the mind that cannot be controlled by conscious effort.

And human experience, though it varies in detail with every individual, is basically the same for each one of us, consisting of sky and earth, day and night, waking and sleeping, man and woman, birth and death. So there is bound to be in the mind of the human race a very large number of inescapable ideas, which are called our natural archetypes.

There are also, however, artificial or cultural archetypes which are not universal or applicable to everyone, but are nevertheless inescapable within the limits of a given culture. Examples of these are the cross in Christianity, and the notion of "escape from the wheel of rebirth" in India. There was a time when these ideas did not exist. And there was a time, too, when the scheme of the Zodiac did not exist. One would not expect the Zodiac to have any influence on remote and primitive peoples, for example, who have never heard of it. If the Zodiac is only an archetype, their horoscopes probably would not work and it would not matter which sign they were born under.

But where the Zodiac is known, and the idea of it has become worked into the collective mind, then there it could well appear to have an influence, even if it has no physical existence. For ideas do not have a physical existence, anyway. No physical basis has yet been discovered for the telepathy that controls an anthill; young swallows migrate before, not after, their parents; and the weaverbird builds its intricate nest without being taught. Materialists suppose, but cannot prove, that "instinct" (as it is called, for no one knows how it works) is controlled by nucleic acid in the chromosomes. This is not a genuine explanation, though, for it only pushes the mystery one stage further back.

Does this mean, then, that the human race, in whose civilization the idea of the twelve signs of the Zodiac has long been embedded, is divided into only twelve types? Can we honestly believe that it is really as simple as that? If so, there must be pretty wide ranges of variation within each type. And if, to explain the variation, we call in heredity and environment, experiences in early childhood, the thyroid and other glands, and also the four functions of the mind mentioned at the beginning of this introduction, and extroversion and introversion, then one begins to wonder if the original classification was worth making at all. No sensible person believes that his favorite system explains everything. But even so, he will not find it much use at all if it does not even save him the trouble of bothering with the others.

Under the Jungian system, everyone has not only a dominant or principal function, but also a secondary or subsidiary one, so that the four can be arranged in order of potency. In the intuitive type, sensation is always the most inefficient function, but the second most inefficient function can be either thinking (which tends to make original thinkers such as Jung himself) or else feeling (which tends to make artistic people). Therefore, allowing for introversion and extroversion, there are at least four kinds of intuitive types, and sixteen types in all. Furthermore, one can see how the sixteen types merge into each other, so that there are no unrealistic or unconvincingly rigid divisions.

In the same way, if we were to put every person under only one sign of the Zodiac, the system becomes too rigid and unlike life. Besides, it was never intended to be used like that. It may be convenient to have only twelve types, but we know that in practice there is every possible gradation between aggressiveness and timidity, or between conscientiousness and laziness. How, then, do we account for this?

The Tyrant and the Saint

Just as the thinking type of man is also influenced to some extent by sensation and intuition, but not very much by emotion, so a person born under Leo can be influenced to some extent by one or two (but not more) of the other signs. For instance, famous persons born under the sign of Gemini include Henry VIII, whom nothing and no-one could have induced to abdicate, and Edward VIII, who did just that. Obviously, then, the sign Gemini does not fully explain the complete character of either of them.

Again, under the opposite sign, Sagittarius, were both Stalin, who was totally consumed with the notion of power, and Charles V, who freely gave up an empire because he preferred to go into a monastery. And we find under Scorpio, many uncompromising characters such as Luther, de Gaulle, Indira Gandhi and Montgomery, but also Petain, a successful commander whose name later became synonymous with collaboration.

A single sign is therefore obviously inadequate to explain the differences between people; it can only explain resemblances, such as the combativeness of the Scorpio group, or the far-reaching devotion of Charles V and Stalin to their respective ideals—the Christian heaven and the Communist utopia.

But very few people are born under one sign only. As well as the month of birth, as was mentioned earlier, the day matters, and, even more, the hour, which ought, if possible, to be noted to the nearest minute. Without this, it is impossible to have an actual horoscope, for the word horoscope means literally, "a consideration of the hour."

The month of birth tells you only which sign of the Zodiac was occupied by the sun. The day and hour tell you what sign was occupied by the moon. And the minute tells you which sign was rising on the eastern horizon. This is called the Ascendant, and it is supposed to be the most important thing in the whole horoscope.

If you were born at midnight, the sun is then in an important position, although invisible. But at one o'clock in the morning the sun is not important, so the moment of birth will not matter much. The important thing then will be the Ascendant, and possibly one or two of the planets. At a given day and hour, say, dawn on January 1st, or 9:00 p.m. on the longest day, the Ascendant will always be the same at any given place. But the moon and planets alter from day to day, at different speeds and have to be looked up in an astronomical table.

The sun is said to signify one's heart, that is to say, one's deepest desires and inmost nature. This is quite different from the moon, which, as we have seen, signifies one's superficial way of behaving. When the ancient Romans referred to the Emperor Augustus as a Capricornian, they meant that he had the moon in Capricorn; they did not pay much attention to the sun, although he was born at sunrise. Or, to take another example, a modern astrologer would call Disraeli a Scorpion because he had Scorpio rising, but most people would call him Sagittarian because he had the sun there. The Romans would have called him Leo because his moon was in Leo.

The sun, as has already been pointed out, is important if one is born near sunrise, sunset, noon or midnight, but is otherwise not reckoned as the principal influence. So if one does not seem to fit one's birth month, it is always worthwhile reading the other signs, for one may have been born at a time when any of them were rising or occupied by the moon. It also seems to be the case that the influence of the sun develops as life goes on, so that the month of birth is easier to guess in people over the age of forty. The young are supposed to be influenced mainly by their Ascendant which characterizes the body and physical personality as a whole.

It should be clearly understood that it is nonsense to assume that all people born at a certain time will exhibit the same characteristics, or that they will even behave in the same manner. It is quite obvious that, from the very moment of its birth, a child is subject to the effects of its environment, and that this in turn will influence its character and heritage to a decisive extent. Also to be taken into account are education and economic conditions, which play a very important part in the formation of one's character as well.

However, it is clearly established that people born under one sign of the Zodiac do have certain basic traits in their character which are different from those born under other signs. It is obvious to every thinking person that certain events produce different reactions in various people. For instance, if a man slips on a banana skin and falls heavily on the pavement, one passer-by may laugh and find this extremely amusing, while another may just walk on, thinking: "What a fool falling down like that. He should look where he is going." A third might also walk away saying to himself: "It's none of my business—I'm glad it wasn't me." A fourth might walk past and think: "I'm sorry for that man, but I haven't the time to be bothered with helping him." And a fifth might stop to help the fallen man to his feet, comfort him and take him home. Here is just one event which could produce entirely different reactions in different people. And, obviously, there are many more. One that comes to mind immediately is the violently opposed views to events such as wars, industrial strikes, and so on. The fact that people have different attitudes to the same event is simply another way of saying that they have different characters. And this is not something that can be put down to background, for people of the same race, religion, or class, very often express quite different reactions to happenings or events. Similarly, it is often the case that members of the same family, where there is clearly uniform background of economic and social standing, education, race and religion, often argue bitterly among themselves over political and social issues.

People have, in general, certain character traits and qualities which, according to their environment, develop in either a positive or a negative manner. Therefore, selfishness (inherent selfishness, that is) might emerge as unselfishness; kindness and consideration as cruelty and lack of consideration towards others. In the same way, a naturally constructive person, may, through frustration, become destructive, and so on. The latent characteristics with which people are born can, therefore, through environment and good or bad training, become something that would appear to be its opposite, and so give the lie to the astrologer's description of their character. But this is not the case. The true character is still there, but it is buried deep beneath these external superficialities.

Careful study of the character traits of different signs can be immeasurable help, and can render beneficial service to the intelligent person. Undoubtedly, the reader will already have discovered that, while he is able to get on very well with some people, he just "cannot stand" others. The causes sometimes seem inexplicable. At times there is intense dislike, at other times immediate sympathy. And there is, too, the phenomenon of love at first sight, which is also apparently inexplicable. People appear to be either sympathetic or unsympathetic towards each other for no apparent reason.

Now if we look at this in the light of the Zodiac, we find that people born under different signs are either compatible or incompatible with each other. In other words, there are good and bad interrelating factors among the various signs. This does not, of course, mean that humanity can be divided into groups of hostile camps. It would be quite wrong to be hostile or indifferent toward people who happen to be born under an incompatible sign. There is no reason why everybody should not, or cannot, learn to control and adjust their feelings and actions, especially after they are aware of the positive qualities of other people by studying their character analyses, among other things.

Every person born under a certain sign has both positive and negative qualities, which are developed more or less according to his free will. Nobody is entirely good or entirely bad, and it is up to each one of us to learn to control himself on the one hand, and at the same time to endeavor to learn about himself and others.

It cannot be repeated often enough that, though the intrinsic nature of man and his basic character traits are born in him, nevertheless it is his own free will that determines whether he will make really good use of his talents and abilities—whether, in other words, he will overcome his vices or allow them to rule him. Most of us are born with at least a streak of laziness, irritability, or some other fault in our nature, and it is up to each one of us to see that we exert sufficient willpower to control our failings so that they do not harm ourselves or others.

Astrology can reveal our inclinations and tendencies. Our weaknesses should not be viewed as shortcomings that are impossible to change. The horoscope of a man may show him to have criminal leanings, for instance, but this does not mean he will definitely become a criminal.

The ordinary man usually finds it difficult to know himself. He is often bewildered. Astrology can frequently tell him more about himself than the different schools of psychology are able to do. Knowing his failings and shortcomings, he will do his best to overcome them, and make himself a better and more useful member of society and a helpmate to his family and friends. It can also save him a great deal of unhappiness and remorse.

And yet it may seem absurd that an ancient philosophy, something that is known as a "pseudo-science," could be a prop to the men and women of the twentieth century. But below the materialistic surface of modern life, there are hidden streams of feeling and thought. Symbology is reappearing as a study worthy of the scholar; the psychosomatic factor in illness has passed from the writings of the crank to those of the specialist; spiritual healing in all its forms is no longer a pious hope but an accepted phenomenon. And it is into this context that we consider astrology, in the sense that it is an analysis of human types.

Astrology and medicine had a long journey together, and only parted company a couple of centuries ago. There still remain in medical language such astrological terms as "saturnine," "choleric," and "mercurial," used in the diagnosis of physical tendencies. The herbalist, for long the handyman of the medical profession, has been dominated by astrology since the days of the Greeks. Certain herbs traditionally respond to certain planetary influences, and diseases must therefore be treated to ensure harmony between the medicine and the disease.

No one expects the most eccentric of modern doctors to go back to the practices of his predecessors. We have come a long way since the time when phases of the moon were studied in illness. Those days were a medical nightmare, with epidemics that were beyond control, and an explanation of the Black Death sought in conjunction with the planets. Nowadays, astrological diagnosis of disease has literally no parallel in modern life. And yet, age-old symbols of types and of the vulnerability of, say, the Saturnian to chronic diseases or the choleric to apoplexy and blood pressure and so on, are still applicable.

But the stars are expected to foretell and not only to diagnose. The astrological forecaster has a counterpart on a highly conventional level in the shape of the weather prophet, racing tipster and stock market forecaster, to name just three examples. All in their own way are aiming at the same result. They attempt to look a little further into the pattern of life and also try to determine future patterns accurately.

Astrological forecasting has been remarkably accurate, but often it is wide of the mark. The brave man who cares to predict world events takes dangerous chances. Individual forecasting is less clear cut; it can be a help or a disillusionment. Then welcome to the nagging question: if it is possible to foreknow, is it right to foretell? A complex point of ethics on which it is hard to pronounce judgment. The doctor faces the same dilemma if he finds that symptoms of a mortal disease are present in his patient and that he can only prognosticate a steady decline. How much to tell an individual in a crisis is a problem that has perplexed many distinguished scholars. Honest and conscientious astrologers in this modern world, where so many people are seeking guidance, face the same problem.

The ancient cults, the symbols of old religions, are eclipsed for the moment. They may return with their old force within a decade or two. But at present the outlook is dark. Human beings badly need assurance, as they did in the past, that all is not chaos. Somewhere, somehow, there is a pattern that must be worked out. As to the why and wherefore, the astrologer is not expected to give judgment. He is just someone who, by dint of talent and training, can gaze into the future.

Five hundred years ago it was customary to call in a learned man who was an astrologer who was probably also a doctor and a philosopher. By his knowledge of astrology, his study of planetary influences, he felt himself qualified to guide those in distress. The world has moved forward at a fantastic rate since then, and in this twentieth century speed has been the keyword everywhere. Tensions have increased, the spur of ambition has been applied indiscriminately. People are uncertain of themselves. At first sight it seems fantastic in the light of modern thinking that they turn to the most ancient of all studies, and get someone to calculate a horoscope for them. But is it *really* so fantastic if you take a second look? For astrology is concerned with tomorrow, with survival. And in a world such as ours, those two things are the keywords of the time in which we live.

HOW TO USE
THESE PREDICTIONS

A person reading the predictions in this book should understand that they are produced from the daily position of the planets for a group of people and are not, of course, individually specialized. To get the full benefit of them he should relate the predictions to his own character and circumstances, co-ordinate them, and draw his own conclusions from them.

If he is a serious observer of his own life he should find a definite pattern emerge that will be a helpful and reliable guide.

The point is that we always retain our free will. The stars indicate certain directional tendencies but we are not compelled to follow. We can do or not do, and wisdom must make the choice.

We all have our good and bad days. Sometimes they extend into cycles of weeks. It is therefore advisable to study daily predictions in a span ranging from the day before to several days ahead; also to re-read the monthly predictions for similar cycles.

Daily predictions should be taken very generally. The word "difficult" does not necessarily indicate a whole day of obstruction or inconvenience. It is a warning to you to be cautious. Your caution will often see you around the difficulty before you are involved. This is the correct use of astrology.

In another section, detailed information is given about the influence of the moon as it passes through the various signs of the Zodiac. It includes instructions on how to use the Moon Tables. This information should be used in conjunction with the daily forecasts to give a fuller picture of the astrological trends.

THE MOON

Moon is the nearest planet to the earth. It exerts more observable influence on us from day to day than any other planet. The effect is very personal, very intimate, and if we are not aware of how it works it can make us quite unstable in our ideas. And the annoying thing is that at these times we often see our own instability but can do nothing about it. A knowledge of what can be expected may help considerably. We can then be prepared to stand strong against the moon's negative influences and use its positive ones to help us to get ahead. Who has not heard of going with the tide?

Moon reflects, has no light of its own. It reflects the sun—the life giver—in the form of vital movement. Moon controls the tides, the blood rhythm, the movement of sap in trees and plants. Its nature is inconstancy and change so it signifies our moods, our superficial behavior—walking, talking and especially thinking. Being a true reflector of other forces, moon is cold, watery like the surface of a still lake, brilliant and scintillating at times, but easily ruffled and disturbed by the winds of change.

The moon takes 28½ days to circle the earth and the Zodiac. It spends just over 2¼ days in each sign. During that time it reflects the qualities, energies and characteristics of the sign and, to a degree, the planet which rules the sign. While the moon in its transit occupies a sign incompatible with our own birth sign, we can expect to feel a vague uneasiness, perhaps a touch of irritableness. We should not be discouraged nor let the feeling get us down, or, worse still, allow ourselves to take the discomfort out on others. Try to remember that the moon has to change signs within 55 hours and, provided you are not physically ill, your mood will probably change with it. It is amazing how frequently depression lifts with the shift in the moon's position. And, of course, when the moon is transiting a sign compatible or sympathetic to yours you will probably feel some sort of stimulation or just plain happy to be alive.

In the horoscope, the moon is such a powerful indicator that competent astrologers often use the sign it occupied at birth as the birth sign of the person. This is done particularly when the sun is on the cusp, or edge, of two signs. Most experienced astrologers, however, coordinate both sun and moon signs by reading and confirming from one to the other and secure a far more accurate and personalized analysis.

For these reasons, the moon tables which follow this section (see pages 28–35) are of great importance to the individual. They show the days and the exact times the moon will enter each sign of the Zodiac for the year. Remember, you have to adjust the indicated times to local time. The corrections, already calculated for most of the main cities, are at the beginning of the tables. What follows now is a guide to the influences that will be reflected to the earth by the moon while it transits each of the twelve signs. The influence is at its peak about 26 hours after the moon enters a sign.

MOON IN ARIES

This is a time for action, for reaching out beyond the usual self-imposed limitations and faint-hearted cautions. If you have plans in your head or on your desk, put them into practice. New ventures, applications, new jobs, new starts of any kind—all have a good chance of success. This is the period when original and dynamic impulses are being reflected onto the earth. The energies are extremely vital and favor the pursuit of pleasure and adventure in practically every form. Sick people should feel an improvement. Those who are well will probably find themselves exuding confidence and optimism. People fond of physical exercise should find their bodies growing with tone and well-being. Boldness, strength, determination should characterize most of your activities with a readiness to face up to old challenges. Yesterday's problems may seem petty and exaggerated—so deal with them. Strike out alone. Self-reliance will attract others to you. This is a good time for making friends. Business and marriage partners are more likely to be impressed with the man and woman of action. Opposition will be overcome or thrown aside with much less effort than usual. CAUTION: Be dominant but not domineering.

MOON IN TAURUS

The spontaneous, action-packed person of yesterday gives way to the cautious, diligent, hardworking "thinker." In this period ideas will probably be concentrated on ways of improving finances. A great deal of time may be spent figuring out and going over schemes and plans. It is the right time to be careful with detail. People will find themselves working longer than usual at their desks. Or devoting more time to serious thought about the future. A strong desire to put order into business and financial arrangements may cause extra work. Loved ones may complain of being neglected and may fail to appreciate that your efforts are for their ultimate benefit. Your desire for system may extend to criticism of arrangements in the home and lead to minor upsets. Health may be affected through overwork. Try to secure a reasonable amount of rest and relaxation, although the tendency will be to "keep going" despite good advice. Work done conscientiously in this period should result in a solid contribution to your future security. CAUTION: Try not to be as serious with people as the work you are engaged in.

MOON IN GEMINI

The humdrum of routine and too much work should suddenly end. You are likely to find yourself in an expansive, quicksilver world of change and self-expression. Urges to write, to paint, to experience the freedom of some sort of artistic outpouring, may be very strong. Take full advantage of them. You may find yourself finishing something you began and put aside long ago. Or embarking on something new which could easily be prompted by a chance meeting, a new acquaintance, or even an advertisement. There may be a yearning for a change of scenery, the feeling to visit another country (not too far away), or at least to get away for a few days. This may result in short, quick journeys. Or, if you are planning a single visit, there may be some unexpected changes or detours on the way. Familiar activities will seem to give little satisfaction unless they contain a fresh element of excitement or expectation. The inclination will be towards untried pursuits, particularly those that allow you to express your inner nature. The accent is on new faces, new places. CAUTION: Do not be too quick to commit yourself emotionally.

MOON IN CANCER

Feelings of uncertainty and vague insecurity are likely to cause problems while the moon is in Cancer. Thoughts may turn frequently to the warmth of the home and the comfort of loved ones. Nostalgic impulses could cause you to bring out old photographs and letters and reflect on the days when your life seemed to be much more rewarding and less demanding. The love and understanding of parents and family may be important, and, if it is not forthcoming you may have to fight against a bit of self-pity. The cordiality of friends and the thought of good times with them that are sure to be repeated will help to restore you to a happier frame of mind. The feeling to be alone may follow minor setbacks or rebuffs at this time, but solitude is unlikely to help. Better to get on the telephone or visit someone. This period often causes peculiar dreams and up-surges of imaginative thinking which can be very helpful to authors of occult and mystical works. Preoccupation with the more person-al world of simple human needs should overshadow any material strivings. CAUTION: Do not spend too much time thinking—seek the company of loved ones or close friends.

MOON IN LEO

New horizons of exciting and rather extravagant activity open up. This is the time for exhilarating entertainment, glamorous and lavish parties, and expensive shopping sprees. Any merrymaking that relies upon your generosity as a host has every chance of being a spectacular success. You should find yourself right in the center of the fun, either as the life of the party or simply as a person whom happy people like to be with. Romance thrives in this heady at-mosphere and friendships are likely to explode unexpectedly into serious attachments. Children and younger people should be at-tracted to you and you may find yourself organizing a picnic or a visit to a fun-fair, the cinema or the seaside. The sunny company and vitality of youthful companions should help you to find some unsuspected energy. In career, you could find an opening for pro-motion or advancement. This should be the time to make a direct approach. The period favors those engaged in original research. CAUTION: Bask in popularity but not in flattery.

MOON IN VIRGO

Off comes the party cap and out steps the busy, practical worker. He wants to get his personal affairs straight, to rearrange them, if necessary, for more efficiency, so he will have more time for more work. He clears up his correspondence, pays outstanding bills, makes numerous phone calls. He is likely to make inquiries, or sign up for some new insurance and put money into gilt-edged invest-ment. Thoughts probably revolve around the need for future secur-ity—to tie up loose ends and clear the decks. There may be a ten-dency to be "finicky," to interfere in the routine of others, particu-larly friends and family members. The motive may be a genuine desire to help with suggestions for updating or streamlining their affairs, but these will probably not be welcomed. Sympathy may be felt for less fortunate sections of the community and a flurry of some sort of voluntary service is likely. This may be accompanied by strong feelings of responsibility on several fronts and health may suffer from extra efforts made. CAUTION: Everyone may not want your help or advice.

MOON IN LIBRA

These are days of harmony and agreement and you should find yourself at peace with most others. Relationships tend to be smooth and sweet-flowing. Friends may become closer and bonds deepen in mutual understanding. Hopes will be shared. Progress by cooperation could be the secret of success in every sphere. In business, established partnerships may flourish and new ones get off to a good start. Acquaintances could discover similar interests that lead to congenial discussions and rewarding exchanges of some sort. Love, as a unifying force, reaches its optimum. Marriage partners should find accord. Those who wed at this time face the prospect of a happy union. Cooperation and tolerance are felt to be stronger than dissension and impatience. The argumentative are not quite so loud in their bellowings, nor as inflexible in their attitudes. In the home, there should be a greater recognition of the other point of view and a readiness to put the wishes of the group before selfish insistence. This is a favorable time to join an art group. CAUTION: Do not be too independent—let others help you if they want to.

MOON IN SCORPIO

Driving impulses to make money and to economize are likely to cause upsets all round. No area of expenditure is likely to be spared the axe, including the household budget. This is a time when the desire to cut down on extravagance can become near fanatical. Care must be exercised to try to keep the aim in reasonable perspective. Others may not feel the same urgent need to save and may retaliate. There is a danger that possessions of sentimental value will be sold to realize cash for investment. Buying and selling of stock for quick profit is also likely. The attention may turn to having a good clean up round the home and at the office. Neglected jobs could suddenly be done with great bursts of energy. The desire for solitude may intervene. Self-searching thoughts could disturb. The sense of invisible and mysterious energies at work could cause some excitability. The reassurance of loves ones may help. CAUTION: Be kind to the people you love.

MOON IN SAGITTARIUS

These are days when you are likely to be stirred and elevated by discussions and reflections of a religious and philosophical nature. Ideas of far-away places may cause unusual response and excitement. A decision may be made to visit someone overseas, perhaps a person whose influence was important to your earlier character development. There could be a strong resolution to get away from present intellectual patterns, to learn new subjects and to meet more interesting people. The superficial may be rejected in all its forms. An impatience with old ideas and unimaginative contacts could lead to a change of companions and interests. There may be an upsurge of religious feeling and metaphysical inquiry. Even a new insight into the significance of astrology and other occult studies is likely under the curious stimulus of the moon in Sagittarius. Physically, you may express this need for fundamental change by spending more time outdoors: sports, gardening or going for long walks. CAUTION: Try to channel any restlessness into worthwhile study.

MOON IN CAPRICORN

Life in these hours may seem to pivot around the importance of gaining prestige and honor in the career, as well as maintaining a spotless reputation. Ambitious urges may be excessive and could be accompanied by quite acquisitive drives for money. Effort should be directed along strictly ethical lines where there is no possibility of reproach or scandal. All endeavors are likely to be characterized by great earnestness, and an air of authority and purpose which should impress those who are looking for leadership or reliability. The desire to conform to accepted standards may extend to sharp criticism of family members. Frivolity and unconventional actions are unlikely to amuse while the moon is in Capricorn. Moderation and seriousness are the orders of the day. Achievement and recognition in this period could come through community work or organizing for the benefit of some amateur group. CAUTION: Dignity and esteem are not always self-awarded.

MOON IN AQUARIUS

Moon in Aquarius is in the second last sign of the Zodiac where ideas can become disturbingly fine and subtle. The result is often a mental "no-man's land" where imagination cannot be trusted with the same certitude as other times. The dangers for the individual are the extremes of optimism and pessimism. Unless the imgination is held in check, situations are likely to be misread, and rosy conclusions drawn where they do not exist. Consequences for the unwary can be costly in career and business. Best to think twice and not speak or act until you think again. Pessimism can be a cruel self-inflicted penalty for delusion at this time. Between the two extremes are strange areas of self-deception which, for example, can make the selfish person think he is actually being generous. Eerie dreams which resemble the reality and even seem to continue into the waking state are also possible. CAUTION: Look for the fact and not just for the image in your mind.

MOON IN PISCES

Everything seems to come to the surface now. Memory may be crystal clear, throwing up long-forgotten information which could be valuable in the career or business. Flashes of clairvoyance and intuition are possible along with sudden realizations of one's own nature, which may be used for self-improvement. A talent, never before suspected, may be discovered. Qualities not evident before in friends and marriage partners are likely to be noticed. As this is a period in which the truth seems to emerge, the discovery of false characteristics is likely to lead to disenchantment or a shift in attachments. However, where qualities are realized it should lead to happiness and deeper feeling. Surprise solutions could bob up for old problems. There may be a public announcement of the solving of a crime or mystery. People with secrets may find someone has "guessed" correctly. The secrets of the soul or the inner self also tend to reveal themselves. Religious and philosophical groups may make some interesting discoveries. CAUTION: Not a time for activities that depend on secrecy.

MOON TABLES

CORRECTION FOR NEW YORK TIME, FIVE HOURS WEST OF GREENWICH

Atlanta, Boston, Detroit, Miami, Washington, Montreal, Ottawa, Quebec, Bogota, Havana, Lima, Santiago .... Same time

Chicago, New Orleans, Houston, Winnipeg, Churchill, Mexico City .... Deduct 1 hour

Albuquerque, Denver, Phoenix, El Paso, Edmonton, Helena .... Deduct 2 hours

Los Angeles, San Francisco, Reno, Portland, Seattle, Vancouver .... Deduct 3 hours

Honolulu, Anchorage, Fairbanks, Kodiak .... Deduct 5 hours

Nome, Samoa, Tonga, Midway .... Deduct 6 hours

Halifax, Bermuda, San Juan, Caracas, La Paz, Barbados .... Add 1 hour

St. John's, Brasilia, Rio de Janeiro, Sao Paulo, Buenos Aires, Montevideo .... Add 2 hours

Azores, Cape Verde Islands .... Add 3 hours

Canary Islands, Madeira, Reykjavik .... Add 4 hours

London, Paris, Amsterdam, Madrid, Lisbon, Gibraltar, Belfast, Rabat .... Add 5 hours

Frankfurt, Rome, Oslo, Stockholm, Prague, Belgrade .... Add 6 hours

Bucharest, Beirut, Tel Aviv, Athens, Istanbul, Cairo, Alexandria, Cape Town, Johannesburg................. Add 7 hours

Moscow, Leningrad, Baghdad, Dhahran, Addis Ababa, Nairobi, Teheran, Zanzibar........................... Add 8 hours

Bombay, Calcutta, Sri Lanka........................... Add 10½ hours

Hong Kong, Shanghai, Manila, Peking, Perth .... Add 13 hours

Tokyo, Okinawa, Darwin, Pusan .... Add 14 hours

Sydney, Melbourne, Port Moresby, Guam .... Add 15 hours

Auckland, Wellington, Suva, Wake .... Add 17 hours

1994 MOON TABLES—NEW YORK TIME

JANUARY		FEBRUARY		MARCH	
Day Moon Enters		**Day Moon Enters**		**Day Moon Enters**	
1. Virgo	3:16 pm	1. Libra		1. Scorpio	9:44 am
2. Virgo		2. Scorpio	2:50 am	2. Scorpio	
3. Libra	6:32 pm	3. Scorpio		3. Sagitt.	11:55 am
4. Libra		4. Sagitt.	6:15 am	4. Sagitt.	
5. Scorpio	9:30 pm	5. Sagitt.		5. Capric.	4:25 pm
6. Scorpio		6. Capric.	11:03 am	6. Capric.	
7. Scorpio		7. Capric.		7. Aquar.	11:16 pm
8. Sagitt.	0:35 am	8. Aquar.	5:17 pm	8. Aquar.	
9. Sagitt.		9. Aquar.		9. Aquar.	
10. Capric.	4:17 am	10. Aquar.		10. Pisces	8:10 am
11. Capric.		11. Pisces	1:24 am	11. Pisces	
12. Aquar.	9:26 am	12. Pisces		12. Aries	7:00 am
13. Aquar.		13. Aries	11:50 am	13. Aries	
14. Pisces	5:05 pm	14. Aries		14. Aries	
15. Pisces		15. Aries		15. Taurus	7:28 am
16. Pisces		16. Taurus	0:21 am	16. Taurus	
17. Aries	3:43 am	17. Taurus		17. Gemini	8:30 pm
18. Aries		18. Gemini	1:06 pm	18. Gemini	
19. Taurus	4:23 pm	19. Gemini		19. Gemini	
20. Taurus		20. Cancer	11:28 pm	20. Cancer	7:55 am
21. Taurus		21. Cancer		21. Cancer	
22. Gemini	4:35 am	22. Cancer		22. Leo	3:40 pm
23. Gemini		23. Leo	5:48 pm	23. Leo	
24. Cancer	1:56 pm	24. Leo		24. Virgo	7:15 pm
25. Cancer		25. Virgo	8:28 am	25. Virgo	
26. Leo	7:39 pm	26. Virgo		26. Libra	7:47 pm
27. Leo		27. Libra	9:07 am	27. Libra	
28. Virgo	10:40 pm	28. Libra		28. Scorpio	7:16 pm
29. Virgo				29. Scorpio	
30. Virgo				30. Sagitt.	7:42 pm
31. Libra	0:35 am			31. Sagitt.	

Summer time to be considered where applicable.

1994 MOON TABLES—NEW YORK TIME

APRIL Day Moon Enters		MAY Day Moon Enters		JUNE Day Moon Enters	
1. Capric.	10:38 pm	1. Aquar.	11:35 am	1. Pisces	
2. Capric.		2. Aquar.		2. Aries	1:32 pm
3. Capric.		3. Pisces	7:48 pm	3. Aries	
4. Aquar.	4:46 am	4. Pisces		4. Aries	
5. Aquar.		5. Pisces		5. Taurus	2:15 am
6. Pisces	1:52 pm	6. Aries	7:02 am	6. Taurus	
7. Pisces		7. Aries		7. Gemini	3:04 pm
8. Pisces		8. Taurus	7:51 pm	8. Gemini	
9. Aries	1:10 am	9. Taurus		9. Gemini	
10. Aries		10. Taurus		10. Cancer	2:23 am
11. Taurus	1:49 pm	11. Gemini	8:44 am	11. Cancer	
12. Taurus		12. Gemini		12. Leo	11:30 am
13. Taurus		13. Cancer	8:28 pm	13. Leo	
14. Gemini	2:49 am	14. Cancer		14. Virgo	6:17 pm
15. Gemini		15. Cancer		15. Virgo	
16. Cancer	2:42 pm	16. Leo	5:59 am	16. Libra	10:49 pm
17. Cancer		17. Leo		17. Libra	
18. Leo	11:46 pm	18. Virgo	12:32 pm	18. Libra	
19. Leo		19. Virgo		19. Scorpio	1:21 am
20. Leo		20. Libra	3:55 pm	20. Scorpio	
21. Virgo	4:59 am	21. Libra		21. Sagitt.	2:33 am
22. Virgo		22. Scorpio	4:52 pm	22. Sagitt.	
23. Libra	6:41 am	23. Scorpio		23. Capric.	3:38 am
24. Libra		24. Sagitt.	4:44 pm	24. Capric.	
25. Scorpio	6:19 am	25. Sagitt.		25. Aquar.	6:11 am
26. Scorpio		26. Capric.	5:18 pm	26. Aquar.	
27. Sagitt.	5:49 am	27. Capric.		27. Pisces	11:45 am
28. Sagitt.		28. Aquar.	8:20 pm	28. Pisces	
29. Capric.	7:06 am	29. Aquar.		29. Aries	9:08 pm
30. Capric.		30. Aquar.		30. Aries	
		31. Pisces	3:04 am		

Summer time to be considered where applicable.

1994 MOON TABLES—NEW YORK TIME

JULY		AUGUST		SEPTEMBER	
Day Moon Enters		**Day Moon Enters**		**Day Moon Enters**	
1. Aries		1. Gemini	6:06 am	1. Cancer	
2. Taurus	9:24 am	2. Gemini		2. Leo	10:38 am
3. Taurus		3. Cancer	5:23 pm	3. Leo	
4. Gemini	10:13 pm	4. Cancer		4. Virgo	3:34 pm
5. Gemini		5. Cancer		5. Virgo	
6. Gemini		6. Leo	1:32 am	6. Libra	5:58 pm
7. Cancer	9:18 am	7. Leo		7. Libra	
8. Cancer		8. Virgo	6:43 am	8. Scorpio	7:27 pm
9. Leo	5:44 pm	9. Virgo		9. Scorpio	
10. Leo		10. Libra	10:08 am	10. Sagitt.	9:26 pm
11. Virgo	11:49 pm	11. Libra		11. Sagitt.	
12. Virgo		12. Scorpio	12:57 pm	12. Sagitt.	
13. Virgo		13. Scorpio		13. Capric.	0:45 am
14. Libra	4:16 am	14. Sagitt.	3:54 pm	14. Capric.	
15. Libra		15. Sagitt.		15. Aquar.	5:43 am
16. Scorpio	7:36 am	16. Capric.	7:19 pm	16. Aquar.	
17. Scorpio		17. Capric.		17. Pisces	12:32 pm
18. Sagitt.	10:10 am	18. Aquar.	11:35 pm	18. Pisces	
19. Sagitt.		19. Aquar.		19. Aries	9:31 pm
20. Capric.	12:31 pm	20. Aquar.		20. Aries	
21. Capric.		21. Pisces	5:28 am	21. Aries	
22. Aquar.	3:39 pm	22. Pisces		22. Taurus	8:48 am
23. Aquar.		23. Aries	1:56 pm	23. Taurus	
24. Pisces	8:57 pm	24. Aries		24. Gemini	9:42 pm
25. Pisces		25. Aries		25. Gemini	
26. Pisces		26. Taurus	1:14 am	26. Gemini	
27. Aries	5:32 am	27. Taurus		27. Cancer	10:13 pm
28. Aries		28. Gemini	2:08 pm	28. Cancer	
29. Taurus	5:14 pm	29. Gemini		29. Leo	7:56 pm
30. Taurus		30. Gemini		30. Leo	
31. Taurus		31. Cancer	2:01 am		

Summer time to be considered where applicable.

1994 MOON TABLES—NEW YORK TIME

OCTOBER		NOVEMBER		DECEMBER	
Day Moon Enters		Day Moon Enters		Day Moon Enters	
1. Leo		1. Libra		1. Scorpio	
2. Virgo	1:40 am	2. Scorpio	3:20 pm	2. Sagitt.	2:14 am
3. Virgo		3. Scorpio		3. Sagitt.	
4. Libra	3:57 am	4. Sagitt.	2:47 pm	4. Capric.	1:43 am
5. Libra		5. Sagitt.		5. Capric.	
6. Scorpio	4:23 am	6. Capric.	3:03 pm	6. Aquar.	2:53 am
7. Scorpio		7. Capric.		7. Aquar.	
8. Sagitt.	4:48 am	8. Aquar.	5:49 pm	8. Pisces	7:25 am
9. Sagitt.		9. Aquar.		9. Pisces	
10. Capric.	6:45 am	10. Aquar.		10. Aries	4:04 pm
11. Capric.		11. Pisces	0:05 am	11. Aries	
12. Aquar.	11:10 am	12. Pisces		12. Aries	
13. Aquar.		13. Aries	9:45 am	13. Taurus	3:57 am
14. Pisces	6:19 pm	14. Aries		14. Taurus	
15. Pisces		15. Taurus	9:45 pm	15. Gemini	5:01 pm
16. Pisces		16. Taurus		16. Gemini	
17. Aries	3:57 am	17. Taurus		17. Gemini	
18. Aries		18. Gemini	10:42 am	18. Cancer	5:26 am
19. Taurus	3:35 pm	19. Gemini		19. Cancer	
20. Taurus		20. Cancer	11:22 pm	20. Leo	4:14 pm
21. Taurus		21. Cancer		21. Leo	
22. Gemini	4:29 am	22. Cancer		22. Leo	
23. Gemini		23. Leo	10:34 am	23. Virgo	1:02 am
24. Cancer	5:16 pm	24. Leo		24. Virgo	
25. Cancer		25. Virgo	7:10 pm	25. Libra	7:28 am
26. Cancer		26. Virgo		26. Libra	
27. Leo	4:05 am	27. Virgo		27. Scorpio	11:18 am
28. Leo		28. Libra	0:23 am	28. Scorpio	
29. Virgo	11:22 am	29. Libra		29. Sagitt.	12:46 pm
30. Virgo		30. Scorpio	2:22 am	30. Sagitt.	
31. Libra	2:47 pm			31. Capric.	12:58 pm

Summer time to be considered where applicable.

1994 PHASES OF THE MOON—NEW YORK TIME

New Moon	First Quarter	Full Moon	Last Quarter
			Jan. 3
Jan. 11	Jan. 18	Jan. 27	Feb. 3
Feb. 10	Feb. 18	Feb. 25	Mar. 4
Mar. 12	Mar. 19	Mar. 26	Apr. 2
Apr. 10	Apr. 17	Apr. 25	May 3
May 10	May 17	May 24	June 1
June 9	June 16	June 22	June 29
July 8	July 15	July 22	July 30
Aug. 7	Aug. 14	Aug. 21	Aug. 29
Sep. 5	Sep. 12	Sep. 19	Sep. 27
Oct. 4	Oct. 11	Oct. 19	Oct. 27
Nov. 3	Nov. 10	Nov. 18	Nov. 25
Dec. 2	Dec. 9	Dec. 17	Dec. 24

1994 PLANTING GUIDE

	Aboveground Crops	Root Crops	Pruning	Weeds Pests
January	2-6-15-25-29	4-11-20-25	9-18-20	13-18-23-27
February	3-12-14-21-26	7-19-24-28	5-14-15	9-14-19-24
March	4-6-21-25-29	2-6-18-29	4-13-14	8-18-23
April	7-17-22-26	2-12-24	9-10-28	5-15-20
May	4-14-19-23-31	9-10-21-27	6-7-25	2-12-17-29
June	1-11-15-20-28	6-17-20-24	3-4-21-22	8-13-26
July	8-12-17-25	3-15-21-30	1-19-27-28	5-10-23
August	4-9-13-22	11-17-27	15-16-24-25	2-19-30
September	1-5-9-18-28	7-14-23	11-12-20-21	3-16-25-30
October	3-7-15-25-30	4-5-11-20	9-18-19	1-13-23-28
November	3-12-21-26	1-7-16-29	5-14-15	9-19-24
December	1-9-19-24-28	5-14-26	3-11-12-30	7-16-21

1994 FISHING GUIDE

	Good	Best
January	4-5-9-13-20-23	6-15-25
February	2-11-16-17-21-22	3-12-19-28
March	2-3-11-12-21-22	4-13-19-20-27
April	5-7-8-9-17-23	4-15-24-28
May	4-9-14-15-21-23-24	2-5-12-21
June	1-10-19-21-26-27-28	3-11-17-20-22
July	8-9-16-23-25-26	7-15-17-21
August	5-10-11-14-22-23	4-13-19-27
September	1-8-9-10-19-28-29	7-9-16-18-20
October	8-16-18-20-22-27	6-15-19-24-26
November	2-3-13-18-23-30	4-12-15-18-21
December	3-12-13-14-18-30	5-9-19-28

MOON'S INFLUENCE OVER DAILY AFFAIRS

The Moon makes a complete transit of the Zodiac every 27 days 7 hours and 43 minutes. In making this transit the Moon forms different aspects with the planets and consequently has favorable or unfavorable bearings on affairs and events for persons according to the sign of the Zodiac under which they were born. Whereas the Sun exclusively represents fire, the Moon rules water. The action of the Moon may be described as fluctuating, variable, absorbent and receptive.

When the Moon is in conjunction with the Sun it is called a New Moon; when the Moon and Sun are in opposition it is called a Full Moon. From New Moon to Full Moon, first and second quarter—which takes about two weeks—the Moon is increasing or waxing. From Full Moon to New Moon, third and fourth quarter, the Moon is decreasing or waning. The Moon Table indicates the New Moon and Full Moon and the quarters.

ACTIVITY	MOON IN
Business:	
buying and selling	Sagittarius, Aries, Gemini, Virgo
new, requiring public support	1st and 2nd quarter
meant to be kept quiet	3rd and 4th quarter
Investigation	3rd and 4th quarter
Signing documents	1st & 2nd quarter, Cancer, Scorpio, Pisces
Advertising	2nd quarter, Sagittarius
Journeys and trips	1st & 2nd quarter, Gemini, Virgo
Renting offices, etc.	Taurus, Leo, Scorpio, Aquarius
Painting of house/apartment	3rd & 4th quarter, Taurus, Scorpio, Aquarius
Decorating	Gemini, Libra, Aquarius
Buying clothes and accessories	Taurus, Virgo
Beauty salon or barber shop visit	1st & 2nd quarter, Taurus, Leo, Libra, Scorpio, Aquarius
Weddings	1st & 2nd quarter

MOON'S INFLUENCE OVER YOUR HEALTH

ARIES	Head, brain, face, upper jaw
TAURUS	Throat, neck, lower jaw
GEMINI	Hands, arms, lungs, shoulders, nervous system
CANCER	Esophagus, stomach, breasts, womb, liver
LEO	Heart, spine
VIRGO	Intestines, liver
LIBRA	Kidneys, lower back
SCORPIO	Sex and eliminative organs
SAGITTARIUS	Hips, thighs, liver
CAPRICORN	Skin, bones, teeth, knees
AQUARIUS	Circulatory system, lower legs
PISCES	Feet, tone of being

Try to avoid work being done on that part of the body when the Moon is in the sign governing that part.

MOON'S INFLUENCE OVER PLANTS

Centuries ago it was established that seeds planted when the Moon is in certain signs and phases called Fruitful will produce more growth than seeds planted when the Moon is in a Barren sign.

FRUITFUL SIGNS	BARREN SIGNS	DRY SIGNS
Taurus	Aries	Aries
Cancer	Gemini	Gemini
Libra	Leo	Sagittarius
Scorpio	Virgo	Aquarius
Capricorn	Sagittarius	
Pisces	Aquarius	

ACTIVITY	MOON IN
Mow lawn, trim plants	**Fruitful sign:** 1st & 2nd quarter
Plant flowers	**Fruitful sign:** 2nd quarter; best in Cancer and Libra
Prune	**Fruitful sign:** 3rd & 4th quarter
Destroy pests; spray	**Barren sign:** 4th quarter
Harvest potatoes, root crops	**Dry sign:** 3rd & 4th quarter; Taurus, Leo, and Aquarius

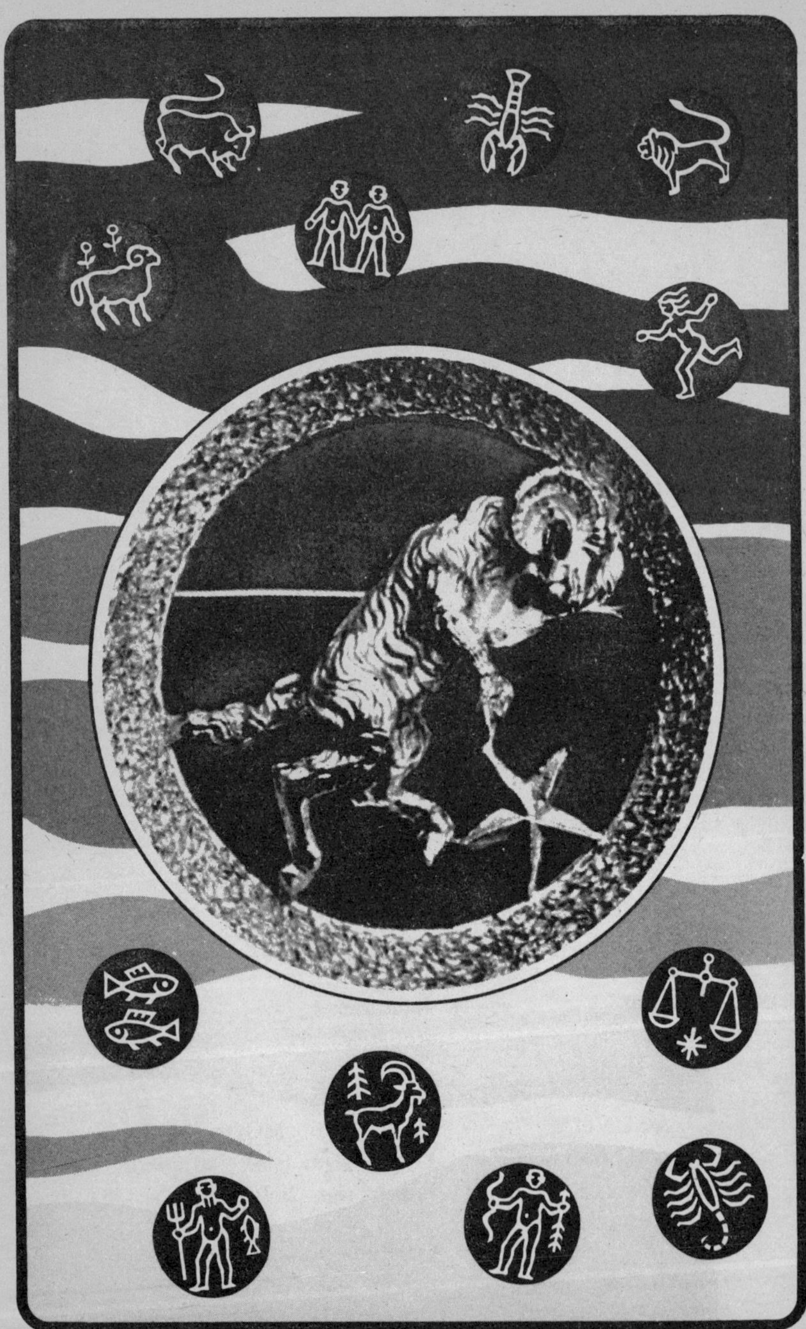

THE SIGNS: DOMINANT CHARACTERISTICS

March 21–April 20

The Positive Side of Aries

The Arien has many positive points to his character. People born under this first sign of the Zodiac are often quite strong and enthusiastic. On the whole, they are forward-looking people who are not easily discouraged by temporary setbacks. They know what they want out of life and they go out after it. Their personalities are strong. Others are usually quite impressed by the Arien's way of doing things. Quite often they are sources of inspiration for others traveling the same route. Aries men and women have a special zest for life that is often contagious; for others, they are often the example of how life should be lived.

The Aries person usually has a quick and active mind. He is imaginative and inventive. He enjoys keeping busy and active. He generally gets along well with all kinds of people. He is interested in mankind, as a whole. He likes to be challenged. Some would say he thrives on opposition, for it is when he is set against that he often does his best. Getting over or around obstacles is a challenge he generally enjoys. All in all, the Arien is quite positive and young-thinking. He likes to keep abreast of new things that are happening in the world. Ariens are often fond of speed. They like things to be done quickly and this sometimes aggravates their slower colleagues and associates.

The Aries man or woman always seems to remain young. Their whole approach to life is youthful and optimistic. They never say die, no matter what the odds. They may have an occasional setback, but it is not long before they are back on their feet again.

The Negative Side of Aries

Everybody has his less positive qualities—and Aries is no exception. Sometimes the Aries man or woman is not very tactful in communicating with others; in his hurry to get things done he is apt to

be a little callous or inconsiderate. Sensitive people are likely to find him somewhat sharp-tongued in some situations. Often in his eagerness to achieve his aims, he misses the mark altogether. At times the Arien is too impulsive. He can occasionally be stubborn and refuse to listen to reason. If things do not move quickly enough to suit the Aries man or woman, he or she is apt to become rather nervous or irritable. The uncultivated Arien is not unfamiliar with moments of doubt and fear. He is capable of being destructive if he does not get his way. He can overcome some of his emotional problems by steadily trying to express himself as he really is, but this requires effort.

April 21–May 20

The Positive Side of Taurus

The Taurus person is known for his ability to concentrate and for his tenacity. These are perhaps his strongest qualities. The Taurus man or woman generally has very little trouble in getting along with others; it's his nature to be helpful toward people in need. He can always be depended on by his friends, especially those in trouble.

The Taurean generally achieves what he wants through his ability to persevere. He never leaves anything unfinished but works on something until it has been completed. People can usually take him at his word; he is honest and forthright in most of his dealings. The Taurus person has a good chance to make a success of his life because of his many positive qualities. The Taurean who aims high seldom falls short of his mark. He learns well by experience. He is thorough and does not believe in short-cuts of any kind. The Taurean's thoroughness pays off in the end, for through his deliberateness he learns how to rely on himself and what he has learned. The Taurus person tries to get along with others, as a rule. He is not overly critical and likes people to be themselves. He is a tolerant person and enjoys peace and harmony—especially in his home life.

The Taurean is usually cautious in all that he does. He is not a person who believes in taking unnecessary risks. Before adopting any one line of action, he will weigh all of the pros and cons. The

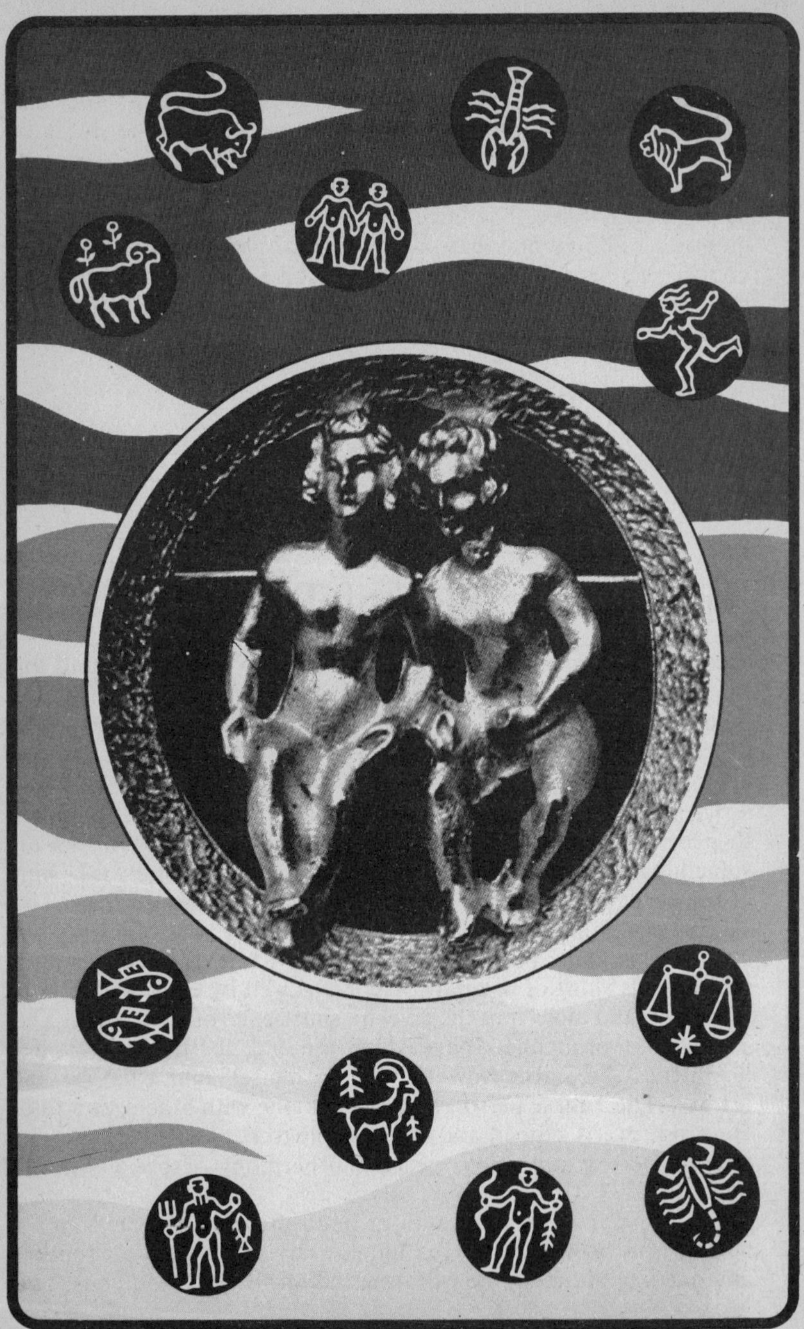

Taurus person is steadfast. Once his mind is made up it seldom changes. The person born under this sign usually is a good family person—reliable and loving.

The Negative Side of Taurus

Sometimes the Taurus man or woman is a bit too stubborn. He won't listen to other points of view if his mind is set on something. To others, this can be quite annoying. The Taurean also does not like to be told what to do. He becomes rather angry if others think him not too bright. He does not like to be told he is wrong, even when he is. He dislikes being contradicted.

Some people who are born under this sign are very suspicious of others—even of those persons close to them. They find it difficult to trust people fully. They are often afraid of being deceived or taken advantage of. The Taurean often finds it difficult to forget or forgive. His love of material things sometimes makes him rather avaricious and petty.

May 21–June 20

The Positive Side of Gemini

The person born under this sign of the Heavenly Twins is usually quite bright and quick-witted. Some of them are capable of doing many different things. The Gemini person very often has many different interests. He keeps an open mind and is always anxious to learn new things.

The Geminian is often an analytical person. He is a person who enjoys making use of his intellect. He is governed more by his mind than by his emotions. He is a person who is not confined to one view; he can often understand both sides to a problem or question. He knows how to reason; how to make rapid decisions if need be.

He is an adaptable person and can make himself at home almost anywhere. There are all kinds of situations he can adapt to. He is a person who seldom doubts himself; he is sure of his talents and his

ability to think and reason. The Geminian is generally most satisfied when he is in a situation where he can make use of his intellect. Never short of imagination, he often has strong talents for invention. He is rather a modern person when it comes to life; the Geminian almost always moves along with the times—perhaps that is why he remains so youthful throughout most of his life.

Literature and art appeal to the person born under this sign. Creativity in almost any form will interest and intrigue the Gemini man or woman.

The Geminian is often quite charming. A good talker, he often is the center of attraction at any gathering. People find it easy to like a person born under this sign because he can appear easygoing and usually has a good sense of humor.

The Negative Side of Gemini

Sometimes the Gemini person tries to do too many things at one time—and as a result, winds up finishing nothing. Some Geminians are easily distracted and find it rather difficult to concentrate on one thing for too long a time. Sometimes they give in to trifling fancies and find it rather boring to become too serious about any one thing. Some of them are never dependable, no matter what they promise.

Although the Gemini man or woman often appears to be well-versed on many subjects, this is sometimes just a veneer. His knowledge may be only superficial, but because he speaks so well he gives people the impression of erudition. Some Geminians are sharp-tongued and inconsiderate; they think only of themselves and their own pleasure.

June 21–July 20

The Positive Side of Cancer

The Cancerians's most positive point is his understanding nature. On the whole, he is a loving and sympathetic person. He would never go out of his way to hurt anyone. The Cancer man or woman

is often very kind and tender; they give what they can to others. They hate to see others suffering and will do what they can to help someone in less fortunate circumstances than themselves. They are often very concerned about the world. Their interest in people generally goes beyond that of just their own families and close friends; they have a deep sense of brotherhood and respect humanitarian values. The Cancerian means what he says, as a rule; he is honest about his feelings.

The Cancer man or woman is a person who knows the art of patience. When something seems difficult, he is willing to wait until the situation becomes manageable again. He is a person who knows how to bide his time. The Cancerian knows how to concentrate on one thing at a time. When he has made his mind up he generally sticks with what he does, seeing it through to the end.

The Cancerian is a person who loves his home. He enjoys being surrounded by familiar things and the people he loves. Of all the signs, Cancer is the most maternal. Even the men born under this sign often have a motherly or protective quality about them. They like to take care of people in their family—to see that they are well loved and well provided for. They are usually loyal and faithful. Family ties mean a lot to the Cancer man or woman. Parents and in-laws are respected and loved. The Cancerian has a strong sense of tradition. He is very sensitive to the moods of others.

The Negative Side of Cancer

Sometimes the Cancerian finds it rather hard to face life. It becomes too much for him. He can be a little timid and retiring, when things don't go too well. When unfortunate things happen, he is apt to just shrug and say, "Whatever will be will be." He can be fatalistic to a fault. The uncultivated Cancerian is a bit lazy. He doesn't have very much ambition. Anything that seems a bit difficult he'll gladly leave to others. He may be lacking in initiative. Too sensitive, when he feels he's been injured, he'll crawl back into his shell and nurse his imaginary wounds. The Cancer woman often is given to crying when the smallest thing goes wrong.

Some Cancerians find it difficult to enjoy themselves in environments outside their homes. They make heavy demands on others, and need to be constantly reassured that they are loved.

July 21–August 21

The Positive Side of Leo

Often Leos make good leaders. They seem to be good organizers and administrators. Usually they are quite popular with others. Whatever group it is that he belongs to, the Leo man is almost sure to be or become the leader.

The Leo person is generous most of the time. It is his best characteristic. He or she likes to give gifts and presents. In making others happy, the Leo person becomes happy himself. He likes to splurge when spending money on others. In some instances it may seem that the Leo's generosity knows no boundaries. A hospitable person, the Leo man or woman is very fond of welcoming people to his house and entertaining them. He is never short of company.

The Leo person has plenty of energy and drive. He enjoys working toward some specific goal. When he applies himself correctly, he gets what he wants most often. The Leo person is almost never unsure of himself. He has plenty of confidence and aplomb. He is a person who is direct in almost everything he does. He has a quick mind and can make a decision in a very short time.

He usually sets a good example for others because of his ambitious manner and positive ways. He knows how to stick to something once he's started. Although the Leo person may be good at making a joke, he is not superficial or glib. He is a loving person, kind and thoughtful.

There is generally nothing small or petty about the Leo man or woman. He does what he can for those who are deserving. He is a person others can rely upon at all times. He means what he says. An honest person, generally speaking, he is a friend that others value.

The Negative Side of Leo

Leo, however, does have his faults. At times, he can be just a bit too arrogant. He thinks that no one deserves a leadership position except him. Only he is capable of doing things well. His opinion of himself is often much too high. Because of his conceit, he is sometimes rather unpopular with a good many people. Some Leos are too materialistic; they can only think in terms of money and profit.

Some Leos enjoy lording it over others—at home or at their place of business. What is more, they feel they have the right to. Egocentric to an impossible degree, this sort of Leo cares little about how others think or feel. He can be rude and cutting.

August 22–September 22

The Positive Side of Virgo

The person born under the sign of Virgo is generally a busy person. He knows how to arrange and organize things. He is a good planner. Above all, he is practical and is not afraid of hard work.

The person born under this sign, Virgo, knows how to attain what he desires. He sticks with something until it is finished. He never shirks his duties, and can always be depended upon. The Virgo person can be thoroughly trusted at all times.

The man or woman born under this sign tries to do everything to perfection. He doesn't believe in doing anything half-way. He always aims for the top. He is the sort of a person who is constantly striving to better himself—not because he wants more money or glory, but because it gives him a feeling of accomplishment.

The Virgo man or woman is a very observant person. He is sensitive to how others feel, and can see things below the surface of a situation. He usually puts this talent to constructive use.

It is not difficult for the Virgoan to be open and earnest. He believes in putting his cards on the table. He is never secretive or under-handed. He's as good as his word. The Virgo person is generally plain-spoken and down-to-earth. He has no trouble in expressing himself.

The Virgo person likes to keep up to date on new developments in his particular field. Well-informed, generally, he sometimes has a keen interest in the arts or literature. What he knows, he knows well. His ability to use his critical faculties is well-developed and sometimes startles others because of its accuracy.

The Virgoan adheres to a moderate way of life; he avoids excesses. He is a responsible person and enjoys being of service.

The Negative Side of Virgo

Sometimes a Virgo person is too critical. He thinks that only he can do something the way it should be done. Whatever anyone else does is inferior. He can be rather annoying in the way he quibbles over insignificant details. In telling others how things should be done, he can be rather tactless and mean.

Some Virgos seem rather emotionless and cool. They feel emo-

tional involvement is beneath them. They are sometimes too tidy, too neat. With money they can be rather miserly. Some try to force their opinions and ideas on others.

September 23–October 22

The Positive Side of Libra

Librans love harmony. It is one of their most outstanding character traits. They are interested in achieving balance; they admire beauty and grace in things as well as in people. Generally speaking, they are kind and considerate people. Librans are usually very sympathetic. They go out of their way not to hurt another person's feelings. They are outgoing and do what they can to help those in need.

People born under the sign of Libra almost always make good friends. They are loyal and amiable. They enjoy the company of others. Many of them are rather moderate in their views; they believe in keeping an open mind, however, and weighing both sides of an issue fairly before making a decision.

Alert and often intelligent, the Libran, always fair-minded, tries to put himself in the position of the other person. They are against injustice; quite often they take up for the underdog. In most of their social dealings, they try to be tactful and kind. They dislike discord and bickering, and most Libras strive for peace and harmony in all their relationships.

The Libra man or woman has a keen sense of beauty. They appreciate handsome furnishings and clothes. Many of them are artistically inclined. Their taste is usually impeccable. They know how to use color. Their homes are almost always attractively arranged and inviting. They enjoy entertaining people and see to it that their guests always feel at home and welcome.

The Libran gets along with almost everyone. He is well-liked and socially much in demand.

The Negative Side of Libra

Some people born under this sign tend to be rather insincere. So eager are they to achieve harmony in all relationships that they will even go so far as to lie. Many of them are escapists. They find facing

the truth an ordeal and prefer living in a world of make-believe.

In a serious argument, some Librans give in rather easily even when they know they are right. Arguing, even about something they believe in, is too unsettling for some of them.

Librans sometimes care too much for material things. They enjoy possessions and luxuries. Some are vain and tend to be jealous.

October 23–November 22

The Positive Side of Scorpio

The Scorpio man or woman generally knows what he or she wants out of life. He is a determined person. He sees something through to the end. The Scorpion is quite sincere, and seldom says anything he doesn't mean. When he sets a goal for himself he tries to go about achieving it in a very direct way.

The Scorpion is brave and courageous. They are not afraid of hard work. Obstacles do not frighten them. They forge ahead until they achieve what they set out for. The Scorpio man or woman has a strong will.

Although the Scorpion may seem rather fixed and determined, inside he is often quite tender and loving. He can care very much for others. He believes in sincerity in all relationships. His feelings about someone tend to last; they are profound and not superficial.

The Scorpio person is someone who adheres to his principles no matter what happens. He will not be deterred from a path he believes to be right.

Because of his many positive strengths, the Scorpion can often achieve happiness for himself and for those that he loves.

He is a constructive person by nature. He often has a deep understanding of people and of life, in general. He is perceptive and unafraid. Obstacles often seem to spur him on. He is a positive person who enjoys winning. He has many strengths and resources; challenge of any sort often brings out the best in him.

The Negative Side of Scorpio

The Scorpio person is sometimes hypersensitive. Often he imagines injury when there is none. He feels that others do not bother to

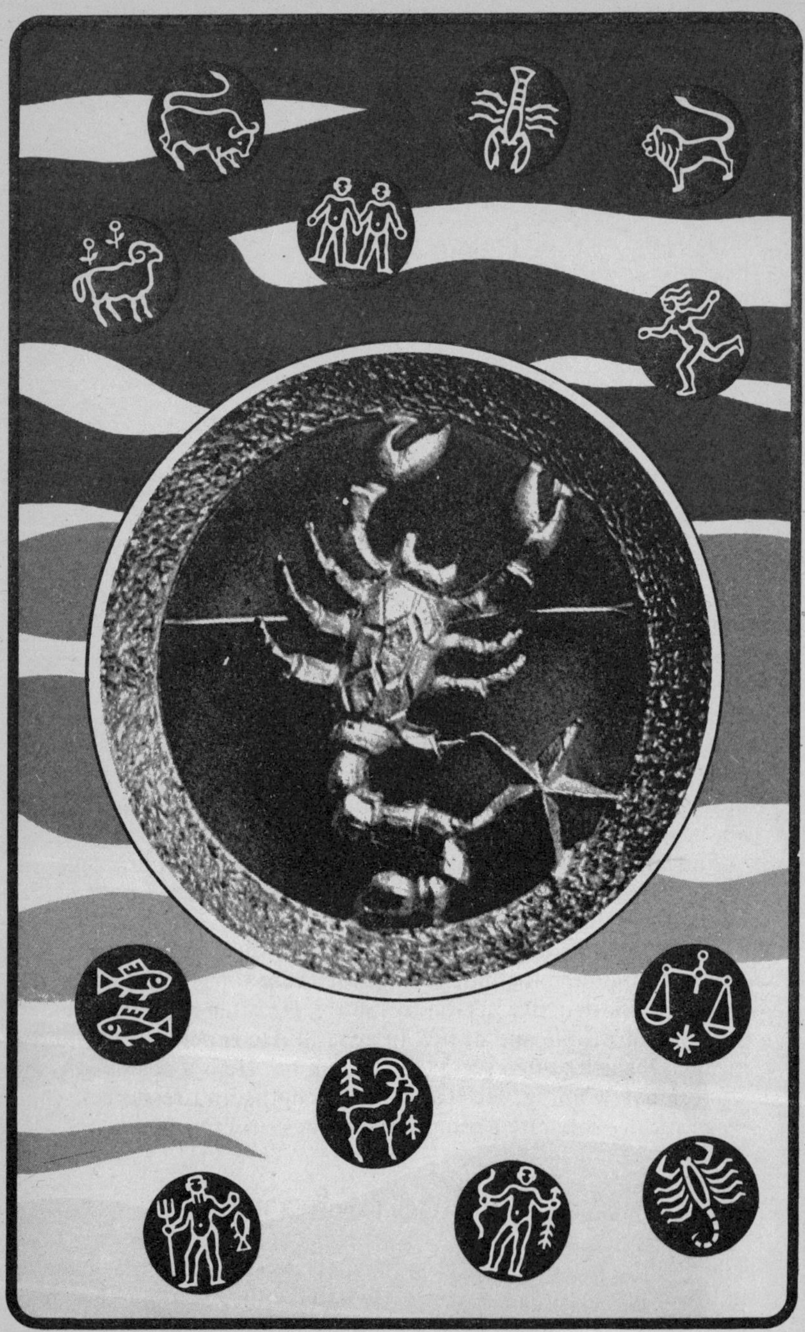

recognize him for his true worth. Sometimes he is given to excessive boasting in order to compensate for what he feels is neglect

The Scorpio person can be rather proud and arrogant. They can be rather sly when they put their minds to it and they enjoy outwitting persons or institutions noted for their cleverness.

Their tactics for getting what they want are sometimes devious and ruthless. They don't care too much about what others may think. If they feel others have done them an injustice, they will do their best to seek revenge. The Scorpion often has a sudden, violent temper; and this person's interest in sex is sometimes quite unbalanced or excessive.

November 23–December 20

The Positive Side of Sagittarius

People born under this sign are often honest and forthright. Their approach to life is earnest and open. The Sagittarian is often quite adult in his way of seeing things. They are broadminded and tolerant people. When dealing with others the person born under the sign of Sagittarius is almost always open and forthright. He doesn't believe in deceit or pretension. His standards are high. People who associate with the Sagittarian, generally admire and respect him.

The Sagittarian trusts others easily and expects them to trust him. He is never suspicious or envious and almost always thinks well of others. People always enjoy his company because he is so friendly and easy-going. The Sagittarius man or woman is often good-humored. He can always be depended upon by his friends, family, and co-workers.

The person born under this sign of the Zodiac likes a good joke every now and then; he is keen on fun and this makes him very popular with others.

A lively person, he enjoys sports and outdoor life. The Sagittarian is fond of animals. Intelligent and interesting, he can begin an animated conversation with ease. He likes exchanging ideas and discussing various views.

He is not selfish or proud. If someone proposes an idea or plan that is better than his, he will immediately adopt it. Imaginative yet practical, he knows how to put ideas into practice.

He enjoys sport and game, and it doesn't matter if he wins or loses. He is a forgiving person, and never sulks over something that has not worked out in his favor.

He is seldom critical, and is almost always generous.

The Negative Side of Sagittarius

Some Sagittarians are restless. They take foolish risks and seldom learn from the mistakes they make. They don't have heads for money and are often mismanaging their finances. Some of them devote much of their time to gambling.

Some are too outspoken and tactless, always putting their feet in their mouths. They hurt others carelessly by being honest at the wrong time. Sometimes they make promises which they don't keep. They don't stick close enough to their plans and go from one failure to another. They are undisciplined and waste a lot of energy.

December 21–January 19

The Positive Side of Capricorn

The person born under the sign of Capricorn is usually very stable and patient. He sticks to whatever tasks he has and sees them through. He can always be relied upon and he is not averse to work.

An honest person, the Capricornian is generally serious about whatever he does. He does not take his duties lightly. He is a practical person and believes in keeping his feet on the ground.

Quite often the person born under this sign is ambitious and knows how to get what he wants out of life. He forges ahead and never gives up his goal. When he is determined about something, he almost always wins. He is a good worker—a hard worker. Although things may not come easy to him, he will not complain, but continue working until his chores are finished.

He is usually good at business matters and knows the value of money. He is not a spendthrift and knows how to put something away for a rainy day; he dislikes waste and unnecessary loss.

The Capricornian knows how to make use of his self-control. He

can apply himself to almost anything once he puts his mind to it. His ability to concentrate sometimes astounds others. He is diligent and does well when involved in detail work.

The Capricorn man or woman is charitable, generally speaking, and will do what is possible to help others less fortunate. As a friend, he is loyal and trustworthy. He never shirks his duties or responsibilities. He is self-reliant and never expects too much of the other fellow. He does what he can on his own. If someone does him a good turn, then he will do his best to return the favor.

The Negative Side of Capricorn

Like everyone, the Capricornian, too, has his faults. At times, he can be over-critical of others. He expects others to live up to his own high standards. He thinks highly of himself and tends to look down on others.

His interest in material things may be exaggerated. The Capricorn man or woman thinks too much about getting on in the world and having something to show for it. He may even be a little greedy.

He sometimes thinks he knows what's best for everyone. He is too bossy. He is always trying to organize and correct others. He may be a little narrow in his thinking.

January 20–February 18

The Positive Side of Aquarius

The Aquarius man or woman is usually very honest and forthright. These are his two greatest qualities. His standards for himself are generally very high. He can always be relied upon by others. His word is his bond.

The Aquarian is perhaps the most tolerant of all the Zodiac personalities. He respects other people's beliefs and feels that everyone is entitled to his own approach to life.

He would never do anything to injure another's feelings. He is never unkind or cruel. Always considerate of others, the Aquarian is always willing to help a person in need. He feels a very strong tie between himself and all the other members of mankind.

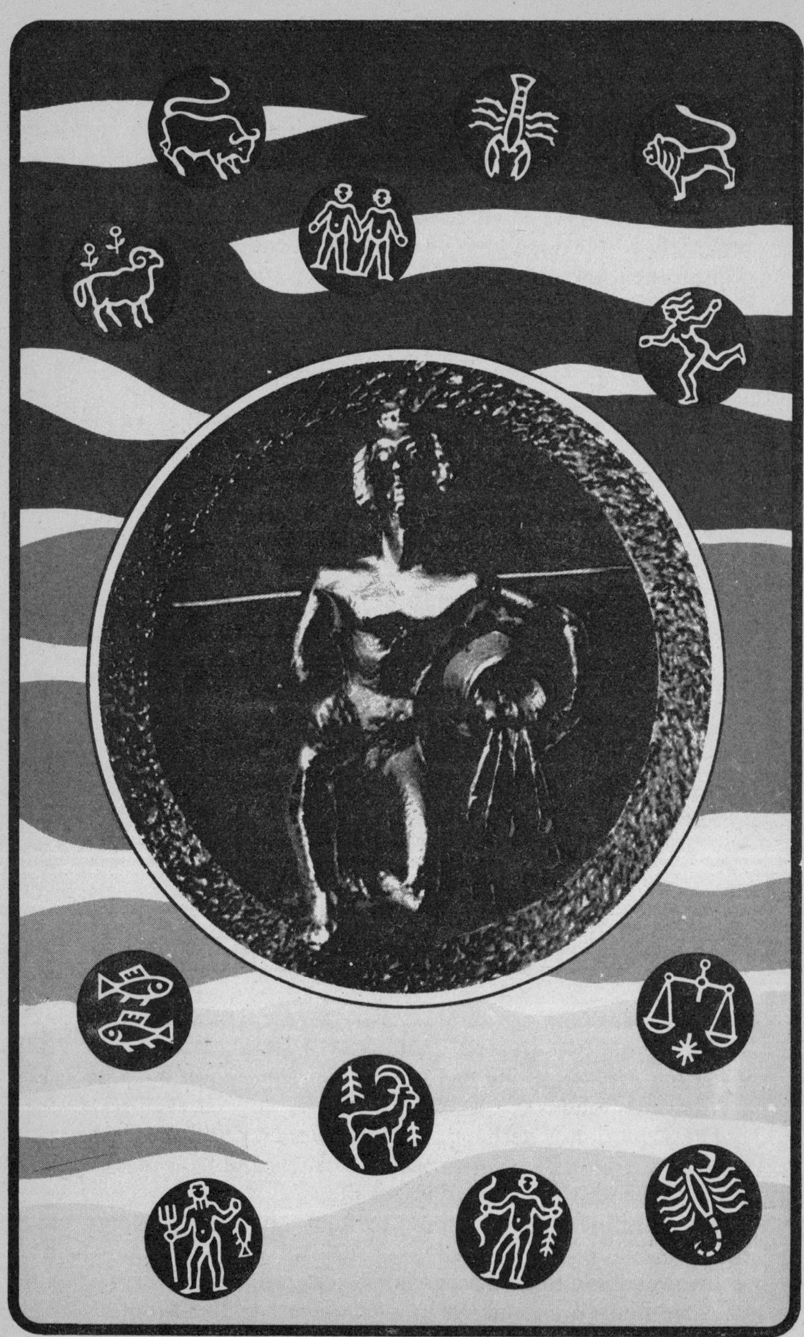

The person born under this sign is almost always an individualist. He does not believe in teaming up with the masses, but prefers going his own way. His ideas about life and mankind are often quite advanced. There is a saying to the effect that the average Aquarian is fifty years ahead of his time.

He is broadminded. The problems of the world concern him greatly. He is interested in helping others no matter what part of the globe they live in. He is truly a humanitarian sort. He likes to be of service to others.

Giving, considerate, and without prejudice, Aquarians have no trouble getting along with others.

The Negative Side of Aquarius

The Aquarian may be too much of a dreamer. He makes plans but seldom carries them out. He is rather unrealistic. His imagination has a tendency to run away with him. Because many of his plans are impractical, he is always in some sort of a dither.

Others may not approve of him at all times because of his unconventional behavior. He may be a bit eccentric. Sometimes he is so busy with his own thoughts, that he loses touch with the realities of existence.

Some Aquarians feel they are more clever and intelligent than others. They seldom admit to their own faults, even when they are quite apparent. Some become rather fanatic in their views. Their criticism of others is sometimes destructive and negative.

February 19–March 20

The Positive Side of Pisces

The Piscean can often understand the problems of others quite easily. He has a sympathetic nature. Kindly, he is often dedicated in the way he goes about helping others. The sick and the troubled often turn to him for advice and assistance.

He is very broadminded and does not criticize others for their faults. He knows how to accept people for what they are. On the whole, he is a trustworthy and earnest person. He is loyal to his

friends and will do what he can to help them in time of need. Generous and good-natured, he is a lover of peace; he is often willing to help others solve their differences. People who have taken a wrong turn in life often interest him and he will do what he can to persuade them to rehabilitate themselves.

He has a strong intuitive sense and most of the time he knows how to make it work for him; the Piscean is unusually perceptive and often knows what is bothering someone before that person, himself, is aware of it. The Pisces man or woman is an idealistic person, basically, and is interested in making the world a better place in which to live. The Piscean believes that everyone should help each other. He is willing to do more than his share in order to achieve cooperation with others.

The person born under this sign often is talented in music or art. He is a receptive person; he is able to take the ups and downs of life with philosophic calm.

The Negative Side of Pisces

Some Pisceans are often depressed; their outlook on life is rather glum. They may feel that they have been given a bad deal in life and that others are always taking unfair advantage of them. The Piscean sometimes feel that the world is a cold and cruel place. He is easily discouraged. He may even withdraw from the harshness of reality into a secret shell of his own where he dreams and idles away a good deal of his time.

The Piscean can be rather lazy. He lets things happen without giving the least bit of resistance. He drifts along, whether on the high road or on the low. He is rather short on willpower.

Some Pisces people seek escape through drugs or alcohol. When temptation comes along they find it hard to resist. In matters of sex, they can be rather permissive.

THE SIGNS AND THEIR KEY WORDS

		POSITIVE	NEGATIVE
ARIES	self	courage, initiative, pioneer instinct	brash rudeness, selfish impetuosity
TAURUS	money	endurance, loyalty, wealth	obstinacy, gluttony
GEMINI	mind	versatility	capriciousness, unreliability
CANCER	family	sympathy, homing instinct	clannishness, childishness
LEO	children	love, authority, integrity	egotism, force
VIRGO	work	purity, industry, analysis	fault-finding, cynicism
LIBRA	marriage	harmony, justice	vacillation, superficiality
SCORPIO	sex	survival, regeneration	vengeance, discord
SAGITTARIUS	travel	optimism, higher learning	lawlessness
CAPRICORN	career	depth	narrowness, gloom
AQUARIUS	friends	human fellowship, genius	perverse unpredictability
PISCES	confinement	spiritual love, universality	diffusion, escapism

THE ELEMENTS AND QUALITIES OF THE SIGNS

ELEMENT	SIGN	QUALITY	SIGN
FIRE..................	ARIES LEO SAGITTARIUS	CARDINAL.........	ARIES LIBRA CANCER CAPRICORN
EARTH...............	TAURUS VIRGO CAPRICORN	FIXED................	TAURUS LEO SCORPIO AQUARIUS
AIR.....................	GEMINI LIBRA AQUARIUS		
WATER..............	CANCER SCORPIO PISCES	MUTABLE.........	GEMINI VIRGO SAGITTARIUS PISCES

Every sign has both an element and a quality associated with it. The element indicates the basic makeup of the sign, and the quality describes the kind of activity associated with each.

Signs can be grouped together according to their *element* and *quality*. Signs of the same element share many basic traits in common. They tend to form stable configurations and ultimately harmonious relationships. Signs of the same quality are often less harmonious, but they share many dynamic potentials for growth as well as profound fulfillment.

THE FIRE SIGNS

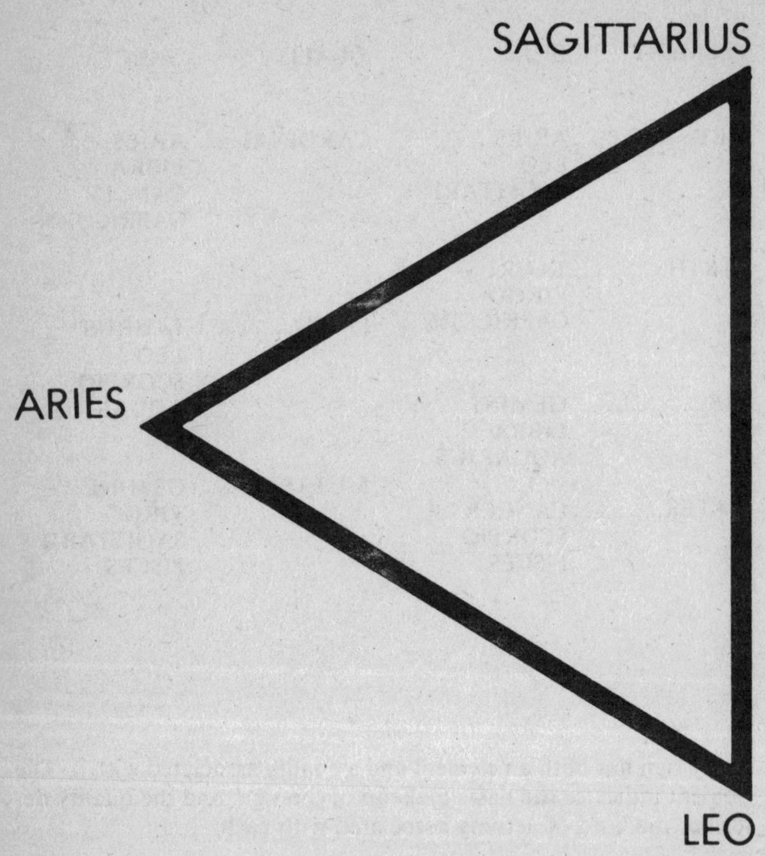

This is the fire group. On the whole these are emotional, volatile types, quick to anger, quick to forgive. They are adventurous, powerful people and .act as a source of inspiration for everyone. They spark into action with immediate exuberant impulses. They are intelligent, self-involved, creative and idealistic. They all share a certain vibrancy and glow that outwardly reflects an inner flame and passion for living.

THE EARTH SIGNS

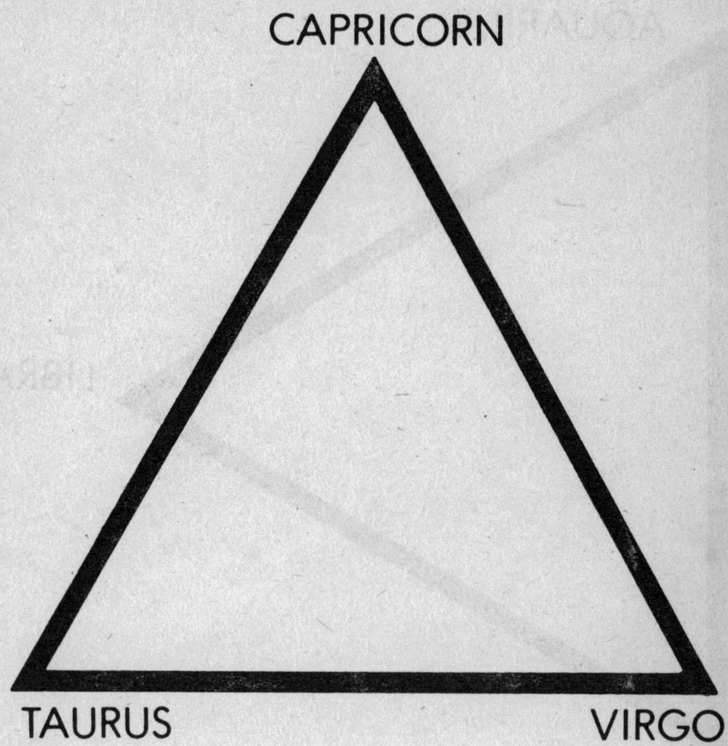

This is the earth group. They are in constant touch with the material world and tend to be conservative. Although they are all capable of spartan self-discipline, they are earthy, sensual people who are stimulated by the tangible, elegant and luxurious. The thread of their lives is always practical, but they do fantasize and are often attracted to dark, mysterious, emotional people. They are like great cliffs overhanging the sea, forever married to the ocean but always resisting erosion from the dark, emotional forces that thunder at their feet.

THE AIR SIGNS

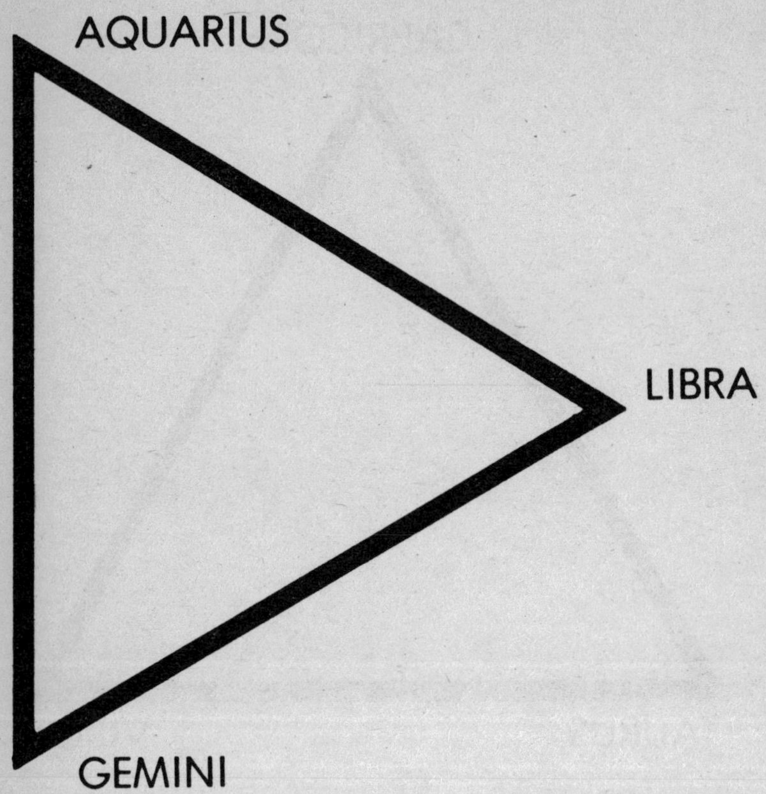

This is the air group. They are light, mental creatures desirous of contact, communication and relationship. They are involved with people and the forming of ties on many levels. Original thinkers, they are the bearers of human news. Their language is their sense of word, color, style and beauty. They provide an atmosphere suitable and pleasant for living. They add change and versatility to the scene, and it is through them that we can explore new territory of human intelligence and experience.

THE WATER SIGNS

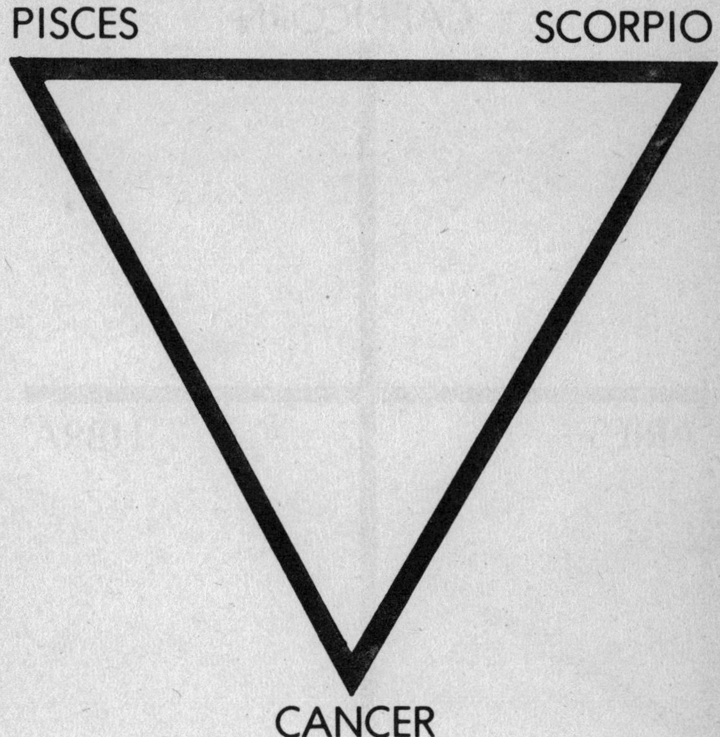

This is the water group. Through the water people, we are all joined together on emotional, non-verbal levels. They are silent, mysterious types whose magic hypnotizes even the most determined realist. They have uncanny perceptions about people and zod are as rich as the oceans when it comes to feeling, emotion or imagination. They are sensitive, mystical creatures with memories that go back beyond time. Through water, life is sustained. These people have the potential for the depths of darkness or the heights of mysticism and art.

THE CARDINAL SIGNS

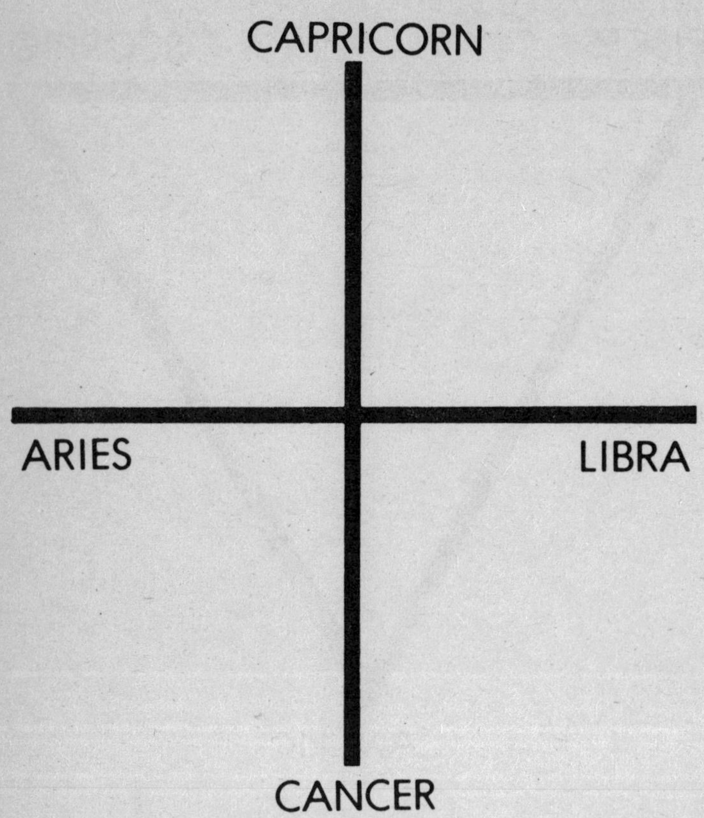

Put together, this is a clear-cut picture of dynamism, activity, tremendous stress and remarkable achievement. These people know the meaning of great change since their lives are often characterized by significant crises and major successes. This combination is like a simultaneous storm of summer, fall, winter and spring. The danger is chaotic diffusion of energy; the potential is irrepressible growth and victory.

THE FIXED SIGNS

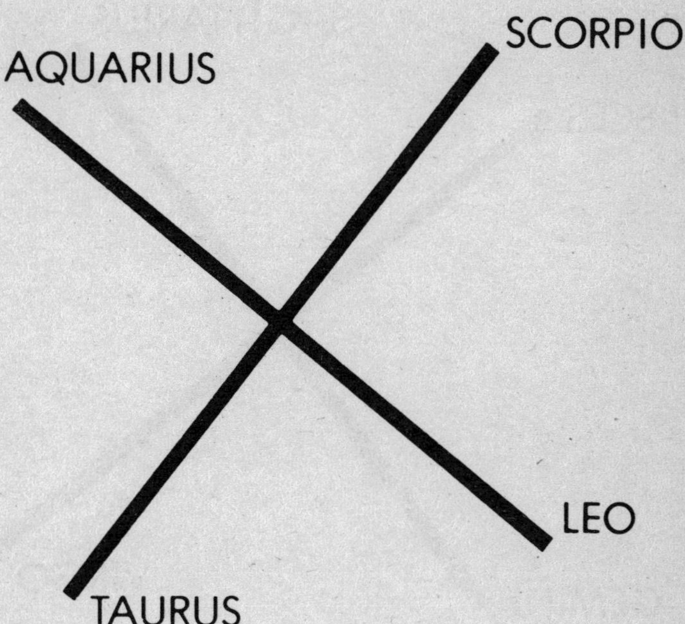

Fixed signs are always establishing themselves in a given place or area of experience. Like explorers who arrive and plant a flag, these people claim a position from which they do not enjoy being deposed. They are staunch, stalwart, upright, trusty, honorable people, although their obstinacy is well-known. Their contribution is fixity, and they are the angels who support our visible world.

THE MUTABLE SIGNS

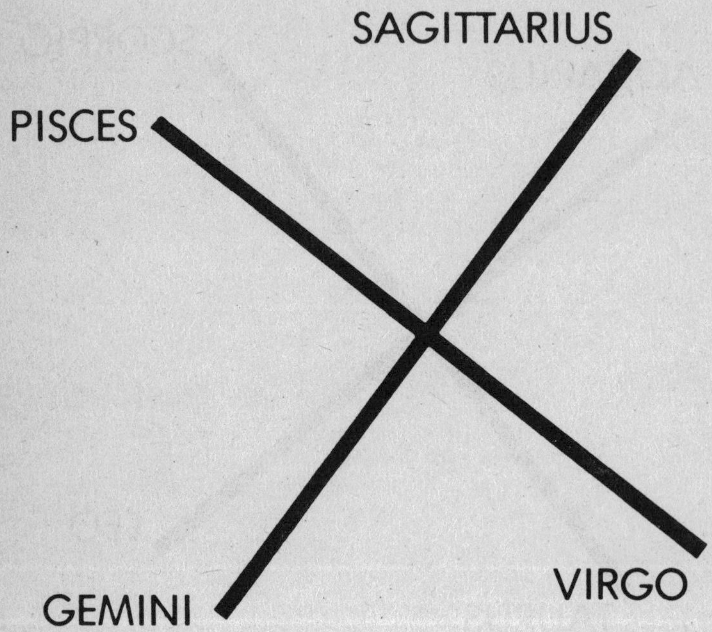

Mutable people are versatile, sensitive, intelligent, nervous and deeply curious about life. They are the translators of all energy. They often carry out or complete tasks initiated by others. Combinations of these signs have highly developed minds; they are imaginative and jumpy and think and talk a lot. At worst their lives are a Tower of Babel. At best they are adaptable and ready creatures who can assimilate one kind of experience and enjoy it while anticipating coming changes.

HOW TO APPROXIMATE YOUR RISING SIGN

Apart from the month and day of birth, the exact *time* of birth is another vital factor in the determination of an accurate horoscope. Not only do the planets move with great speed, but one must know how far the Earth has turned during the day. That way you can determine exactly where the planets are located with respect to the precise birthplace of an individual. This makes *your* horoscope *your* horoscope. In addition to these factors, another grid is laid upon that of the Zodiac and the planets: the houses. After all three have been considered, specific planetary relationships can be measured and analyzed in accordance with certain ordered procedures. It is the skillful translation of all this complex astrological language that a serious astrologer strives for in his attempt at coherent astrological synthesis. Keep this in mind.

The horoscope sets up a kind of framework around which the life of an individual grows like wild ivy, this way and that, weaving its way around the trellis of the natal positions of the planets. The year of birth tells us the positions of the distant, slow-moving planets like Jupiter, Saturn, Uranus and Pluto. The month of birth indicates the Sun sign, or birth sign as it is commonly called, as well as indicating the positions of the rapidly moving planets like Venus, Mercury and Mars. The day of birth locates the position of our Moon, and the moment of birth determines the houses through what is called the Ascendant, or Rising Sign.

As the Earth rotates on its axis once every 24 hours, each one of the twelve signs of the Zodiac appears to be "rising" on the horizon, with a new one appearing about every two hours. Actually it is the turning of the Earth that exposes each sign to view, but you will remember that in much of our astrological work we are discussing "apparent" motion. This *Rising Sign* marks the Ascendant and it colors the whole orientation of a horoscope. It indicates the sign governing the first house of the chart, and will thus determine which signs will govern all the other houses. The idea is a bit complicated at first, and we needn't dwell on complications in this introduction, but if you can imagine two color wheels with twelve divisions superimposed upon each other, one moving slowly and the other remaining still, you will have some idea of how the signs keep shifting the "color" of the houses as the Rising Sign continues to change every two hours.

The important point is that the birth chart, or horoscope, actually does define specific factors of a person's makeup. It contains a picture of being, much the way the nucleus of a tiny cell contains the potential for an entire elephant, or a packet of seeds contains a rosebush. If there were no order or continuity to the world, we could plant roses and get elephants. This same order that gives continuous flow to our lives often annoys people if it threatens to determine too much of their lives. We must grow from what we were planted, and there's no reason why we can't do that magnificently. It's all there in the horoscope. Where there is limitation, there is breakthrough; where there is crisis, there is transformation. Accurate analysis of a horoscope can help you find these points of breakthrough and transformation, and it requires knowledge of subtleties and distinctions that demand skillful judgment in order to solve even the simplest kind of personal question.

It is still quite possible, however, to draw some conclusions based upon the sign occupied by the Sun alone. In fact, if you're just being introduced to this vast subject, you're better off keeping it simple. Otherwise it seems like an impossible jumble, much like trying to read a novel in a foreign language without knowing the basic vocabulary. As with anything else, you can progress in your appreciation and understanding of astrology in direct proportion to your interest. To become really good at it requires study, experience, patience and above all—and maybe simplest of all—a fundamental understanding of what is actually going on right up there in the sky over your head. It is a vital living process you can observe, contemplate and ultimately understand. You can start by observing sunrise, or sunset, or even the full Moon.

In fact you can do a simple experiment after reading this introduction. You can erect a rough chart by following the simple procedure below:

1. Draw a circle with twelve equal segments.

2. Starting at what would be the nine o'clock position on a clock, number the segments, or houses, from 1 to 12 in a *counterclockwise direction*.

3. Label house number 1 in the following way: 4 A.M.-6 A.M.

4. In a counterclockwise direction, label the rest of the houses: 2 A.M.-4 A.M., MIDNIGHT-2 A.M., 10 P.M-MIDNIGHT, 8 P.M.-10 P.M., 6 P.M.-8 P.M., 4 P.M.-6 P.M., 2 P.M.-4 P.M., NOON-2 P.M., 10 A.M.-NOON, 8 A.M.-10 A.M., and 6 A.M.-8 A.M.

5. Now find out what time you were born and place the sun in the appropriate house.

6. Label the edge of that house with your Sun sign. You now have a description of your basic character and your fundamental drives. You can also see in what areas of life on Earth you will be most likely to focus your constant energy and center your activity.

7. If you are really feeling ambitious, label the rest of the houses with the signs, starting with your Sun sign, in order, still in a *counterclockwise direction*. When you get to Pisces, start over with Aries and keep going until you reach the house behind the Sun.

8. Look to house number 1. The sign that you have now labeled and attached to house number 1 is your Rising sign. It will color your self-image, outlook, physical constitution, early life and whole orientation to life. Of course this is a mere approximation, since there are many complicated calculations that must be made with respect to adjustments for birth time, but if you read descriptions of the sign preceding and the sign following the one you have calculated in the above manner, you may be able to identify yourself better. In any case, when you get through labeling all the houses, your drawing should look something like this:

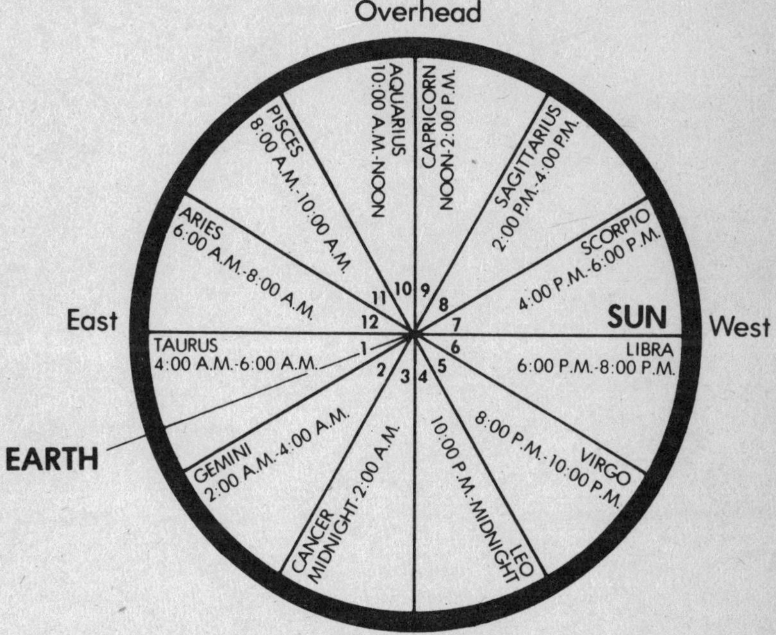

Basic chart illustrating the position of the Sun in Scorpio, with the Ascendant Taurus as the Rising Sign.

This individual was born at 5:15 P.M. on October 31 in New York City. The Sun is in Scorpio and is found in the 7th house. The Rising sign, or the sign governing house number 1, is Taurus, so this person is a blend of Scorpio and Taurus.

Any further calculation would necessitate that you look in an ephemeris, or table of planetary motion, for the positions of the rest of the planets for your particular birth year. But we will take the time to define briefly all the known planets of our Solar System and the Sun to acquaint you with some more of the astrological vocabulary that you will be meeting again and again. (See page 21 for a full explanation of the Moon in all the Signs.)

THE PLANETS AND SIGNS THEY RULE

The signs of the Zodiac are linked to the planets in the following way. Each sign is governed or ruled by one or more planets. No matter where the planets are located in the sky at any given moment, they still rule their respective signs, and when they travel through the signs they rule, they have special dignity and their effects are stronger.

Following is a list of the planets and the signs they rule. After looking at the list, go back over the definitions of the planets and see if you can determine how the planet ruling *your* Sun sign has affected your life.

SIGNS	RULING PLANETS
Aries	Mars, Pluto
Taurus	Venus
Gemini	Mercury
Cancer	Moon
Leo	Sun
Virgo	Mercury
Libra	Venus
Scorpio	Mars, Pluto
Sagittarius	Jupiter
Capricorn	Saturn
Aquarius	Saturn, Uranus
Pisces	Jupiter, Neptune

THE PLANETS
OF THE
SOLAR SYSTEM

Here are the planets of the Solar System. They all travel around the Sun at different speeds and different distances. Taken with the Sun, they all distribute individual intelligence and ability throughout the entire chart.

The planets modify the influence of the Sun in a chart according to their own particular natures, strengths and positions. Their positions must be calculated for each year and day, and their function and expression in a horoscope will change as they move from one area of the Zodiac to another.

Following, you will find brief statements of their pure meanings.

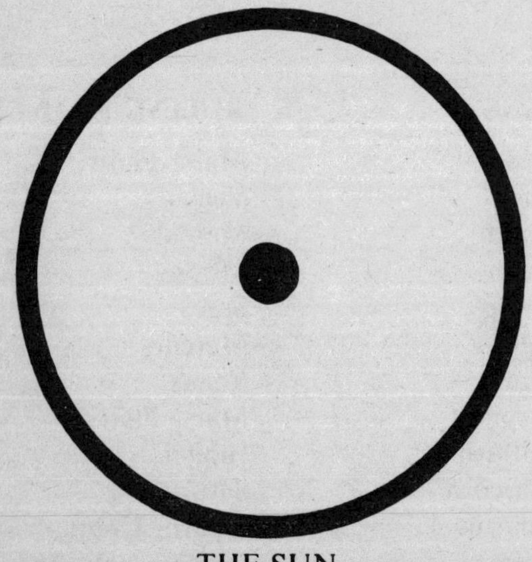

THE SUN

SUN

This is the center of existence. Around this flaming sphere all the planets revolve in endless orbits. Our star is constantly sending out its beams of light and energy without which no life on Earth would be possible. In astrology it symbolizes everything we are trying to become, the center around which all of our activity in life will always revolve. It is the symbol of our basic nature and describes the natural and constant thread that runs through everything that we do from birth to death on this planet.

To early astrologers, the sun seemed to be another planet because it crossed the heavens every day, just like the rest of the bodies in the sky.

It is the only star near enough to be seen well—it is, in fact, a dwarf star. Approximately 860,000 miles in diameter, it is about ten times as wide as the giant planet Jupiter. The next nearest star is nearly 300,000 times as far away, and if the Sun were located as far away as most of the bright stars, it would be too faint to be seen without a telescope.

Everything in the horoscope ultimately revolves around this singular body. Although other forces may be prominent in the charts of some individuals, still the Sun is the total nucleus of being and symbolizes the complete potential of every human being alive. It is vitality and the life force. Your whole essence comes from the position of the Sun.

You are always trying to express the Sun according to its position by house and sign. Possibility for all development is found in the Sun, and it marks the fundamental character of your personal radiations all around you.

It is the symbol of strength, vigor, wisdom, dignity, ardor and generosity, and the ability for a person to function as a mature individual. It is also a creative force in society. It is consciousness of the gift of life.

The underdeveloped solar nature is arrogant, pushy, undependable and proud, and is constantly using force.

MERCURY

Mercury is the planet closest to the Sun. It races around our star, gathering information and translating it to the rest of the system. Mercury represents your capacity to understand the desires of your own will and to translate those desires into action.

In other words it is the planet of Mind and the power of communication. Through Mercury we develop an ability to think, write, speak and observe—to become aware of the world around us. It colors our attitudes and vision of the world, as well as our capacity to communicate our inner responses to the outside world. Some people who have serious disabilities in their power of verbal communication have often wrongly been described as people lacking intelligence.

Although this planet (and its position in the horoscope) indicates your power to communicate your thoughts and perceptions to the world, intelligence is something deeper. Intelligence is distributed throughout all the planets. It is the relationship of the planets to each other that truly describes what we call intelligence. Mercury rules speaking, language, mathematics, draft and design, students, messengers, young people, offices, teachers and any pursuits where the mind of man has wings.

VENUS

Venus is beauty. It symbolizes the harmony and radiance of a rare
and elusive quality: beauty itself. It is refinement and delicacy,
softness and charm. In astrology it indicates grace, balance and the
aesthetic sense. Where Venus is we see beauty, a gentle drawing in
of energy and the need for satisfaction and completion. It is a special touch that finishes off rough edges. It is sensitivity, and affection, and it is always the place for that other elusive phenomenon:
love. Venus describes our sense of what is beautiful and loving.
Poorly developed, it is vulgar, tasteless and self-indulgent. But its
ideal is the flame of spiritual love—Aphrodite, goddess of love, and
the sweetness and power of personal beauty.

MARS

This is raw, crude energy. The planet next to Earth but outward from the Sun is a fiery red sphere that charges through the horoscope with force and fury. It represents the way you reach out for new adventure and new experience. It is energy and drive, initiative, courage and daring. The power to start something and see it through. It can be thoughtless, cruel and wild, angry and hostile, causing cuts, burns, scalds and wounds. It can stab its way through a chart, or it can be the symbol of healthy spirited adventure, well-channeled constructive power to begin and keep up the drive. If you have trouble starting things, if you lack the get-up-and-go to start the ball rolling, if you lack aggressiveness and self-confidence, chances are there's another planet influencing your Mars. Mars rules soldiers, butchers, surgeons, salesmen—any field that requires daring, bold skill, operational technique or self-promotion.

JUPITER

This is the largest planet of the Solar System. Scientists have recently learned that Jupiter reflects more light than it receives from the Sun. In a sense it is like a star itself. In astrology it rules good luck and good cheer, health, wealth, optimism, happiness, success and joy. It is the symbol of opportunity and always opens the way for new possibilities in your life. It rules exuberance, enthusiasm, wisdom, knowledge, generosity and all forms of expansion in general. It rules actors, statesmen, clerics, professional people, religion, publishing and the distribution of many people over large areas.

Sometimes Jupiter makes you think you deserve everything, and you become sloppy, wasteful, careless and rude, prodigal and lawless, in the illusion that nothing can ever go wrong. Then there is the danger of over-confidence, exaggeration, undependability and over-indulgence.

Jupiter is the minimization of limitation and the emphasis on spirituality and potential. It is the thirst for knowledge and higher learning.

SATURN

Saturn circles our system in dark splendor with its mysterious rings, forcing us to be awakened to whatever we have neglected in the past. It will present real puzzles and problems to be solved, causing delays, obstacles and hindrances. By doing so, Saturn stirs our own sensitivity to those areas where we are laziest.

Here we must patiently develop *method,* and only through painstaking effort can our ends be achieved. It brings order to a horoscope and imposes reason just where we are feeling least reasonable. By creating limitations and boundary, Saturn shows the consequences of being human and demands that we accept the changing cycles inevitable in human life. Saturn rules time, old age and sobriety. It can bring depression, gloom, jealousy and greed, or serious acceptance of responsibilities out of which success will develop. With Saturn there is nothing to do but face facts. It rules laborers, stones, granite, rocks and crystals of all kinds.

The Outer Planets

The following three are the outer planets. They liberate human beings from cultural conditioning, and in that sense are the law breakers. In early times it was thought that Saturn was the last planet of the system—the outer limit beyond which we could never go. The discovery of the next three planets ushered in new phases of human history, revolution and technology.

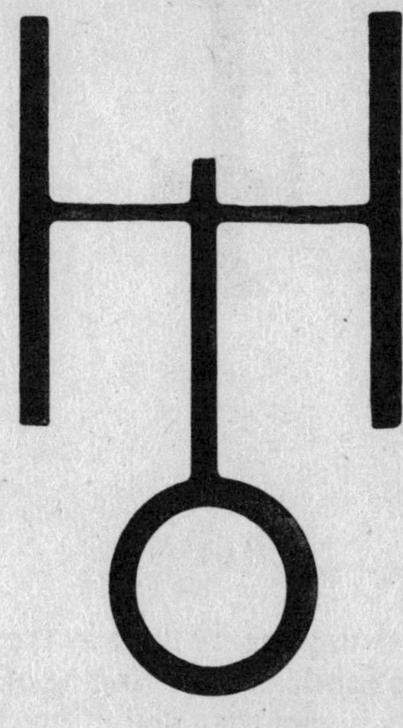

URANUS

Uranus rules unexpected change, upheaval, revolution. It is the symbol of total independence and asserts the freedom of an individual from all restriction and restraint. It is a breakthrough planet and indicates talent, originality and genius in a horoscope. It usually causes last-minute reversals and changes of plan, unwanted separations, accidents, catastrophes and eccentric behavior. It can add irrational rebelliousness and perverse bohemianism to a personality or a streak of unaffected brilliance in science and art. It rules technology, aviation and all forms of electrical and electronic advancement. It governs great leaps forward and topsy-turvy situations, and *always* turns things around at the last minute. Its effects are difficult to ever really predict, since it rules sudden last-minute decisions and events that come like lightning out of the blue.

NEPTUNE

Neptune dissolves existing reality the way the sea erodes the cliffs beside it. Its effects are subtle like the ringing of a buoy's bell in the fog. It suggests a reality higher than definition can usually describe. It awakens a sense of higher responsibility often causing guilt, worry, anxieties or delusions. Neptune is associated with all forms of escape and can make things seem a certain way so convincingly that you are absolutely sure of something that eventually turns out to be quite different.

It is the planet of illusion and therefore governs the invisible realms that lie beyond our ordinary minds, beyond our simple factual ability to prove what is "real." Treachery, deceit, disillusionment and disappointment are linked to Neptune. It describes a vague reality that promises eternity and the divine, yet in a manner so complex that we cannot really fathom it at all. At its worst Neptune is a cheap intoxicant; at its best it is the poetry, music and inspiration of the higher planes of spiritual love. It has dominion over movies, photographs and much of the arts.

PLUTO

Pluto lies at the outpost of our system and therefore rules finality in a horoscope—the final closing of chapters in your life, the passing of major milestones and points of development from which there is no return. It is a final wipeout, a closeout, an evacuation. It is a distant, subtle but powerful catalyst in all transformations that occur. It creates, destroys, then recreates. Sometimes Pluto starts its influence with a minor event or insignificant incident that might even go unnoticed. Slowly but surely, little by little, everything changes, until at last there has been a total transformation in the area of your life where Pluto has been operating. It rules mass thinking and the trends that society first rejects, then adopts and finally outgrows.

Pluto rules the dead and the underworld—all the powerful forces of creation and destruction that go on all the time beneath, around and above us. It can bring a lust for power with strong obsessions.

It is the planet that rules the metamorphoses of the caterpillar into a butterfly, for it symbolizes the capacity to change totally and forever a person's life style, way of thought and behavior.

FAMOUS PERSONALITIES

ARIES: Hans Christian Andersen, Pearl Bailey, Marlon Brando, Wernher Von Braun, Charlie Chaplin, Joan Crawford, Da Vinci, Bette Davis, Doris Day, W. C. Fields, Alec Guinness, Adolf Hitler, William Holden, Thomas Jefferson, Nikita Khrushchev, Elton John, Arturo Toscanini, J. P. Morgan, Paul Robeson, Gloria Steinem, Lowell Thomas, Vincent van Gogh, Tennessee Williams

TAURUS: Fred Astaire, Charlote Brontë, Carol Burnett, Irving Berlin, Bing Crosby, Salvador Dali, Tchaikovsky, Queen Elizabeth II, Duke Ellington, Ella Fitzgerald, Henry Fonda, Sigmund Freud, Orson Welles, Joe Louis, Lenin, Karl Marx, Golda Meir, Eva Peron, Bertrand Russell, Shakespeare, Kate Smith, Benjamin Spock, Barbra Streisand, Shirley Temple, Harry Truman

GEMINI: Mikhail Baryshnikov, Boy George, Igor Stravinsky, Carlos Chavez, Walt Whitman, Bob Dylan, Ralph Waldo Emerson, Judy Garland, Paul Gauguin, Allen Ginsberg, Benny Goodman, Bob Hope, Burl Ives, John F. Kennedy, Peggy Lee, Marilyn Monroe, Joe Namath, Cole Porter, Laurence Olivier, Harriet Beecher Stowe, Queen Victoria, John Wayne, Frank Lloyd Wright

CANCER: "Dear Abby," David Brinkley, Yul Brynner, Pearl Buck, Marc Chagall, Jack Dempsey, Mildred (Babe) Zaharias, Mary Baker Eddy, Henry VIII, John Glenn, Ernest Hemingway, Lena Horne, Oscar Hammerstein, Helen Keller, Ann Landers, George Orwell, Nancy Reagan, Rembrandt, Richard Rodgers, Ginger Rogers, Rubens, Jean-Paul Sartre, O. J. Simpson

LEO: Neil Armstrong, Russell Baker, James Baldwin, Emily Brontë, Wilt Chamberlain, Julia Child, Cecil B. De Mille, Ogden Nash, Amelia Earhart, Edna Ferber, Arthur Goldberg, Dag Hammarskjöld, Alfred Hitchcock, Mick Jagger, George Meany, George Bernard Shaw, Napoleon, Jacqueline Onassis, Henry Ford, Francis Scott Key, Andy Warhol, Mae West, Orville Wright

VIRGO: Ingrid Bergman, Warren Burger, Maurice Chevalier, Agatha Christie, Sean Connery, Lafayette, Peter Falk, Greta Garbo, Althea Gibson, Arthur Godfrey, Goethe, Buddy Hackett, Michael Jackson, Lyndon Johnson, D. H. Lawrence, Sophia Loren, Grandma Moses, Arnold Palmer, Queen Elizabeth I, Walter Reuther, Peter Sellers, Lily Tomlin, George Wallace

LIBRA: Brigitte Bardot, Art Buchwald, Truman Capote, Dwight D. Eisenhower, William Faulkner, F. Scott Fitzgerald, Gandhi, George Gershwin, Micky Mantle, Helen Hayes, Vladimir Horowitz, Doris Lessing, Martina Navratalova, Eugene O'Neill, Luciano Pavarotti, Emily Post, Eleanor Roosevelt, Bruce Springsteen, Margaret Thatcher, Gore Vidal, Barbara Walters, Oscar Wilde

SCORPIO: Vivien Leigh, Richard Burton, Art Carney, Johnny Carson, Billy Graham, Grace Kelly, Walter Cronkite, Marie Curie, Charles de Gaulle, Linda Evans, Indira Gandhi, Theodore Roosevelt, Rock Hudson, Katherine Hepburn, Robert F. Kennedy, Billie Jean King, Martin Luther, Georgia O'Keeffe, Pablo Picasso, Jonas Salk, Alan Shepard, Robert Louis Stevenson

SAGITTARIUS: Jane Austen, Louisa May Alcott, Woody Allen, Beethoven, Willy Brandt, Mary Martin, William F. Buckley, Maria Callas, Winston Churchill, Noel Coward, Emily Dickinson, Walt Disney, Benjamin Disraeli, James Doolittle, Kirk Douglas, Chet Huntley, Jane Fonda, Chris Evert Lloyd, Margaret Mead, Charles Schulz, John Milton, Frank Sinatra, Steven Spielberg

CAPRICORN: Muhammad Ali, Isaac Asimov, Pablo Casals, Dizzy Dean, Marlene Dietrich, James Farmer, Ava Gardner, Barry Goldwater, Cary Grant, J. Edgar Hoover, Howard Hughes, Joan of Arc, Gypsy Rose Lee, Martin Luther King, Jr., Rudyard Kipling, Mao Tse-tung, Richard Nixon, Gamal Nasser, Louis Pasteur, Albert Schweitzer, Stalin, Benjamin Franklin, Elvis Presley

AQUARIUS: Marian Anderson, Susan B. Anthony, Jack Benny, Charles Darwin, Charles Dickens, Thomas Edison, John Barrymore, Clark Gable, Jascha Heifetz, Abraham Lincoln, John McEnroe, Yehudi Menuhin, Mozart, Jack Nicklaus, Ronald Reagan, Jackie Robinson, Norman Rockwell, Franklin D. Roosevelt, Gertrude Stein, Charles Lindbergh, Margaret Truman

PISCES: Edward Albee, Harry Belafonte, Alexander Graham Bell, Frank Borman, Chopin, Adelle Davis, Albert Einstein, Jackie Gleason, Winslow Homer, Edward M. Kennedy, Victor Hugo, Mike Mansfield, Michelangelo, Edna St. Vincent Millay, Liza Minelli, John Steinbeck, Linus Pauling, Ravel, Diana Ross, William Shirer, Elizabeth Taylor, George Washington

PISCES

CHARACTER ANALYSIS

Quite often people born under the sign of Pisces are rather dreamy in their ways. Generally speaking, they are responsive and impressionable. Theirs is a sensitive nature. They usually approach life in serious, yet somewhat unrealistic way. The sign of Pisces—the two fish—indicates a double nature. Indeed, there often seems to be more to someone born under this twelfth sign of the zodiac than meets the eye. His behavior is often a riddle to others. He may seem secretive about the smallest, most unimportant things, yet open in important matters when perhaps he should not be. Chances are he is a gentle and kind person. He would never do anything that would injure someone's feelings. Although he can be purposeful when it is necessary, he is apt to impress some as being unable to grapple with some of the routine problems of life. He can appear to be a bit helpless and lacking in self-confidence. He may not always speak up when he should. Uncertain, he may take an extraordinarily long time to make up his mind about the smallest thing.

People generally like the person born under Pisces. He can be trusted; he is conscientious in all that he undertakes. Others can depend on him no matter what the situation. His word is usually his bond. Likeable and pleasant, others usually feel comfortable when in his company. He is a person who likes peace and quiet. His personality is usually such that others feel calm and even-tempered when in his presence. Because he is so easy-going, opportunists usually try to take advantage of his good nature. He is not a fighter by nature; if others abuse his generosity and openness, he is not likely to put up a fight. The Piscean is usually a very sensitive person. His feelings are easily injured. Sometimes he takes offense when none is intended.

The person born under the sign of Pisces is usually methodical in his work. He may seem a bit lazy to others; but, in fact, he will live up to his responsibilities at home or at work if he sees that it is necessary for keeping peace and order. He usually takes life as it comes. He doesn't generally complain. He adapts himself to what ever situation he finds himself in.

The Piscean is not afraid of changes. In fact, he welcomes them, especially if others can benefit from them. Anything that he feels will make the world a better place in which to live is something he will support.

The Piscean is a person who sympathizes readily with people who are in dire straights. He is always prepared to help someone in need if he can. In a rather uncanny way, he seems to know how other people are feeling before they say anything. He is very perceptive and is familiar with the problems of the world. He is generally imaginative, and his thoughts are usually concerned with bettering the world situation. However, he tends to be too much of a dreamer to put his plans and hopes into action. He lacks that driving force to turn plans into reality.

When he does go about finishing up his work and completing his plans, he can usually make an important contribution to others. He is generous, sometimes to a fault. He thinks more of others, at times, than he does of himself. He can be quite self-sacrificing. In general, though, he seldom gets around to realizing his plans. He's too much of a dreamer, and is afraid of encountering frustration once he commits himself to action

The person born under this sign is usually interested in the arts. In the world of music, painting, or poetry, he can lose himself to his heart's content and forget about the hard realities of life. Mysterious things attract him. Unknown realms seem to lure him on; at the same time this sort of interest clashes with his basic personality, making it rather difficult for him to adjust to the facts of life. He is the kind of a person who when he takes up something goes all the way. He is very susceptible. Subjects that interest him have a complete hold on him until he knows them inside-out. Theories, beliefs, and the like interest him greatly. While he may know a great deal about them, he may be somewhat saddened, for he feels that his knowledge cuts him off from others. Some Piceans feel superior in their intellectual isolation.

The person born under this sign is sometimes moody. He can go from feeling high to low in a remarkably short time if he isn't careful. At times he feels rather sorry for himself; he feels that his talents are not really appreciated. The strong Piscean, however, knows how to put such thoughts out of his mind and to forge ahead. Sometimes he can inspire others better than he can inspire himself. He is somewhat afraid of conflict and frustration and will do his best to avoid them. When forced to face harsh reality, he sometimes finds himself at loose ends. It is too much for him. He would rather hear a pleasant lie than the cold, hard truth. If things become too difficult to manage, he may try to neglect his responsibilities. He feels good when he is in the company of strong, purposeful people. He is not the kind of person who does very well alone. When others encourage him, he may try harder to realize his plans.

Health

The average Piscean may not look very strong or healthy. However, his constitution is usually quite good and he can recover from an illness fairly quick. In general, his health is good; the great out of doors is likely to be good for him. He needs plenty of sunshine and fresh air in order to feel fit. He should also see to it that he gets plenty of exercise; on the other hand, he should not do anything that might cause him to strain himself. Quite often the person born under the sign of Pisces looks younger than he really is.

The average Piscean is rather slim and delicate. Many of the world's best dancers are born under this sign. His eyes and his feet are usually the weak points of his anatomy. He should do what he can to guard against chills and cold.

It is important that the Piscean be moderate in his behavior. Overindulgence is apt to be bad for his constitution. A well-balanced diet should help him to keep in shape. Plenty of green vegetables and fresh fruit are necessary. The person born under this sign may have a weakness for anything that stimulated him physically. He will have to watch out that he does not abuse his good health through the use of alcohol or drugs. The Piscean who knows what is good for him will live to a ripe old age, generally. Some Pisceans are rather stubborn, however, and do the things that please them most without giving much thought to the consequences. If he does become addicted to drugs or to alcohol, he may have a difficult time trying to break the habit. His will is often not very strong. Sometimes he likes others to feel sorry for him, so he does his best to appear pitiful and vicitimized.

Occupation

The Piscean does well in any kind of work that involves helping others. This is his main interest in life. He likes doing what he can for others. The sick and needy can always depend on him for help. Quite often Pisces people make good doctors, psychiatrists, teachers, and accountants. Social work is another profession that often attracts someone born under this sign. On the whole, he is a sympathetic person. He often knows what is wrong with someone before the person knows it himself. Others often turn to him when in trouble and in need of advice. He can easily put himself in someone else's place. He has a certain charm, generally, and may do well in diplomatic work.

The Piscean's strong point is his ability to understand others—his insight into the problems of others. When choosing a job or career, he should try to make use of this gift that he has.

The average Piscean is generally quite flexible. He can take on many different roles if need be. There are two sides to his nature; he usually has many interests. He can move in any direction with equal skill. Sometimes he does well in the world of film or theater. He often has remarkable dramatic talents. This is usually because of his flexible personality. He understands others and knows how to express himself as if he is the character he portrays. Sometimes he does well as a playwright.

Whatever he does, the Piscean is happiest if he has a chance to exercise his many interests. He likes a lot of variety in his work. If he finds the position that is cut out for his talents, he is usually a very happy person. In the right job, he is not afraid of encountering frustration or opposition for he is well equipped to deal with it.

Work that requires a great deal of concentration and bother about small details seldom interests him. However, he can apply himself to anything that completely absorbs his imagination and spirit. He is the kind of worker who can always be depended on to do his best. He is methodical and industrious. At times, he is clever enough to think up a way of cutting his work time in half, much to the surprise of those who work with him. He is generally well liked by his co-workers. He is easy to get along with and always ready to listen to another's problems or troubles.

The weaker sort of Piscean can be quite lazy at times. As soon as he meets with the slightest upset he is ready to call it quits. He does not have much faith in himself or what he can do. Confusion completely ruins him—he can become disorganized when confronted with frustration. He may have difficulty in putting his thoughts in order.

The Piscean is a bit of a sensualist. He likes to pamper himself. He likes his comfort. He is fond of material things which make him feel good. Money does not interest him for what it is but for what it can do. He is fond of the security that money can bring. Many Pisceans are a bit afraid of growing old, and they want to see to it that they have a nest-egg they can draw on when they become senior citizens. If he does not have as much money as he thinks he needs, he may worry about it constantly. In fact, he may worry about it so much that it prevents him from making the headway he so desperately desires. When he becomes involved with others and tries to help them solve their problems he may become more generous than he should. He sometimes spends money to help others when he should really save it to help himself. Chances are that the average Piscean will never become a millionaire. However, this does not bother him, as long as he has enough money to adequately provide for himself and those he cares for. If he does come into a lot of money unexpectedly, opportunists will probably find a way to take it away from him. He is the kind of person who finds it difficult to say no, especially if someone is in dire need.

Sometimes the average Piscean does not really know what he wants in life. He may find it difficult to direct himself toward any one particular goal. However, once he finds his niche in life, he can go far on sheer will and determination. The strong Piscean has a good sense of direction and will work hard to attain those things he desires. Some people born under this sign are rather lucky and attain financial success without working hard for it. The well-heeled Piscean would be wise to invest his money in real estate or something secure. He should avoid risks as much as possible.

Some Pisceans make good businessmen, even though they may not have a very competitive nature. Somehow or other, they manage to hold their own through determination. In a partnership situation the Piscean can do well, if his partner has those business qualities he lacks.

Home and Family

The Piscean is very susceptible to his environment. If he is to succeed, he has to be in an environment that encourages success. He likes a home where he can relax in comfort—a place where he can let his imagination roam. Home and family are important to the Piscean who wants to get far in life. It gives him the kind of stability he needs.

The Pisces person is a home-lover by nature. Nothing pleases him as much as the warm and peaceful atmosphere of home. His tastes are generally simple and plain. Comfort is important. His home may contain some art objects that mean a lot to him. Art plays an important part in his life. At times it means more to him than so-called practical things. He likes a home that is neat and tidy. A home in the country would please him very much. He likes the wide open spaces—a place where he can wander about freely without having to worry about traffic or crowds. The countryside gives him a chance to relax and to let his imagination run free.

People enjoy visiting the Pisces man or woman because he or she knows how to make guests feel at home. The Piscean is a good conversationalist. When others talk about themselves, he is never bored, but listens to them carefully, interrupting every now and again to make a helpful suggestion.

He is a romantic kind of person. Marriage appeals to him in that it gives him a chance to explore the romantic side of his nature. Both men and women born under this sign are rather fond of domestic life and do what they can to have a happy home.

Social Relationships

The Piscean is perhaps the most sensitive kind of person in existence. He is very gentle, considerate, and kind. He does not want to hurt others and does what he can to avoid injury to himself. Romance and love mean a great deal to him. In general, he is open and sincere. He does not like people who are mean or petty. He is earnest in expressing his affections.

Most of the time, his standards are pretty high. He is looking for someone who is well-groomed and intelligent; someone who probably has as great an interest in the arts as he does. When he has found the person of his dreams, he may become rather possessive. He is the kind of person who may suspect his loved one of infidelity when he really has no grounds. He easily becomes jealous and this could emotionally destroy him if he is not careful. The happy Piscean is someone who can take a person for what he or she is and not long for perfection; someone who is realistic when looking for a friend or a mate.

Naturally affectionate himself, the average Piscean man likes a woman who is free in expressing herself as far as her affection for him is concerned. He has to be reassured that his loved one really loves him. He likes to be complimented—to be told what a good lover he is. Flattery is music to his ears. His feelings are too sensitive at times, and this may cause him to end an affair. He may imagine he has been slighted when that is not the case at all. The strong Piscean guards against becoming a victim to this sort of illusion. He does what he can to keep his romance alive and healthy.

The weak Piscean does not really know what he wants in romance, and he may stumble from one affair to an other not knowing how to make up his mind.

The dreamy Pisces person often has very high ideals. If he has the right person behind him he is bound to go far. He needs someone who understands his weaknesses as well as his strengths. The Piscean needs love. If he does not have it, his life may seem useless and empty to him.

He can be the dreamy sort of lover, thinking more about the kind of romance he would like to have and doing very little to make this a reality. Alone, he is not very strong, He has little confidence in his thoughts, whims, or fancies. They amuse him and make him feel safe. He is not a strong-willed person as far as character is concerned. He does best when in company of strong people—people who know their own minds; their self-confidence seems to rub off on him. He is an adaptable person and can easily take on the character of the people he associates with. Therefore, it is very important that he mix with the right people. When looking for a mate, he should try to find someone who has those qualities he lacks—someone who is positive-thinking with a firm grip on reality.

LOVE AND MARRIAGE

The Piscean feels deeply. When he gives his love, it usually is for good. He doesn't believe in playing with the affections of others; love is too important to him for that. He must watch out for stronger people. If someone is in love with him and makes definite advances, he may be too weak to resist; he then finds himself in a love affair he neither wished nor willed. At times, the average Piscean may shuttle from one mood to another without warning and this is apt to puzzle his loved one. It is possible for him to be passionate one moment and cool the next—and for no apparent reason. Someone who loves him must learn to accept this. Another thing; it is sometimes difficult for even his most intimate friend to really know how he feels. His lover may feel she has reason to doubt his love even when he professes it. Others find it difficult to know whether or not the Piscean really means what he says, at times.

The intelligent Pisces person takes stock of himself and tries to do something about his weak points. He tries to correct his personality faults and quirks. He may even try to appear tougher than he really is as a sort of protection against people who would like to take advantage of his kind nature. He may fool many—but not the people who really know him. While exhibiting a hard-bitten exterior, he is likely to be as soft as cotton candy inside. The person who loves him will accept him for his faults and good qualities. She will not be put off by his mask of toughness and hard-boiledness.

Home means a lot to the person born under the sign of Pisces. It is a place where he can relax in comfort and be himself without fear of being taken advantage of. The Pisces woman generally makes a good housewife; she likes the domestic life. She keeps things in order. Romance after marriage also means a lot to the average Piscean. He or she is affectionate and warm and likes love to be returned. Pisces makes a very considerate mate—someone who will do all he can to see to it that his partner is comfortable and well-provided for. He is easy to get along with most of the time. The Pisces woman cries readily if she has a disagreement or argument.

Romance and the Pisces Woman

Of all the women of the Zodiac, the Piscean is the most sensitive and the most loving. She is very giving by nature and does what she can to make those she loves happy and content. Marriage means a lot to her. She is sincere and affectionate. The man who wins her is a lucky fellow.

She is usually interested in a sensitive sort of man. Someone who is intelligent and has an understanding and appreciation of the arts. She cannot abide a man who is mean or petty. She likes someone who is expansive and strong, someone she can depend on at all times. She may find it difficult to make up her own mind at times, so it is important for her to have someone who knows what he wants in life, someone she can lean upon and ask for advice when she needs it.

Some Pisces women really don't know what they want in a man and may drift from one romance to another, somewhat in a daze. She is a romantic and may spend her waking hours day-dreaming about the kind of love life she would like to have; but then she may just keep it a dream, a bit afraid to go out and do something about it. She likes her loved one to make a fuss over her; to tell her how lovely and desirable she is. She has to be assured that her man really loves her. Small gifts from time to time and compliments tend to keep her spirits up.

The Pisces woman is rather sensitive and may imagine that someone has insulted her when she has no real reason for thinking so. She can become very jealous at times. If she suspects her lover of being unfaithful, it could mean the end of the relationship. Although her lover may be innocent of the accusation, he may find it impossible to convince his Piscean sweetheart that this is so. The strong Pisces woman acknowledges this weakness she has and does her best to brush imagined jealousy out of her mind.

She is a good wife and likes taking care of things at home. She may not have a good head for figures; she may spend more money than is really necessary. A practical husband can bring her to reason as far as this is concerned.

She loves children and makes a tender and permissive mother. Her tendency is to spoil children. She may give them too much love and attention when a firmer hand is needed. There is always a strong tie between a Pisces mother and her child.

Romance and the Pisces Man

The Pisces man is a romantic. He is sincere in his affections and does not tend to move from one romance to another. He believes in being true to just one woman. He likes an artistic and intelligent woman—someone with whom he can discuss his interests as an equal. He likes a woman who is apt to fuss over him. He likes being flattered even if there is not a grain of truth in what is said. He has to be constantly reassured. He has to have a woman who is kind and considerate someone who is able to put up with his changing moods.

A woman who has a strong character is well-suited to the Piscean man. He must not have someone who is weaker than himself. He is the kind of a man who has to be in love. Without love, he is apt to feel lonely and unwanted. He may try to make up for this by drinking rather heavily or abusing his health in other ways. However, too strong or forceful a woman may be too much for him. He may find it impossible to avoid her advances and may later find himself involved with someone he does not really love.

He likes to know where his loved one is every moment of the day. He can be rather possessive even before marriage. His loved one may find some of his demands rather excessive at times. Jealousy could easily destroy him and his romance. The wise Pisces man knows how to put foolish thoughts out of his head and to trust the woman he loves when he has no reason to do otherwise.

His love is deep. When he marries and settles down, it's usually for good. He makes a faithful husband. He does what he can to provide for his family. A happy, well-run home is important to him and he does what he can to make his wife and children feel loved and needed. Security is also important to him, and he will always do what he can to keep his home together.

Children love him. He may be too easy-going as a father, letting his children do as they please. It is fine if his wife is a bit firmer in handling the offspring, for then they have a chance of turning out well.

Woman—Man

PISCES WOMAN
ARIES MAN

Although it's possible that a Pisces woman could find happiness with a man born under the sign of the Ram, it's uncertain as to how long that happiness would last.

An Arien who has made his mark in the world and is somewhat steadfast in his outlook and attitude could be quite a catch for you. On the other hand, men under this sign are often swift-footed and quick-minded; their industrious mannerisms may fail to impress you, especially if you feel that much of their get-up-and-go often leads nowhere.

When it comes to a fine romance, you want someone with a nice, broad shoulder to lean on. You are likely to find a relationship with someone who doesn't like to stay put for too long somewhat upsetting.

The Arien may have a little trouble in understanding you, too—at least, in the beginning of the relationship. He may find you a bit too shy and moody. Ariens tend to speak their minds; he's liable to criticize you at the drop of a hat.

You may find a man born under this sign too demanding. He may give you the impression that he expects you to be at his constant beck and call. You have a lot of patience at your disposal, and he may try every last bit of it. He is apt to be not as thorough as you in everything he does. In order to achieve success or a goal quickly, he is liable to overlook small but important details—and regret it when it is far too late.

Being married to an Arien does not mean that you'll have a secure and safe life as far as finances are concerned. Not all Ariens are rash with cash, but they lack the sound head you perhaps have for putting away something for that inevitable rainy day. He'll do his best, however, to see that you're adequately provided for—even though his efforts may leave something to be desired as far as you're concerned.

With an Aries man for a mate, you'll find yourself constantly among people. Ariens generally have many friends—and you may not heartily approve of them all. People born under this sign are often more interested in "interesting" people than they are in influential ones. Although there may be a family squabble from time to time, you are stable enough to be able to take it in your stride.

Aries men love children. They make wonderful fathers. Kids take to them like ducks to water. Their quick minds and behavior appeal to the young.

PISCES WOMAN
TAURUS MAN

Some Taurus men are strong and silent. They do all they can to protect and provide for the women they love. The Taurus man will never let you down. He's steady, sturdy, and reliable. He's pretty honest and practical, too. He says what he means and means what he says. He never indulges in deceit and will always put his cards on the table.

The Taurean is a very affectionate man. Being loved, appreciated and understood are very important for his well-being. Like you, he is also looking for peace and security in his life. If you both work toward these goals together, you'll find that they are easily attained.

If you should marry a Taurus man, you can be sure that the wolf will never darken your door. They are notoriously good providers, and do everything they can to make their families comfortable and happy.

He'll appreciate the way you have of making a home warm and inviting. Slippers and pipe, and the evening papers are essential ingredients in making your Taurus husband happy at the end of the workday. Although he may be a big lug of a guy, you'll find that he's pretty fond of gentleness and soft things, If you puff up his pillow and tuck him in at night, he won't complain. He'll eat it up and ask for more.

You probably won't complain about his friends. The Taurean tends to seek out friends who are successful or prominent. You admire people, too, who work hard and achieve what they set out for. It helps to reassure your way of life and the way you look at things.

The Taurus man doesn't care too much for change. He's a stay-at-home of the first-order. Chances are that the house you move into after you're married will be the house you'll live in for the rest of your life.

You'll find that the man born under this sign is easy to get along with. It's unlikely that you'll have many quarrels or arguments.

Although he'll be gentle and tender with you, your Taurus man is far from being a sensitive type. He's a man's man. Chances are he loves sports like fishing and football. He can be earthy, as well as down-to-earth.

Taureans love their children very much but do everything they can not to spoil them. They believe in children staying in their places. They make excellent disciplinarians. Your children will be polite and respectful.

PISCES WOMAN
GEMINI MAN

The Gemini man is quite a catch. Many a woman has set her cap for him and failed to bag him. Generally, Gemini men are intelligent, witty, and outgoing. Many of them tend to be versatile.

On the other hand, some of them seem to lack that sort of common sense that you set so much store in. Their tendencies to start a half-dozen projects, then toss them up in the air out of boredom may do nothing more than exasperate you.

One thing that causes a Twin's mind and affection to wander is a bore, and it is unlikely that an active woman like you would ever allow herself to be accused of being that. The Gemini man who has caught your heart will admire you for your ideas and intellect—perhaps even more than for your home-making talents and good looks.

A strong-willed woman could easily fill the role of rudder for her Gemini's ship-without-a-sail. The intelligent Gemini is often aware of his shortcomings and doesn't mind if someone with better bearings gives him a shove in the right direction—when it's needed. The average Gemini doesn't have serious ego-hangups and will even accept a well-deserved chewing out from his mate or girl friend gracefully.

A successful and serious-minded Gemini could make you a very happy woman, perhaps, if you gave him half the chance. Although he may give you the impression that he has a hole in his head, the Gemini man generally has a good head on his shoulders and can make efficient use of it when he wants. Some of them, who have learned the art of being steadfast, have risen to great heights in their professions. President John F. Kennedy was a Gemini, as was writer Thomas Mann and poet William Butler Yeats.

Once you convince yourself that not all people born under the sign of the Twins are witless grasshoppers, you won't mind dating a few—to test your newborn conviction. If you do wind up walking down the aisle with one, accept the fact that married life with him will mean your taking the bitter with the sweet.

Life with a Gemini man can be more fun than a barrel of clowns. You'll never be allowed to experience a dull moment. Don't leave money matters to him or you'll both wind up behind the eight ball.

Gemini men are always attractive to the opposite sex. You'll perhaps have to allow him an occasional harmless flirt—it will seldom amount to more than that if you're his proper mate.

The Gemini father is a pushover for children. See to it that you keep them in line otherwise they'll be running the house.

PISCES WOMAN
CANCER MAN

The man born under the sign of Cancer may very well be the man after your own heart. Generally, Cancerians are steady people. They are interested in security and practicality. Despite their seemingly grouchy exterior sometimes, men born under the sign of the Crab are rather sensitive and kind individuals. They are almost always hard workers and are very interested in making successes of themselves in business as well as socially. You'll find that his conservative outlook on many things often agrees with yours. He'll be a man on whom you can depend come rain or come shine. He'll never shirk his responsibilities as a provider, and he'll always see to it that his wife and family never want.

Your patience will come in handy if you decide it's a Cancerian you want for a mate. He isn't the type that rushes headlong into romance. He wants to be as sure about love as you do. If after the first couple of months of dating, he suggests that you take a walk with him down lovers' lane, don't jump to the conclusion that he's about to make his "great play." Chances are he'll only hold your hand and seriously observe the stars. Don't let his coolness fool you, though. Beneath his starched reserve lies a very warm heart. He's just not interested in showing off as far as affection is concerned. Don't think his interest is wandering if he doesn't kiss you goodnight at the front door; that just isn't his style. For him, affection should only be displayed for two sets of eyes—yours and his. He's passionate only in private.

He will never step out of line. He's too much of a gentleman for that. When you're all alone with him and there's no chance of you being disturbed or spied upon, he'll pull out an engagement ring (that used to belong to his grandmother) and slip it on your trembling finger.

Speaking of relatives, you'll have to get pretty much used to the fact that Cancerians are overly fond of their mothers. When he says his mother's the most wonderful woman in the world, you'd better agree with him—that is, if you want to become his wife.

He'll always be a faithful husband; Cancerians never pussyfoot around after they've taken that marriage vow. They don't take marriage responsibilities lightly. He'll see to it that everything in the house runs smoothly and that bills are paid promptly—never put aside. He's liable to take all kinds of insurance polices out on his family and property. He'll arrange it so that when retirement time rolls around, you'll both be very well off.

Men under this sign make patient and understanding fathers.

PISCES WOMAN
LEO MAN

To know a man born under the sign of the Lion is not necessarily to love him—even though the temptation may be great. When he fixes most girls with his leonine double-whammy, it causes their hearts to pitter-pat and their minds to cloud over.

You are a little too sensible to allow yourself to be bowled over by a regal strut and a roar. Still, there's no denying that Leo has a way with women—even sensible women like yourself. Once he's swept a girl off her feet, it may be hard for her to scramble upright again. Still, you are no pushover for romantic charm—especially if you feel it's all show.

He'll wine you and dine you in the fanciest places. He'll croon to you under the moon and shower you with diamonds if he can get a hold of them. Still, it would be wise to find out just how long that shower is going to last before consenting to be his wife.

Lions in love are hard to ignore, let alone brush off. Your no's will have a way of nudging him on until he feels he has you completely under his spell. Once mesmerized by this romantic powerhouse, you will most likely find yourself doing things you never dreamed of. Leos can be like vain pussycats when involved romantically. They like to be cuddled, curried, and tickled under the chin. This may not be your cup of tea exactly, still when you're romantically dealing with a man born under the sign of Leo, you'll find yourself doing all kinds of things to make him purr.

Although he may be big and magnanimous while trying to win you, he'll let out a blood-curdling roar if he thinks he's not getting the tender love and care he feels is his due. If you keep him well supplied with affection, you can be sure his eyes will never look for someone else and his heart will never wander.

Leo men often tend to be authoritarian—they are bound to lord it over others in one way or another it seems. If he is the top banana at his firm, he'll most likely do everything he can to stay on top. If he's not number one, he's most likely working on it and will be sitting on the throne before long.

You'll have more security than you can use if he is in a position to support you in the manner to which he feels you should be accustomed. He is apt to be too lavish, though—at least, by your standards.

You'll always have plenty of friends when you have a Leo for a mate. He's a natural-born friend-maker and entertainer. He just loves to let his hair down at parties.

As fathers, Leos tend to spoil their children no end.

PISCES WOMAN
VIRGO MAN

Although the Virgo man may be a bit of a fuss-budget at times, his seriousness and dedication to common sense may help you to overlook his tendency to sometimes be overly critical about minor things.

Virgo men are often quiet, respectable types who set great store in conservative behavior and level-headedness. He'll admire you for your practicality and tenacity, perhaps even more than for your good looks. He's seldom bowled over by a glamour-puss. When he gets his courage up, he turns to a serious and reliable girl for romance. He'll be far from a Valentino while dating. In fact, you may wind up making all the passes. Once he does get his motor running, however, he can be a warm and wonderful fellow—to the right girl.

He's gradual about love. Chances are your romance with him will most likely start out looking like an ordinary friendship. Once he's sure you're no fly-by-night flirt and have no plans of taking him for a ride, he'll open up and spread sunshine all over your heart.

Virgo men tend to marry late in life. He believes in holding out until he's met the right girl. He may not have many names in his little black book; in fact, he may not even have a black book. He's not interested in playing the field, leaving that to men of the more flamboyant signs. The Virgo man is so particular that he may remain romantically inactive for a long period. His girl has to be perfect or it's no go. If you find yourself feeling weak-kneed for a Virgo, do your best to convince him that perfection is not so important when it comes to love; help him to realize that he's missing out on a great deal by not considering the near-perfect or whatever it is you consider yourself to be. With your sure-fire perseverance, you will most likely be able to make him listen to reason and he'll wind up reciprocating your romantic interests.

The Virgo man is no block of ice. He'll respond to what he feels to be the right feminine flame. Once your love-life with a Virgo man starts to bubble, don't give it a chance to fall flat. You may never have a second chance at winning his heart.

If you should ever have a falling out with him, forget about patching it up. He'd prefer to let the pieces lie scattered. Once married, though, he'll stay that way—even if it hurts. He's too conscientious to try to back out of a legal deal of any sort.

The Virgo man is as neat as a pin. He's thumbs down on sloppy housekeeping. Keep everything bright, neat, and shiny, and that goes for the children, too, at least by the time he gets home from work. Chocolate-coated kisses from Daddy's little girl go over like a lead balloon with him.

PISCES WOMAN
LIBRA MAN

You are apt to find men born under the sign of Libra too wrapped up in their own private dreams to be really interesting as far as love and romance are concerned. Quite often, he is a difficult person to bring back down to earth; it is hard for him to face reality at times. Although he may be very cautious about weighing both sides of an argument, he may never really come to a reasonable decision about anything. Decision-making is something that often makes the Libra man uncomfortable; he'd rather leave that job to someone else. Don't ask him why for he probably doesn't know himself.

Qualities such as permanence and constancy are important to you in a love relationship. The Libra man may be quite a puzzlement for you. One moment he comes on hard and strong with declarations of his love; the next moment you find he's left you like yesterday's mashed potatoes. It does no good to wonder what went wrong. Chances are nothing, really. It's just one of Libra's strange ways.

He is not exactly what you would call an ambitious person; you are perhaps looking for a mate or friend with more drive and fidelity. You are the sort of person who is interested in getting ahead—in making some headway in the areas that interest you; the Libran is often contented just to drift along. He does have drive, however, but it's not the long-range kind. It is not that he's shiftless or lazy. He's interested in material things; he appreciates luxuries and the like, but he may not be willing to work hard enough to obtain them. Beauty and harmony interest him. He'll dedicate a lot of time to arranging things so that they are aesthetically pleasing. It would be difficult to accuse the Libra man of being practical; nine times out of ten, he isn't.

If you do begin a relationship with a man born under this sign, you will have to coax him now and again to face various situations in a realistic manner. You'll have your hands full, that's for sure. But if you love him, you'll undoubtedly do your best to understand him—no matter how difficult this may be.

If you take up with a Libra man, either temporarily or permanently, you'd better take over the task of managing his money. Often he has little understanding of financial matters; he tends to spend without thinking, following his whims.

PISCES WOMAN
SCORPIO MAN

Some people have a hard time understanding the man born under the sign of Scorpio; few, however, are able to resist his fiery charm. When angered, he can act like an overturned wasps' nest; his sting can leave an almost permanent mark. If you find yourself interested in the Scorpio man, you'd better learn how to keep on his good side.

The Scorpio man can be quite blunt when he chooses; at times, he may seem rather hard-hearted. He can be touchy every now and then, and this is apt to get on your nerves after a while. When you feel like you can't take it anymore, you'd better tiptoe away from the scene rather than chance an explosive confrontation. He's capable of giving you a sounding-out that will make you pack your bags and go back to Mother—for good.

If he finds fault with you, he'll let you know. He's liable to misinterpret your patience and think it a sign of indifference. Still and all, you are the kind of woman who can adapt to almost any sort of relationship or circumstance if you put your heart and mind to it.

Scorpio men are all quite perceptive and intelligent. In some respects, they know how to use their brains more effectively than most. They believe in winning, in whatever they do; second place holds no interest for them. In business, they usually achieve the position they want through drive and use of intellect.

Your interest in home-life is not likely to be shared by him. No matter how comfortable you've managed to make the house, it will have very little influence on him with regard to making him aware of his family responsibilities. He does not like to be tied down, generally, and would rather be out on the battlefield of life, belting away at what he feels to be a just and worthy cause. Don't try to keep the homefires burning too brightly while you wait for him to come home from work—you may just run out of firewood.

The Scorpio man is passionate in all things—including love. Most women are easily attracted to him, and you are perhaps no exception. Those who allow themselves to be swept off their feet by a Scorpio man, shortly find that they're dealing with a carton of romantic fireworks. The Scorpio man is passionate with a capital

P, make no mistake about that. Some women may find that he's just too love-happy, but that's their problem.

Scorpio men are straight to the point. They can be as sharp as a razor blade and just as cutting to anyone that crosses them.

Scorpio fathers like large families, generally.

PISCES WOMAN
SAGITTARIUS MAN

The woman who has set her cap for a man born under the sign of Sagittarius may have to apply an awful amount of strategy before she can get him to drop down on bended knee. Although some Sagittarians may be marriage-shy, they're not ones to skitter away from romance. A high-spirited woman may find a relationship with a Sagittarian—whether a fling or "the real thing"—a very enjoyable experience.

As a rule, Sagittarians are bright, happy, and healthy people. They have a strong sense of fair play. Often they're a source of inspiration to others. They're full of ideas and drive.

You'll be taken by the Sagittarian's infectious grin and his light-hearted, friendly nature. If you do wind up being the woman in his life, you'll find that he's apt to treat you more like a buddy than the love of his life. It's just his way. Sagittarians are often chummy instead of romantic.

You'll admire his broadmindedness in most matters—including those of the heart. If, while dating you, he claims that he still wants to play the field, he'll expect you to enjoy the same liberty. Once he's promised to love, honor, and obey, however, he does just that. Marriage for him, once he's taken that big step, is very serious business.

A woman who has a keen imagination and a great love of freedom will not be disappointed if she does tie up with a Sagittarian. The Sagittarius man is often quick-witted. Men of this sign have a genuine interest in equality. They hate prejudice and injustice.

If he does insist on a night out with the boys once a week, he won't scowl if you decide to let him shift for himself in the kitchen once a week while you pursue some of your own interests. He believes in fairness.

He's not much of a homebody. Quite often he's occupied with far away places either in his dreams or in reality. He enjoys—just as you do—being on the go or on the move. He's got ants in his pants and refuses to sit still for long stretches at a time. Humdrum routine—especially at home—bores him. At the drop of a hat, he may ask you to whip off your apron and dine out for a change. He likes surprising people. He'll take great pride in showing you off to his friends. He'll always be a considerate mate; he will never embarrass or disappoint you intentionally.

He's very tolerant when it comes to friends, and you'll most likely spend a lot of time entertaining people.

Sagittarians become interested in their children when they're out of the baby stage.

PISCES WOMAN
CAPRICORN MAN

A with-it girl like you is likely to find the average Capricorn man a bit of a drag. The man born under the sign of the Goat is often a closed person and difficult to get to know. Even if you do get to know him, you may not find him very interesting.

In romance, Capricorn men are a little on the rusty side. You'll probably have to make all the passes.

You may find his plodding manner irritating and his conservative, traditional ways downright maddening. He's not one to take chances on anything. "If it was good enough for my father, it's good enough for me" may be his motto. He follows a way that is tried and true. Whenever adventure rears its tantalizing head, the Goat will turn the other way; he's just not interested.

He may be just as ambitious as you are—perhaps even more so—but his ways of accomplishing his aims are more subterranean or, at least, seem so. He operates from the background a good deal of the time. At a gathering you may never even notice him, but he's there, taking in everything, sizing everyone up, planning his next careful move.

Although Capricorns may be intellectual to a degree, it is not generally the kind of intelligence you appreciate. He may not be as quick or as bright as you; it may take him ages to understand a simple joke.

If you do decide to take up with a man born under this sign, you should be pretty good in the "cheering up" department. The Capricorn man often acts as though he's constantly being followed by a cloud of gloom.

The Capricorn man is most at ease when in the comfort and privacy of his own home. The security possible within four walls can make him a happy man. He'll spend as much time as he can at home. If he is loaded down with extra work, he'll bring it home instead of working overtime at the office.

You'll most likely find yourself frequently confronted by his relatives. Family is very important to the Capricorn—his family, that is. They had better have a pretty important place in your life, too, if you want to keep your home a happy one.

Although his caution in most matters may all but drive you up the wall, you'll find that his concerned way with money is justified most of the time. He'll plan everything right down to the last penny.

He can be quite a scold with children. You'll have to step in and smooth things out.

PISCES WOMAN
AQUARIUS MAN

You are liable to find the Aquarius man the most broadminded man you have ever met; on the other hand, you are also liable to find him the most impractical. Often he's more of a dreamer than a doer. If you don't mind putting up with a man whose heart and mind are as wide as the Missouri but whose head is almost always up in the clouds, then start dating that Aquarian who has somehow captured your fancy. Maybe you, with your good sense, can bring him back down to earth when he gets too starry-eyed.

He's no dumb bell; make no mistake about that. He can be busy making some very complicated and idealistic plans when he's got that out-to-lunch look in his eyes. But more than likely, he'll never execute them. After he's shared one or two of his progressive ideas with you, you are liable to ask yourself, "Who is this nut?" But don't go jumping to conclusions. There's a saying that Aquarians are a half-century ahead of everybody else in the thinking department.

If you decide to answer "Yes" to his "Will you marry me?" you'll find out how right his zany whims are on or about your 50th anniversary. Maybe the waiting will be worth it. Could be that you have an Einstein on your hands—and heart.

Life with an Aquarian won't be one of total despair if you can learn to temper his airiness with your down-to-earth practicality. He won't gripe if you do. The Aquarian always maintains an open mind; he'll entertain the ideas and opinions of everybody. He may not agree with all of them.

Don't go tearing your hair out when you find that it's almost impossible to hold a normal conversation with your Aquarius friend at times. He's capable of answering your "how-are-you-feeling" with a run down on the price of Arizona sugar beets. Always try to keep in mind that he means well.

His broadmindedness doesn't stop when it comes to you and your personal freedom. You won't have to give up any of your hobbies or projects after you're married; he'll encourage you to continue in your interests.

He'll be a kind and generous husband. He'll never quibble over petty things. Keep track of the money you both spend. He can't. Money burns a hole in his pocket.

At times, you may feel like calling it quits. Chances are, though, that you'll always give him another chance.

He's a good family man. He understands children as much as he loves them.

PISCES WOMAN
PISCES MAN

The man born under Pisces is quite a dreamer. Sometimes he's so wrapped up in his dreams that he's difficult to reach. To the average, active woman, he may seem a little sluggish.

He's easy-going most of the time. He seems to take things in his stride. He'll entertain all kinds of views and opinions from just about everyone, nodding or smiling vaguely, giving the impression that he's with them one hundred percent while that may not be the case at all. His attitude may be "why bother" when he's confronted with someone wrong who thinks he's right. The Pisces man will seldom speak his mind if he thinks he'll be rigidly opposed.

The Pisces man is oversensitive at times—he's afraid of getting his feelings hurt. He'll sometimes imagine a personal affront when none's been made. Chances are you'll find this complex of his maddening; at times you may feel like giving him a swift kick where it hurts the most. It wouldn't do any good, though. It would just add fuel to the fire of his complex.

One thing you'll admire about this man is his concern for people who are sickly or troubled. He'll make his shoulder available to anyone in the mood for a good cry. He can listen to one hard-luck story after another without seeming to tire. When his advice is asked, he is capable of coming across with some words of wisdom. He often knows what is bugging someone before that person is aware of it himself. It's almost intuitive with Pisceans, it seems. Still, at the end of the day, this man will want some peace and quiet. If you've got a problem when he comes home, don't unload it in his lap. If you do, you are liable to find him short-tempered. He's a good listener but he can only take so much.

Pisceans are not aimless although they may seem so at times. The positive sort of Pisces man is quite often successful in his profession and is likely to wind up rich and influential. Material gain, however, is never a direct goal for a man born under this sign.

The weaker Pisces are usually content to stay on the level where they find themselves. They won't complain too much if the roof leaks or if the fence is in need of repair.

Because of their seemingly laissez-faire manner, people under this sign—needless to say—are immensely popular with children. For tots they play the double role of confidant and playmate. It will never enter his mind to discipline a child, no matter how spoiled or incorrigible that child becomes.

Man—Woman

PISCES MAN
ARIES WOMAN

The Aries woman may be a little too bossy and busy for you. Generally speaking, Ariens are ambitious creatures. They can become a little impatient with people who are more thorough and deliberate than they are—especially if they feel they're taking too much time. The Aries woman is a fast worker. Sometimes she's so fast she forgets to look where she's going. When she stumbles or falls, it would be nice if you were there to catch her. Ariens are proud women. They don't like to be told "I told you so" when they err. Tongue lashings can turn them into blocks of ice. Don't begin to think that the Aries woman frequently gets tripped up in her plans. Quite often they are capable of taking aim and hitting the bull's-eye. You'll be flabbergasted at times by their accuracy as well as by their ambition. On the other hand, you're apt to spot a flaw in your Arien's plans before she does.

You are perhaps somewhat slower than the Arien in attaining your goals. Still, you are not apt to make mistakes along the way; you're almost always well-prepared.

The Aries woman is rather sensitive at times. She likes to be handled with gentleness and respect. Let her know that you love her for her brains as well as for her good looks. Never give her cause to become jealous. When your Aries date sees green, you'd better forget about sharing a rosy future together. Handle her with tender loving care and she's yours.

The Aries woman can be giving if she feels her partner is deserving. She is no iceberg; she responds to the proper masculine flame. She needs a man she can look up to and feel proud of. If the shoe fits, put it on. If not, better put your sneakers back on and quietly tiptoe out of her sight. She can cause you plenty of heartache if you've made up your mind about her but she hasn't made up hers about you. Aries women are very demanding at times.

Some of them tend to be high-strung; they can be difficult if they feel their independence is being hampered.

The cultivated Aries woman makes a wonderful homemaker and hostess. You'll find she's very clever in decorating and using color. Your house will be tastefully furnished; she'll see to it that it radiates harmony. The Aries wife knows how to make guests feel at home.

Although the Aries woman may not be keen on burdensome responsibilities, she is fond of children and the joy they bring.

PISCES MAN
TAURUS WOMAN

A Taurus woman could perhaps understand you better than most women. She is very considerate and loving. She is thorough and methodical in whatever she does. She knows how to take her time in doing things; she is anxious to avoid mistakes. She is a careful person. She never skips over things that may seem unimportant; she goes over everything with a fine-tooth comb.

Home is very important to the Taurus woman. She is an excellent homemaker. Although your home may not be a palace, it will become, under her care, a comfortable and happy abode. She'll love it when friends drop by for the evening. She is a good cook and enjoys feeding people well. No one will ever go away from your house with an empty stomach.

The Taurus woman is serious about love and affection. When she has taken a tumble for someone, she'll stay by him—for good, if possible. She will try to be practical in romance, to some extent. When she sets her cap for a man, she keeps after him until he's won her. Generally, the Taurus woman is a passionate lover, even though she may appear otherwise at first glance. She is on the look-out for someone who can return her affection fully. Taureans are sometimes given to fits of jealousy and possessiveness. They expect fair play in the area of marriage; when it doesn't come about, they can be bitingly sarcastic and mean.

The Taurus woman is generally an easy-going person. She's fond of keeping peace. She won't argue unless she has to. She'll do her best to keep your love relationship on an even keel.

Marriage is generally a one-time thing for Taureans. Once they've made the serious step, they seldom try to back out of it. Marriage is for keeps. They are fond of love and warmth. With the right man, they turn out to be ideal wives.

The Taurus woman will respect you for your steady ways; she'll have confidence in your common sense.

Taurus women seldom put up with nonsense from their children. They are not so much strict as concerned. They like their children to be well-behaved and dutiful. Nothing pleases a Taurus mother more than a compliment from a neighbor or teacher about her child's behavior. Although some children may inwardly resent the iron hand of a Taurus mother, in later life they are often thankful that they were brought up in such an orderly and conscientious way.

PISCES MAN
GEMINI WOMAN

You may find a romance with a woman born under the sign of the Twins a many-splendored thing. In her you can find the intellectual companionship you often look for in a friend or mate. A Gemini girl friend can appreciate your aims and desires because she travels pretty much the same road as you do intellectually. . . that is, at least part of the way. She may share your interests but she will lack your tenacity.

She suffers from itchy feet. She can be here, there, all over the place and at the same time, or so it would seem. Her eagerness to move about may make you dizzy, still you'll enjoy and appreciate her liveliness and mental agility.

Geminians often have sparkling personalities; you'll be attracted by her warmth and grace. While she's on your arm you'll probably notice that many male eyes are drawn to her—she may even return a gaze or two, but don't let that worry you. All women born under this sign have nothing against a harmless flirt once in a while. They enjoy this sort of attention; if she feels she is already spoken for, however, she will never let it get out of hand.

Although she may not be as handy as you'd like in the kitchen, you'll never go hungry for a filling and tasty meal. The gemini girl is always in a rush; she won't feel like she's cheating by breaking out the instant mashed potatoes or the frozen peas. She may not be much of a good cook but she is clever; with a dash of this and a suggestion of that, she can make an uninteresting tv dinner taste like something out of a James Beard cookbook. Then, again, maybe you've struck it rich and have a Gemini girl friend who finds complicated recipes a challenge to her intellect. If so, you'll find every meal a tantalizing and mouth-watering surprise.

When you're beating your brains out over the Sunday crossword puzzle and find yourself stuck, just ask your Gemini girlie; she'll give you all the right answers without batting an eyelash.

Like you, she loves all kinds of people. You may even find that you're a bit more particular than she. Often all that a Geminian requires is that her friends be interesting—and stay interesting.

One thing she's not able to abide is a dullard.

Leave the party-organizing to your Gemini sweetheart or mate, and you'll never have a chance to know what a dull moment is. She'll bring out the swinger in you if you give her half the chance.

A Gemini mother enjoys her children. Like them, she's often restless, adventurous, and easily bored.

PISCES MAN
CANCER WOMAN

The girl born under the sign of Cancer needs to be protected from the cold, cruel world. She'll love you for your masculine, yet gentle manner; you make her feel safe and secure. You don't have to pull any he-man or heroic stunts to win her heart; that's not what interests her. She's more likely to be impressed by your sure, steady ways—that way you have of putting your arm around her and making her feel that she's the only girl in the world. When she's feeling glum and tears begin to well up in her eyes, you have that knack of saying just the right thing—you know how to calm her fears, no matter how silly some of them may seem.

The girl born under this sign is inclined to have her ups and downs. You have that talent for smoothing out the ruffles in her sea of life. She'll most likely worship the ground you walk on or put you on a terribly high pedestal. Don't disappoint her if you can help it. She'll never disappoint you. This is the kind of woman who will take great pleasure in devoting the rest of her natural life to you. She'll darn your socks, mend your overalls, scrub floors, wash windows, shop, cook, and do just about anything short of murder in order to please you and to let you know that she loves you. Sounds like that legendary good old-fashioned girl, doesn't it? Contrary to popular belief, there are still a good number of them around—and many of them are Cancerians.

Of all the signs of the zodiac, the women under the Cancer sign are the most maternal. In caring for and bringing up children, they know just how to combine the right amount of tenderness with the proper dash of discipline. A child couldn't ask for a better mother. Cancer women are sympathetic, affectionate, and patient with their children.

While we're on the subject of motherhood, there's one thing you should be warned about: never be unkind to your mother-in-law. It will be the only golden rule your Cancerian wife will probably expect you to live up to. No mother-in-law jokes in the presence of your Mrs., please. With her, they'll go over like a lead balloon. Mother is something pretty special for her. She may be the crankiest, nosiest old bat this side of the Great Divide, still she's your wife's mother; you'd better treat her like she's one of the landed gentry. Sometimes this may be difficult to swallow, but if you want to keep your home together and your wife happy, you'd better learn to grin and bear it.

Treat your Cancer wife like a queen, and she'll treat you royally.

PISCES MAN
LEO WOMAN

The Leo woman can make most men roar like lions. If any woman in the zodiac has that indefinable something that can make men lose their heads and find their hearts, it's the Leo woman.

She's got more than a fair share of charm and glamour and she knows how to make the most of her assets, especially when she's in the company of the opposite sex. Jealous men are apt to lose their cool or their sanity when trying to woo a woman born under the sign of the Lion. She likes to kick up her heels quite often and doesn't care who knows it. She often makes heads turn and tongues wag. You don't necessarily have to believe any of what you hear—it's most likely jealous gossip or wishful thinking. Needless to say, other women in her vicinity turn green with envy and will try anything short of shoving her into the nearest lake in order to put her out of the running.

Although this vamp makes the blood rush to your head and makes you momentarily forget all the things you thought were important and necessary in your life, you may feel differently when you come back down to earth and the stars are out of your eyes. You may feel that she isn't the kind of girl you planned to bring home to Mother. Not that your mother might disapprove of your choice—but you might after the shoes and rice are a thing of the past. Although the Leo woman may do her best to be a good wife for you, chances are she'll fall short of your idea of what a good wife should be like.

If you're planning on not going as far as the altar with that Leo woman who has you flipping your lid, you'd better be financially equipped for some very expensive dating. Be prepared to shower her with expensive gifts and to take her dining and dancing to the smartest spots in town. Promise her the moon if you're in a position to go that far. Luxury and glamour are two things that are bound to lower a Leo's resistance. She's got expensive tastes, and you'd better cater to them if you expect to get to first base with this femme.

If you've got an important business deal to clinch and you have doubts as to whether you can swing it or not, bring your Leo girlie along to the business luncheon. Chances are that with her on your arm, you'll be able to win any business battle with both hands tied. She won't have to say or do anything—just being there at your side is enough. The grouchiest oil magnate can be transformed into a gushing, obedient schoolboy if there's a charming Leo woman in the room.

Leo mothers are blind to the faults of their children. They make very loving and affectionate parents and tend to spoil their offspring.

PISCES MAN
VIRGO WOMAN

The Virgo woman may be a little too difficult for you to understand at first. Her waters run deep. Even when you think you know her, don't take any bets on it. She's capable of keeping things hidden in the deep recesses of her womanly soul—things she'll only release when she's sure that you're the man she's been looking for. It may take her some time to come around to this decision. Virgo girls are finicky about almost everything; everything has to be letter-perfect before they're satisfied. Many of them have the idea that the only people who can do things right are Virgos.

Nothing offends a Virgo woman more than slovenly dress, sloppy character, or a careless display of affection. Make sure your tie is not crooked and your shoes sport a bright shine before you go calling on this lady. Keep your off-color jokes for the locker-room; she'll have none of that. Take her arm when crossing the street. Don't rush the romance. Trying to corner her in the back of a cab may be one way of striking out. Never criticize the way she looks—in fact, the best policy would be to agree with her as much as possible. Still, there's just so much a man can take; all those dos and don'ts you'll have to observe if you want to get to first base with a virgo may be just a little too much to ask of you. After a few dates, you may come to the conclusion that she just isn't worth all that trouble. However, the Virgo woman is mysterious enough, generally speaking, to keep her men running back for more. Chances are you'll be intrigued by her airs and graces.

If lovemaking means a lot to you, you'll be disappointed at first in the cool ways of your Virgo girlie. However, under her glacial facade there lies a hot cauldron of seething excitement. If you're patient and artful in your romantic approach, you'll find that all that caution was well worth the trouble. When Virgos love, they don't stint. It's all or nothing as far as they're concerned. once they're convinced that they love you, they go all the way, right off the bat, tossing all cares to the wind.

One thing a Virgo woman can't stand in love is hypocrisy. They don't give a hoot about what the neighbors say, if their hearts tell them "Go ahead!" They're very concerned with human truths—so much so that if their hearts stumble upon another fancy, they're liable to be true to that new heart-throb and leave you standing in the rain. She's honest to her heart and will be as true to you are you are with her, generally. Do her wrong once, however, and it's farewell.

Both strict and tender, she tries to bring out the best in her children.

PISCES MAN
LIBRA WOMAN

As the song goes, it's a woman's prerogative to change her mind. The lyricist must have had the Libra woman in his thoughts when he jotted this ditty out. Her changeability, in spite of its undeniable charm (sometimes) could actually drive even a man of your patience up the wall. She's capable of smothering you with love and kisses one day and on the next, avoid you like the plague. If you think you're a man of steel nerves then perhaps you can tolerate her sometimey-ness without suffering too much. However, if you own up to the fact that you're only a mere mortal who can only take so much, then you'd better fasten your attention on a girl who's somewhat more constant.

But don't get the wrong idea: a love affair with a Libran is not bad at all. In fact, it can have an awful lot of plusses to it. Libra women are soft, very feminine, and warm. She doesn't have to vamp all over the place in order to gain a man's attention. Her delicate presence is enough to warm the cockles of any man's heart. One smile and you're like a piece of putty in the palm of her hand.

She can be fluffy and affectionate—things you like in a girl. On the other hand, her indecision about which dress to wear, what to cook for dinner, or whether to redo the rumpus room or not could make you tear your hair out. What will perhaps be more exasperating is her flat denial to the accusation that she cannot make even the simplest decision. The trouble is that she wants to be fair or just in all matters; she'll spend hours weighing pros and cons. Don't make her rush into a decision; that will only irritate her.

The Libra woman likes to be surrounded by beautiful things. Money is no object when beauty is concerned. There will always be plenty of flowers in the house. She'll know how to arrange them tastefully, too. Women under this sign are fond of beautiful clothes and furnishings. They will run up bills without batting an eye—if given the chance.

Once she's cottoned to you, the Libra woman will do everything in her power to make you happy. She'll wait on you hand and foot when you're sick and bring you breakfast in bed on Sundays. She'll be very thoughtful and devoted. If anyone dares suggest you're not the grandest man in the world, your Libra wife will give that person a good sounding-out.

Librans work wonders with children. Gentle persuasion and affection are all she uses in bringing them up, and it works.

PISCES MAN
SCORPIO WOMAN

When the Scorpio woman chooses to be sweet, she's apt to give the impression that butter wouldn't melt in her mouth . . . but, of course, it would. When her temper flies, so will everything else that isn't bolted down. She can be as hot as a *tamale* or as cool as a cucumber when she wants. Whatever mood she's in, you can be sure it's for real. She doesn't believe in poses or hypocrisy.

The Scorpio woman is often seductive and sultry. Her femme fatale charm can pierce through the hardest of hearts like a laser ray. She doesn't have to look like Mata Hari (many of them resemble the tomboy next door), but once you've looked into those tantalizing eyes, you're a goner.

The Scorpio woman can be a whirlwind of passion. Life with a girl born under this sign will not be all smiles and smooth-sailing. If you think you can handle a woman who can purr like a pussycat when handled correctly but spit bullets once her fur is ruffled, then try your luck. Your stable and steady nature will most likely have a calming effect on her. You're the kind of man she can trust and rely on. But never cross her—even on the smallest thing; if you do, you'd better tell Fido to make room for you in the doghouse —you'll be his guest for the next couple of days.

Generally, the Scorpio woman will keep family battles within the walls of your home. When company visits, she's apt to give the impression that married life with you is one big joy-ride. It's just her way of expressing her loyalty to you—at least, in front of others. She believes that family matters are and should stay private. She'll certainly see to it that others have a high opinion of you both. She'll be right behind you whatever it is you want to do. Although she's an individualist, after she has married, she'll put her own interests aside for those of the man she loves. With a woman like this behind, you can't help but go far. She'll never try to take over your role as boss of the family. She'll give you all the support you need in order to fulfill that role. She won't complain if the going gets rough. She is a courageous woman. She's as anxious as you to find that place in the sun for you both. She's as determined a person as you are.

Although she may love her children, she may not be very affectionate toward them. She'll make a devoted mother, though. She'll be anxious to see them develop their talents. She'll teach the children to be courageous and steadfast.

PISCES MAN
SAGITTARIUS WOMAN

You'll most likely never come across a more good-natured girl than the one born under the sign of Sagittarius. Generally, they're full of bounce and good cheer. Their sunny dispositions seem almost permanent and can be relied upon even on the rainiest of days.

Women born under this sign are almost never malicious. If ever they seem to be, it is only seeming. Sagittarians are often a little short on tact and say literally anything that comes into their pretty little heads—no matter what the occasion. Sometimes the words that tumble out of their mouths seem downright cutting and cruel. Still, no matter what she says, she means well. The Sagittarius woman is quite capable of losing some of her friends—and perhaps even some of yours—through a careless slip of the lip.

On the other hand, you are liable to appreciate her honesty and good intentions. To you, qualities of this sort play an important part in life. With a little patience and practice, you can probably help cure your Sagittarian of her loose tongue; in most cases, she'll give in to your better judgement and try to follow your advice to letter.

Chances are, she'll be the outdoor-type of girl friend. Long hikes, fishing trips, and white-water canoeing will most likely appeal to her. She's a busy person; no one could ever call her a slouch. She sets great store in mobility. She won't sit still for one minute if she doesn't have to.

She is great company most of the time and, generally, lots of fun. Even if your buddies drop by for poker and beer, she won't have any trouble fitting in.

On the whole, she is a very kind and sympathetic woman. If she feels she's made a mistake, she'll be the first to call your attention to it. She's not afraid to own up to her own faults and shortcomings.

You might lose your patience with her once or twice. After she's seen how upset her shortsightedness or tendency to blabbermouth has made you, she'll do her best to straighten up.

The Sagittarius woman is not the kind who will pry into your business affairs. But she'll always be there, ready to offer advice if you need it.

The Sagittarius woman is seldom suspicious. Your word will almost always be good enough for her.

She is a wonderful and loving friend to her children.

PISCES MAN
CAPRICORN WOMAN

The Capricorn woman may not be the most romantic of the zodiac, but she's far from frigid when she meets the right man. She believes in true love; she doesn't appreciate getting involved in flings. To her, they're just a waste of time. She's looking for a man who means "business"—in life as well as in love. Although she can be very affectionate with her boy friend or mate, she tends to let her head govern her heart. That is not to say she is a cool, calculating cucumber. On the contrary, she just feels she can be more honest about love if she consults her brain first. She wants to size up the situation before throwing her heart in the ring. She wants to make sure it won't get stepped on.

The Capricorn woman is faithful, dependable, and systematic in just about everything she undertakes. She is quite concerned with security and sees to it that every penny she spends is spent wisely. She is very economical about using her time, too. She does not believe in whittling away her energy on a scheme that is bound not to pay off.

Ambitious themselves, Capricorns are quite often attracted to ambitious men—men who are interested in getting somewhere in life. If a man of this sort wins her heart, she'll stick by him and do all she can to help him get to the top.

The Capricorn woman is almost always diplomatic. She makes an excellent hostess. She can be very influential when your business acquaintances come to dinner.

The Capricorn woman is likely to be very concerned, if not downright proud, about her family tree. Relatives are pretty important to her, particularly if they're socially prominent. Never say a cross word about her family members. That can really go against her grain, and she'll punish you by not talking to you for days.

She's generally thorough in whatever she does. Capricorn women are well-mannered and gracious, no matter what their backgrounds. They seem to have it in their natures to always behave properly.

If you should marry a woman born under this sign, you need

never worry about her going on a wild shopping spree. They understand the value of money better than most women. If you turn over your paycheck to her at the end of the week, you can be sure that a good hunk of it will wind up in the bank.

The Capricorn mother is loving and correct.

PISCES MAN
AQUARIUS WOMAN

If you find that you've fallen head over heels for a woman born under the sign of the Water Bearer, you'd better fasten your safety belt. It may take you quite a while to actually discover what this girl is like—and even then, you may have nothing to go on but a string of vague hunches. The Aquarian is like a rainbow, full of bright and shining hues; she's like no other girl you've ever known. There is something elusive about her, something difficult to put your finger on.

The Aquarius woman can be pretty odd and eccentric at times. Some say this is the source of her mysterious charm. You are liable to think she's just a plain screwball; you may be 50 percent right.

Aquarius women often have their heads full of dreams. By nature, they're often unconventional; they have their own ideas about how the world should be run. Sometimes their ideas may seem pretty weird—chances are they're just a little bit too progressive. There is a saying that runs "The way the Aquarian thinks, so will the world in 50 years." She'll most likely be the most tolerant and open-minded woman you've ever encountered.

If you find that she's too much mystery and charm for you to handle, just talk it out with her and say that you think it would be better to call it quits. She'll most likely give you a peck on the cheek and say, "Okay, but let's still be friends." Aquarius women are like that. Perhaps you'll both find it easier to get along in a friendship than in a romance.

It is not difficult for her to remain buddy-buddy with an ex-lover. For many Aquarians, the line between friendship and romance is a pretty fuzzy one.

She is not a jealous person and, while you're romancing her, she won't expect you to be, either. You'll find her a pretty free spirit most of the time. Just when you think you know her inside-out, you'll discover that you don't really know her at all.

She's a very sympathetic and warm person; she is often helpful to those in need of assistance and advice.

She'll seldom be suspicious, even when she has every right to be. If the man she loves makes a little slip, she's liable to forgive and forget it.

She makes a fine mother. Her positive and big-hearted qualities are easily transmitted to her offspring.

PISCES MAN
PISCES WOMAN

Many a man dreams of a Piscean kind of girl. You're perhaps no exception. She's soft and cuddly and very domestic. She'll let you be the brains of the family; she's contented to just lean on your shoulder and let you be the master of the household.

She can be very ladylike and proper. Your business associates and friends will be dazzled by her warmth and femininity. Although she's a charmer, there is a lot more to her than just a pretty exterior. There is a brain ticking away behind that soft, womanly facade. You may never become aware of it—that is, until you're married to her. It's no cause for alarm, however; she'll most likely never use it against you.

If she feels you're botching up your married life through careless behavior or if she feels you could be earning more money than you do, she'll tell you about it. But any wife would, really. She will never try to usurp your position as head and breadwinner of the family.

No one had better dare say one uncomplimentary word about you in her presence. It's liable to cause her to break into tears. Pisces women are usually very sensitive beings. Their reaction to adversity, frustration, or anger is just a plain, good, old-fashioned cry. They can weep buckets when inclined.

She'll have an extra-special dinner prepared for you when you make a new conquest in your profession. Don't bother to go into details, though, at the dinner table; she doesn't have much of a head for business matters, usually, and is only too happy to leave that up to you.

Treat her with tenderness, and your relationship will be an enjoyable one. She's most likely fond of chocolates. A bunch of beautiful flowers will never fail to make her eyes light up. See to it that you never forget her birthday or your anniversary. These things are very important to her. If you let them slip your mind, you'll send her into a crying fit that could last a considerable length of time. If you are patient and kind, you can keep a Pisces woman happy for a lifetime. She, however, is not without her faults. Her "sensitivity" may get on your nerves after a while; you may find her lacking in imagination and zest; you may even feel that she uses her tears as a method of getting her own way. She makes a strong, self-sacrificing mother.

PISCES

YEARLY FORECAST: 1994

*Forecast for 1994 Concerning Business
and Financial Affairs, Job Prospects,
Travel, Health, Romance and Marriage
for Those Born with the Sun
in the Zodiacal Sign of Pisces.
February 19–March 20*

Pisces will be pulled in different directions and have to make some tough choices in the year ahead. You can trust your intuition when facts conflict and decisions are unclear. Your sensitive nature makes you aware of more possibilities than others may notice. You are ready and willing to make some changes based on altered circumstances. Not being tied to the past, you can move ahead with confidence and never look back with regrets. Someone you have been associated with for a long time is ready to give you extra responsibility. The balance of power is shifting in your direction, affecting other relationships as well. Family members and friends may not adapt quite as readily as you to these changes. Be patient and tolerant of their views even if you do not agree with them. You have the opportunity to develop underutilized talents in a way that pleases you. Throughout the year you will be inclined to give away what is too precious to sell. Rely on an adviser to negotiate on your behalf so that you get what you rightfully deserve. There is a strong element of luck that goes hand in hand with your actions. This comes about partly through chance, but much of your good fortune is based on your abilities and self-confidence. You will not settle for dabbling in a new technology or anything else that interests you. Once you become involved it is all or nothing, which makes 1994 especially promising for the Pisces-born person. By year's end your reputation will be enhanced as the result of your own determination.

The first half of 1994 will be more pressure-packed than the last six months. Job-related activities will keep you on the go when you would rather be at home. Family members are likely to grow accustomed to evening meals when you are not able to join them and to out-of-town trips that are unscheduled. You will also be doing more entertaining than usual, often for business as well as social reasons. There is a strong indication of a new assignment that might lead to relocating. Teamwork is a vital ingredient for success. As part of a group you have extra power and strength as well as strong backing when you are tempted to give in or give up. Money matters also require team effort. Work hand in hand with a banker or broker you trust. This is a good year for a major purchase such as a home or other property. Even the experienced Pisces financial dealer should not negotiate the final price alone. You can get a better result working through a neutral third party whom you are directing from the sidelines. Health should not be a problem during most of the year. In the second quarter, however, it is important to pay more attention to diet and exercise. The rush of your schedule could lead to ignoring a warning sign. From July through December is the happiest time for romance and home life. You may be welcoming a newcomer into your family circle or making a new beginning at that time.

Business and employment prospects this year are especially bright for Pisces ready to move up the ladder of success. There is more opportunity than you may even be able to accept. It is important to emphasize cooperation even while developing your own special abilities. Be wary of becoming too much of a specialist. You do not want to limit yourself or your options in any way. There is a strong emphasis on originality that will help you take one person's idea and make it uniquely your own. Build on what has been successful in the past without being bound by it. Extra effort produces extra rewards. You cannot be chained to a timeclock and expect to make much of an impact or a good impression. Overtime may be required more frequently than last year, and probably without extra pay. The social aspects of business are also very important. Getting to know co-workers and higher-ups on a personal basis can benefit your career. It is useful to understand their motivation and expectations so that you can gauge how you are measuring up. Guard against becoming anyone's right-hand helper. If you tie your success to theirs you limit your ability to catch a ride with the next rising star on the work scene. For Pisces students and recent graduates, a job with a large corporation can provide more opportunity and better training than can be offered in a smaller organization.

Self-employment is a definite possibility because of your good organizational ability and far-reaching ideas. You can hire someone to handle the details that do not particularly appeal. Pisces tend to think in broad sweeps and along varied lines. You can be the person in charge one minute and then quickly change roles to pitch in where needed under the direction of another person. Your creativity combines well with a desire to reach out and help people. Pisces can have a major impact as counselors, advisers and religious leaders. You are also a natural using your talents to entertain and amuse in front of an audience. Give some time this year to a charitable cause that is important to you. You are happiest utilizing your basic nature for the good of other people and not merely to make a living.

Travel is foreseen primarily in connection with work and business. You will have frequent occasions to go out of town in order to seal a deal or negotiate the last remaining points. Face-to-face you can be most persuasive; by letter or phone you lose some of your natural enthusiasm that is useful in overcoming resistance. There are indications of relocating due to a job change. However, you may choose to commute a long distance if family members object to pulling up stakes and making a new start during the school year. January, February, May and July are best for long-distance trips; June and September favor vacation travel. Combining business with pleasure is the ideal. A companion not only makes being away from home more bearable but also helps in providing an extra pair of eyes and ears to take in all that is going on. Dealing with people at a distance demands intuiting their wishes when you cannot get a straight answer. The primary warning this year is to avoid being away from your normal base of operations merely because you grow restless. When you are under stress you have to keep your fingers on the switches.

Health should not be much of a worry in 1994. Emotions may not be too stable, however, at varying times during the year. Use exercise as an outlet for stress. Consider joining a team that engages in strenuous competition for the fun of it. Or a health club can give you the framework for a regular exercise regimen that would be difficult on your own. You may have to begin wearing glasses or have your current prescription strengthened during the year. Schedule a checkup if you begin to have blurry vision or recurring headaches. You have the willpower during the last half of 1994 to give up a habit you know is unhealthy. Becoming part of a group dedicated to the same goal can be helpful. In all of your activities there is strength in numbers. Whatever can be accomplished individually can be that much easier and more effective if you are working toward a mutual goal.

Home and family may take a backseat to your outside interests more often than you would like this year. You cannot get ahead by shortchanging your job responsibilities, although the pull of home life may be hard to resist. The first six months are the most hectic time for Pisces in business as an employee or self-employed. Try to arrange your schedule so that you do not have to be out of town too frequently, and then so that overnight stays are spaced. Family members will give you the encouragement you need to branch out in a new direction. Partnership with a relative is favored, although this may amount to a financial arrangement rather than a close working union. Love is the one sure and steady force. Your mate or date knows how important it is to you to use your talents in productive ways. While they may wish for more of your time and attention, they will not turn their desires into demands. Pay them back with undivided attention when you are with them. Children, too, need extra doses of love. Be wary of becoming an authoritarian; treat loved ones with the same courtesy and respect that you show everyone else. For the single Pisces, this is a year that makes marriage more appealing than ever before. Someone you know as a co-worker or team member is apt to become more dominant in your personal life. Romance that starts with a firm foundation of friendship will endure the longest. It is a positive year to add to your family circle, whether it be through marriage, birth or adoption.

You will have more income this year than last, but also higher expenses. Budgeting is the key to not feeling poor. Work out a financial plan with your mate or partner to establish spending boundaries and savings guidelines. Pay cash except for a major purchase that is normally bought on time. If you do not have money in the bank for what you want, postpone buying. Look for ways to turn a hobby into a money-making proposition. Your creative abilities do not have to be confined to pleasing family and friends; opportunity exists for you to branch out. You have to take some risks in order to make money, but be sure they are well calculated. Through regular work you stand the best chance of a steady paycheck. It is not a good year to give up this security unless you have financial backing from a family member or potential partner. The risks you are willing to take in money matters as well as all other affairs have to be weighed in the balance. To move ahead in 1994, say yes to those changes that are most promising. Then proceed to put them in motion.

DAILY FORECAST
January–December 1994
JANUARY

1. SATURDAY. Changeable.   The year gets off to a lively start but not as sure-footed as you would like. Getting along with family members requires that you cater to their wishes or they are likely to pout. Those your own age and older are apt to act like youngsters. Someone is trying to wriggle out of a promise made to you only a short time ago. Their excuses will not fool you, but you may decide for the sake of harmony to pretend that you understand. Do not allow one of your own New Year's resolutions to trip you up. Keep busy and you have less time to think about what you would rather be doing. Stay warm tonight; it is a tricky month and weather patterns are unpredictable.

2. SUNDAY. Cautious.   Be gentle with a relative or neighbor who does not have to say much to get on your nerves. Caution is the watchword in all relationships. You may feel boxed in and yearn to be away from your usual surroundings. But if you convey this message you could hurt the feelings of someone who is trying to make you happy. Be wary of making empty promises or idle threats. Keep future plans to yourself until certain what you want. Only then can you begin rounding up support and finding out who is definitely on your side. It is not prudent to make any long-term commitment that would be difficult to get out of in the year ahead. Take time to check out your options before deciding.

3. MONDAY. Inactive.   Keep a low profile at home, and if you must be back on the job steer clear of the boss. Certain things are best left unsaid now. You could wind up supporting the wrong side if you flip a coin to decide. Ferret out more information before making a major decision. Facts are not as reliable as the source is indicating. Check with independent people who have no ax to grind pro or con. A new partnership appears promising. First, however, ask around to determine past performance. Pisces students should have no trouble scoring on a test based on current studies. But you may have to shake off lessons of the past that are no longer applicable.

4. TUESDAY. Good.   What comes as a surprise to other people should not startle you. Your insight is especially valuable. A trend just beginning to emerge seems crystal clear to the Pisces ready for change. Grab the opportunity to get in on the ground floor of new opportunity. Do not hesitate to join with a group of like-minded people. There is special power through an organization that can rally support. It is a good day to apply for a loan or scholarship. Money managers understand your needs and may bend rules for you. Answer questions factually without embroidering the truth. You could fine yourself trapped in a web of deceit even if you tell a very small lie.

5. WEDNESDAY. Satisfactory.   A current project holds great promise for the future. Patience is mandatory now so that you do not make any major errors as you proceed. Double-check not only the work done by others but also your own output. A basic miscalculation can lead to results that are out of whack. Test out a new idea in a small way. Borrow or rent necessary equipment until you determine if you will need it. It could be that you will soon be applying for a copyright or patent. By evening you will be ready for a quiet dinner and fantasy programming on television. Your mind can transport you to a land of make-believe that you wish you could never leave.

6. THURSDAY. Pleasant.   Enjoy spending some of your hard-earned pay on a gift for someone you love or for yourself. Select an item of lasting value such as jewelry or a painting. This is also a good day to bargain hunt at an advertised sale. If you come across a sale on items you use regularly, stock up. A family member is anxious to please you. Be sure to show your appreciation and love in return. If planning a trip, shop around for the best price in transportation and accommodations. A package deal could save you a lot, particularly if you can plan well in advance. There is opportunity to learn from a master by observing from a special vantage point.

7. FRIDAY. Useful.   Although you know that improvement is necessary in a certain area, you can see progress being made on almost a daily basis. Continue to learn, or to teach. Do not hesitate to share what you know for fear you may be passing on information to a competitor. Pisces have more self-confidence than that; whatever you do to help someone else will come back to you in a different but equally valuable form. Make decisions today based on information currently available. If it proves outdated later in the year, you can upgrade a plan or make modifications then. The boss may let you off early to get a head start on weekend plans if you have to travel.

8. SATURDAY. Cautious.   Proceed with caution in all activities where cooperation is necessary. It is all too easy for Pisces to take over and wind up alienating just those people whose help you want most. Guard against volunteering too readily; wait to be asked. The time has come to concentrate on a problem of your own and allow other people to sort theirs out independently. It is often easier to offer advice to a friend or family member and ignore a situation in your own life that would benefit from analysis. Holding a grudge is only hurting you, not the other person involved. Forgive and forget is a valuable motto to strive to uphold, but you could find it hard at times.

9. SUNDAY. Difficult.   Keep negative thoughts to yourself even though you may have to bite your tongue in order to do so. Speaking up can land you in trouble with your mate or another loved one. They will not appreciate hearing the obvious from you; they are not stupid, only stubborn. If you make any threats you must be prepared to back them up with action. It is best to stay free and clear of a family dispute. Taking sides lands you in trouble, and trying to act as arbitrator can inspire both people to turn on you. Go over family finances looking for ways to make small cutbacks. Then you will not have to eliminate eating out or entertainment from your financial allotments.

10. MONDAY. Variable.   Look for clues in what you read as you travel. A solution to a problem that has been bothering you for some time is close at hand. You can come up with a special use for an item that you have at home and utilize daily. It is a starred day for getting to the bottom of a matter by having a frank discussion with the other people who feel as strongly about it as you do. Nothing should be taken for granted; any promise made now ought to be put in writing. Appearances may belie the true facts of the matter. But the more you worry, the harder it is to come up with an answer. Find a private place to meditate and to develop positive thoughts, which can lead to a workable remedy.

11. TUESDAY. Fortunate. Do not settle for partial answers or a quick brush-off to your questions. Persevere until you are satisfied that you understand. No question is too basic or simple to ask. It is important to catch up with technological wizards who talk in a language all their own. There is a strong element of good fortune hovering around Pisces today. Be true to yourself and you will receive special benefits not available to other Signs. Grasp opportunity without stopping to wonder if other people have ulterior motives in trying to help you. Although patience can be important, this is a time for action. You and your mate can communicate tonight without a word being said.

12. WEDNESDAY. Mixed. Doing a good turn for someone will make you feel good. Share what you have and what you know. Be generous in responding to an appeal to aid a neighbor with a health problem. You may want to prepare a meal, drop by to offer some cheerful conversation or work on a fund-raiser. Pisces parents have an opportunity now to become more involved in educational matters. Find a way to volunteer for a school function. Also pay more attention to homework so that a youngster does not fall behind in studies. Pisces students may have to go back to basics to comprehend the current lesson. Another student is the best tutor available, provided he or she is willing.

13. THURSDAY. Exciting. A chance meeting could be the beginning of an exciting new relationship. Look your best from the time you get up until you collapse into bed at the end of the day. Wear a color that makes you stand out in a crowd. Your determination to succeed will see you over the humps and bumps on the road to success. Self-confidence is soaring, helping you attract the favorable attention that is a key to success. Once you have acquired the necessary skills, getting ahead depends to a large degree on who you know and how much of an impression you make. Initial success is apt to bring a wealth of new offers. Someone who has been keeping an eye on your progress may be considering an offer you will find too good to refuse.

14. FRIDAY. Successful. Pisces have their fingers on the right buttons. Timing is the secret ingredient leading to success. Your ability to select the precise moment to act gives you an edge over all competitors. There is no reason to play hard to get. Positive attention is focusing on you. Enjoy being in the spotlight and reaping the rewards as your reputation grows. A quick trip gives you a firsthand glimpse of what you have only heard about through interested persons. When you see for yourself you will know how to react. Your greatest satisfaction comes from taking over a project that is not going well and revamping it in order to achieve the success you know is possible. You delight in any challenge.

15. SATURDAY. Manageable. Family members are likely to be scattering in all directions during the day. Whatever you are able to accomplish around the house has to be done primarily on your own. Creative work is starred; your imagination is in full throttle as you put together your own combination of color and materials. A new technique is worth trying for the fun of it. Check out a book from the library before spending your hard-earned money to buy it. Read it and then decide if you want a copy of your own. Sound advice may come from a parent or in-law. The older generation helps you meld the best from the new and the old. Be sure you have enough money to cover expenses.

16. SUNDAY. Variable. Pisces are energetic and industrious throughout the day. Lack of cooperation, however, can hamper your efforts. Focus on tying up loose ends instead of beginning anything new. This is not a day to make any hasty decisions. Information currently available to you is apt to be incomplete. When you discover what someone has been holding back you could have a complete change of heart. Promises are unreliable although intentions are good. It is healthier to voice a complaint to the other person involved than to go off and complain to someone else. The direct approach is the most effective as it can usually resolve a problem quickly.

17. MONDAY. Exciting. An unusual turn of events takes a project off the shelf and gives it star billing. What you have believed all along is now gaining the prominence you know it deserves. You will tend to be in the right place at the right time just by following your inner sixth sense. Pisces intuition is right on target. People who have been listening to you, but not paying much attention, are now apt to be glued on your every word. It is tempting to say I told you so; resist if possible. Push through a deal that others want far more than you. Strike while the iron is hot is an appropriate motto to follow. A private rendezvous can be arranged tonight with little effort.

18. TUESDAY. Changeable. Do not turn down a chance to become part of a rather exclusive group. You do not have to drop old friends and acquaintances as you scale the ladder of success. Treat everyone as a respected equal, no matter what their status or position. The health of a family member could necessitate taking some time off to accompany them to a medical appointment. Ask those questions that they may not want to ask or may not be thinking about. Be sure you understand doctor's orders to avoid confusion when you get home. It may be worth getting a second opinion. Work will wait for you; it is clear where your priorities lie today. Get in touch with a distant relative.

19. WEDNESDAY. Tricky. Some nagging doubts may make you wonder if you have made the right decision. But there is no turning back at this point. Proceed as though you had all the confidence in the world. Your attitude affects the people around you. Resist extravagant impulses geared to please a loved one. Your time and attention are more valuable than anything you could buy. There could be some signs of jealousy among family members or in the neighborhood. You do not have anything to apologize for, but you may nevertheless feel guilty about having a lot while others are going without. Find a way to contribute through an organized charity.

20. THURSDAY. Disconcerting. You could have some explaining to do if your mate or partner discovers a bank withdrawal that they knew nothing about. Careful accounting is mandatory to keep a business relationship intact. Pisces handling money that is not entirely their own cannot make independent decisions. Even if you have to postpone a purchase or miss out on opportunity, you must secure permission before spending joint money. Children are likely to be in a rebellious or mischievous mood. Pisces parents may be called to the school for a conference. An appeal to the child's intelligence and sense of fair play can be more effective than any punishment.

21. FRIDAY. Lucky. Deal with the backlog of letters waiting for your reply. In going through them you may stumble upon an offer overlooked at first. Act on it without delay; luck is on your side today. Follow through on a promise made earlier in the month even though it may not be too convenient to do so. You will feel better for it, and your reputation will remain intact. This is not a time when you have to be falsely modest. Blow your own horn about recent accomplishments. Let everyone know that you are pleased with results. Be sure to spread the praise to those who may have helped in the least significant ways. Socializing tonight could lead to new love, but could be a fiasco, too.

22. SATURDAY. Outstanding. Possibilities are excellent for receiving the answer you want to an important question. Do not waste any more time worrying about what others are thinking; find out directly, simply by asking. The happiest combination is to be in love with your best friend. Conditions are lively but not hectic. You know you are appreciated for all of your Pisces talents and abilities. It is not necessary to put on any airs or to pretend to be who you are not. Travel could be enjoyable if you are accompanied by someone you want to have a heart-to-heart talk with. Two strangers in a foreign land can cut to the emotion of a situation without masquerading.

23. SUNDAY. Pleasant. A cash windfall can help you pay for tickets to a show or sports event. Discovering that you have more in your wallet than expected, or finding a little money stuffed into a pocket, brightens the entertainment outlook today. Be sure to include younger family members in all of your activities. It is also a starred day for taking a small gamble by playing a game of chance. An idea that you have been mulling over for a while could be transformed into a money-maker; teaming up with a friend or neighbor could be the impetus you need. You should be feeling in control and on top of things. Your positive approach gives you a definite advantage.

24. MONDAY. Variable. Morning hours are the time for direct action. By afternoon you may begin to have some doubts, and this evening you could be questioning almost everything. Strike while ideas are hot. Prove that what you are planning has a good probability of working out as you envision. It is much better to air complaints than to keep them bottled up inside. Tactfully explain changes you would like to see made. You could get your way on some; others may be explained to your satisfaction. Straightforward talk about joint finances can ward off problems just beginning to develop. Equal partners must have an equal say in all decision making of any consequence.

25. TUESDAY. Changeable. A personal invitation makes you realize you are being noticed and appreciated. Respond quickly so that there are no doubts about reserving room for you. It is a good day to plan a future trip to attend a conference or other gathering of people who share a common interest. In fact, you may be asked to speak or present a paper or put on a display. Keep conversation on the light, neutral side. Anything negative that you say could come back to haunt you later in the year. Ideas are changing rapidly; by the time you finish what you are now planning you may wonder why you ever started it. A family member wants to apologize in order to get back in your good graces; accept without holding a grudge.

26. WEDNESDAY. Easygoing. Check up on all that is being done without actually rolling up your sleeves and pitching in. It is important now for Pisces to delegate as much responsibility as possible. Your mind is active and your ideas are good, but physically you may lack energy. Pass out compliments as though they were candy. There could be some useful discussion with colleagues or family members. Their views should be factored into your own. You can rely on people who know you well to tell the truth even though it may hurt a little. They know you are looking for information, not a pat on the back. Invite a few friends to be your guests tonight for an impromptu party.

27. THURSDAY. Buoyant. Personal ambitions can be brought closer to being realized. Conditions are perfect for taking a giant leap instead of baby steps. Run, do not walk, when opportunity presents itself. You are exerting maximum personal magnetism today. People are eager to be on your team and help out in whatever way you want. Through business and professional contact you can develop new friendships. Diversify within limits; if you spread yourself too thin you lose track of what is going on. You will make a strong impression on important people by acting naturally. Plan a special outing with your mate or date that will make you the envy of your friends.

28. FRIDAY. Quiet. Catch up with paperwork put aside during busier periods. Be sure to write a letter in reply to a note from someone who was once a schoolmate or a work associate. Keeping in touch is important to your long-range plans as well as theirs. Pay bills in full if possible. You can save a lot by not being saddled with high interest charges on a monthly basis. It can be worthwhile to put away credit cards and only buy with cash. If you cannot afford what you want, postpone the purchase. An interesting tidbit of news could bring out your creative talent. Work being done by a person you admire can be the starting point for your own project. You needed just that stimulus to motivate you.

29. SATURDAY. Mixed. An outing planned for today may have to be canceled due to weather or other factors. Take advantage of the unexpected free time to catch up with work around the house. Pull everything out of a bulging closet or a bureau drawer so stuffed you can barely close it. Make a pile of items to be given away because they no longer fit or are out of style or are just not what you want now. When one area is in spic and span order you feel more in control of everything. A minor difference with a family member could escalate into a major argument if you do not restrain your comments. Someone who is trying hard deserves a second chance. It may take even more than one.

30. SUNDAY. Tranquil. Listen to advice being offered without making any decision about it. Suggestions made by other people might seem right to them but be all wrong for you. There is insufficient energy today to formulate your plans. You can release some pent-up stress by exercising indoors or out. Avoid competition, even with yourself. A romance that has had its ups and downs is back on track. Relax and enjoy the companionship without making long-range plans. A new start can be happy providing you do not attempt to orchestrate every move. Check out the help-wanted advertisements; you may come across one that seems written with you in mind.

31. MONDAY. Stimulating. Stand up for what you believe in and you can overcome opposition quite easily. There are few people willing to cross your path now. The ball is in your court; take it and run. Determination can help you get what you want even if your chances were slim at the start. Choose words with care. People are hanging on what you say and will remember long after you have forgotten. It is a promising day for new investment. A company just starting out can return a large dividend if you are a patient investor rather than a speculator. The Moon now in Libra favors open communications and makes this a starred time for property negotiations direct with the owner.

FEBRUARY

1. TUESDAY. Pleasant. A romance is brewing that could lead straight to the altar. Pisces may not be directly involved, but you tend to feel that you have shot Cupid's arrow. Any effort to bring together people who you believe are a perfect match is likely to be successful. You can also excel as a mediator or arbitrator to settle a dispute. A worry has loosened its grip on you, giving you renewed energy and enthusiasm. What has been viewed as a problem is now only a fading memory. This is a good day to check into what other people are doing and find a way to help if assistance is needed. Do not wait to be asked. Your basic instincts are a reliable guide.

2. WEDNESDAY. Good. Thanks to a family member you may wind up with more money in the bank. An inheritance is possible, or a prize or other windfall. You know immediately what you want to buy, but wait a few days at least before making a major purchase. Pisces who handle money belonging to clients or other people can win praise for their astute investment decisions. What is going up is not apt to come down for a while. Put some spare cash into a company with a good track record for earnings and management. You can please your mate or partner without having to spend a lot. Time and attention are what they crave. Show that you care by way of the little things that you do for them.

3. THURSDAY. Stimulating. Working as part of a team is more stimulating than shutting yourself off behind a closed door. In one group you may be a leader while in another you are working to achieve someone else's plans. Try something new that appeared recently in a popular magazine or newspaper. Creative pursuits are especially worthwhile. What you have been doing primarily as a hobby can become a source of extra income for you. Your sense of adventure makes travel high on your list of priorities. Plan a trip to a destination that is frequently bypassed by tourists. Being able to combine work with pleasure is ideal. Jump at a chance to attend a conference or other meeting in a distant city, perhaps even a foreign one.

4. FRIDAY. Variable. Morning hours are excellent for seeking a bargain at an advertised sale. Arriving before the crowds gives you the best selection and the least hassle. This is not a time for Pisces to spend freely. Whatever you need can be found at a discount if you shop around. Know what you want and settle for nothing less. A cheaper brand may not act as well as its better known counterpart. You get what you pay for, but you do not have to pay full retail price. By afternoon you are ready to handle paperwork so that you have a clean slate for the weekend ahead. Be sure to repay a loan from a friend before your regular bills.

5. SATURDAY. Disturbing. Misleading statements are being passed from one person to the next as though they were absolute truth. Bring a halt to these rumors by refusing to tell anyone else. You can stop the chain of innuendo that could be damaging a person's reputation and good name. If you happen to be the object of some gossip, keep your head high and ride through the storm. A family member could begin questioning something you have long regarded as fact. It may come down to a matter of basic beliefs that cannot be resolved with talk and argument. Turn your humanitarian impulses into positive action by collecting money, food or clothing for people in need; and try to interest others to help.

6. SUNDAY. Rewarding. Take part in an activity with family members spanning the generations. Both young and old are eager to go along with you. You can learn a great deal from their outlook, which is likely to be slightly different from your own. Rewards come from looking at a problem as though you had never thought about it before. A fresh approach points the way to a solution that has so far escaped your notice. Opportunity may spring up in the most unexpected places. What is stored in a family member's attic could be a most welcome surprise. Learning more about your family heritage gives you a greater sense of who you are and what direction you might take next.

7. MONDAY. Demanding. Pisces are in a very demanding mood. Nothing done by others will totally satisfy you. For peace of mind, important work should be handled personally so that results are all your own; then you have only yourself to blame if you wish for more. Even the best of plans is apt to be fouled up in some way today. Misunderstandings are difficult to avoid. You could be left waiting at the wrong restaurant or on the wrong street corner. Assurances made by a repairman or other person providing a service may not be realized. Take into account that promises are not ironclad guarantees. Be ready to make adjustments at the last minute to avoid disappointment. Love relationships are apt to falter due to lack of sharing or failure to express affection.

8. TUESDAY. Hectic. Working at a fast clip demands that you pay more attention than usual to minor matters. Focus completely on the project at hand; do not allow your mind to wander off to what is coming next on your schedule. You are right on the ball today, able to analyze and make quick decisions. What is decided in the heat of the moment is likely to work out just as well as a decision that takes days or weeks and many committee meetings. Facts and figures that have been forgotten by other people will pop into your mind when you need them. Utilize your full memory potential, particularly in a social setting. Be sure to get a person's name correctly when you are introduced and then remember it.

9. WEDNESDAY. Unsettling. Guard against mixing business judgment with personal feelings. Pisces bosses may have to reprimand or even fire someone who has been a guest in their home or a long-time acquaintance. Money matters could also cause difficulties among business partners who happen to be friends. You need to remain calm and level-headed when negotiating even the simplest agreement. Terms agreed to now cannot be changed at a later date on a whim. You can be overly judgmental and critical. Give people the benefit of the doubt until you definitely have facts to support a different view. Do not be too overbearing with family members either, contradicting or mocking them.

10. THURSDAY. Satisfactory. There is not much chance today that someone can put something over on you. Your wits are sharp, and your tongue is likely to be the same. Keep negative thoughts to yourself unless uttering them might do some good. A promise made to you may not be fulfilled, leaving you holding the bag and having to explain. Quiet pursuits do not appeal now. You are in demand as a leader. Your ideas are quick to win acceptance. Hanging onto the familiar can stymie your progress; venture into an unknown area, particularly one that is considered high-tech. Learn as you go from someone who recently completed a course or is just a natural at the skill.

11. FRIDAY. Important. Turn to someone older, or at least wiser, if you need personal advice about a family matter. Be sure your confidant is not the type of person to repeat what you say in confidence. A decision has to be made soon about accepting a new assignment or a totally new job. Relocation questions could be holding you back or causing a family member to pull the reins on you. A trip could ease your mind and make the decision less stressful. This is a starred day to let your ambitions lead you forward. If you are only marching in place you will never get ahead. A well-calculated risk is worth the short-term disruption that might possibly result. If you don't try, you will never know.

12. SATURDAY. Pleasant. Casual conversation could conjure up an idea that comes as a complete surprise. A thought that you have been trying to ignore could suddenly refuse to be suppressed any longer. You cannot run away from a problem situation; face it squarely and the threat evaporates. Conditions are pleasant for a family get-together. Those you love understand your moods and are willing to cater to them. Your Pisces luck can help you come out a winner in a game of chance; if skill is also involved you may not be quite as fortunate. Someone is hoping you will call this evening. It is up to you to be the pursuer in romance at this particular time. If you succeed, all will change.

13. SUNDAY. Easygoing. A new relationship is beginning to take you or another family member away from home more often. This easygoing day favors welcoming a newcomer into the family circle without obviously quizzing them. It is also a fine time to acquire a kitten or puppy. Although you may be bursting to tell a secret, keep it to yourself a little while longer. You will know the moment is right when you can no longer contain your excitement. Past experience has direct relevance to a current project. Avoid following a pattern or rules to the letter; put a touch of your own creativity into everything that you are doing. Whether or not it pleases others does not worry you.

14. MONDAY. Rewarding. You cannot solve all the problems of the world, but you can make a difference in your own small corner of the universe. Help a friend or co-worker who does not seem to know which way to turn next. Just listening without offering advice can be useful. If you are asked for an opinion, be honest and straightforward. The most useful help might be to state bluntly that in your opinion they are overstating the magnitude of a problem. Humor can be a great appeaser. Be sure your savings are at work for you. This is a starred time to buy a savings bond or other insured investment. An accountant or financial adviser can assist you in cutting your end-of-year tax liability.

15. TUESDAY. Uncertain. Pisces are likely to be confused and lacking in direction today. Conditions are not quite as they seem. There is so much going on that you have to sort through it all to get to the crux of any matter. Extra effort is not necessarily going to improve the situation. The harder you try, the more likely you are to miscalculate. People who control what you do, and when you do it, are giving contradictory orders. When you start one project you may be called away to work on another. Loose ends make you nervous and uncomfortable. Home can be a haven of peace and tranquillity. That special person in your life is the one certainty you can count on at this stage. So you feel secure and needed.

16. WEDNESDAY. Difficult. Conditions remain difficult but not without glimmers of hope for a happy resolution of conflict. A heart-to-heart talk with a person who has been causing you grief can help iron out the problem. It could be a case of misunderstanding or of different goals. Beware of following a false trail. What has worked in the past is not automatically the best course to follow now. Although duty may call, you cannot drop everything to answer it. A friend or family member will understand if you set a time and place to get together later in the week when your schedule opens up. Tonight you need extra rest and quiet relaxation; it will help you ward off germs.

17. THURSDAY. Demanding. Someone is looking over your shoulder as you work through the day. Try to avoid being nervous or showing off. Keep to a steady schedule as though you had only yourself to please. The mistakes recently made by a co-worker should serve as an incentive for you to be on guard. You cannot excuse away sloppy or incomplete work. Flippant remarks and so-called jokes are unlikely to find an appreciative audience. Your words are likely to be analyzed and questioned. Devote some time to going over your personal or business finances in search of an error you know was made. Use a calculator so you do not make a mathematical miscomputation a second time. You need the peace and quiet of home tonight.

18. FRIDAY. Frustrating. Help and cooperation from higher-ups cannot be assumed. In fact, they may leave you to fend for yourself to see how you perform under pressure. Frustrations mount as a friend backs out of an arrangement at the last minute. As a sympathetic Pisces, you would never dream of canceling a date on a whim; some other Signs are practically oblivious to a commitment. Listen closely to your inner voice; it will not steer you wrong. A hunch could pay off in the long run. However, do not go looking for immediate results or you may begin to wonder if you have made a mistake of judgment. Nostalgic thoughts can be stopped short by a burst from the present.

19. SATURDAY. Difficult. Relationships remain rocky, although someone is being more honest than you are giving them credit for. There is a definite tilt putting the Pisces person on the bottom rung of the ladder now. You may have to take instructions or direct orders from someone you still think of as a child. Tension with neighbors should be resolved if possible. If you get into a continuing hassle with them you only hurt yourself and your family. You will be more persuasive if you talk with someone rather than to them. Avoid making any threats you cannot enforce. Channel creative impulses into something useful rather than as just other items to stick away on a shelf.

20. SUNDAY. Enjoyable. After the past few troubling days, this welcome respite does not come any too soon. Stay in bed as late as possible; dawdle over a second cup of coffee and the Sunday newspaper. An intimate setting helps problems with your mate become a thing of the past. You do not have to say a lot in order to have perfect mutual understanding. It is a fine day for considering ways to lighten and brighten your home. Slipcovers or an area rug could do the trick; translucent window coverings let the sunshine in. A bouquet of flowers or a potted plant is a welcome touch on the kitchen table. Enjoy being a guest later in the day and not having to lift a finger.

21. MONDAY. Disconcerting. Conditions are not encouraging for buying or selling anything of value. You can be duped by a fast-talker and not realize it until it is too late. Stay away from stores that offer only sales and no service or guarantees of satisfaction. What you save in price you can easily spend in frustration or even heartache later. Cultivate a can-do attitude. Although you may be a novice at a certain skill, you are a quick learner. Check out a book from the library, or buy your own copy at a bookstore, so that you can soak up knowledge that the boss or another higher-up thinks you already possess. A late phone call could disrupt your sleep tonight, but you forgive this caller.

22. TUESDAY. Mixed. Reduce spending so that you do not have to write a check or use a credit card today. Resist an urge to buy an item on sale that you like but do not need. It is important to display your work skills while the boss is around. If you appear lackadaisical you could be loaded down with extra tasks no one else wants. Pisces with few current assignments can find ways to string out the job so that it takes the time you have available. Avoid making any important commitments for the future. Finish up what you have already promised first. A drop-by visitor has good news to share about a family event and you will be one of the first to know, which delights you.

23. WEDNESDAY. Satisfactory. Be alert for an opportunity to make a difference at home or on the job. Handle priorities first thing this morning so that by afternoon you can delve into some optional jobs. Exceed minimum standards that are expected of everyone. You want to impress higher-ups with your ability and dedication. Standing out from the crowd puts you in line for a promotion or pay raise later in the year. Do not wait for other people to catch up with you; push forward according to your own timetable. Quicker ways of completing work can be found by looking for the second time at current methods. Question why a certain routine is being followed; you can come up with a more efficient procedure that saves time and money.

24. THURSDAY. Variable. Enthusiasm is at a high peak now, but Pisces can get carried away and miss the finer points of a project. Those little details are vital for long-term success. Double-check facts and figures; do not trust your memory. Work under way should be understated so that expectations are not out of line with reality. A higher-up is not considering an important factor in setting deadlines. Try to help him or her see the light in a tactful manner. If you must take a direct order that you disagree with, at least put your objections in writing so that you are covered in the future. A romantic attraction makes the evening both entertaining and memorable.

25. FRIDAY. Changeable. Someone who talks a lot does not necessarily have all the facts or all the answers. The person in the background of current affairs may be much more knowledgeable but not willing to step forward without being asked. You can get into trouble if your judgment is off the mark today; take a consensus immediately. Check basic facts with an independent source that does not have a stake in the outcome of the project you are finishing. Body language can help you separate sincere emotion from a hyped-up sales pitch. Pisces who have self-confidence stemming from previous success stand the best chance of overcoming obstacles in an innovative way.

26. SATURDAY. Cautious. Make a search for potential hazards around your home or yard, then find a way to take care of them. Safety should be today's prime consideration in all activities. Wear clothing appropriate for the weather. Extra layers help you keep warm, and you can peel off a few if the temperature rises. Insist that young family members keep you informed of their whereabouts throughout the day. For the Pisces searching for love, be wary of mistaking infatuation for the real thing. Avoid rushing a relationship that is growing out of the friendship stage into something more intense. Take nothing for granted when it comes to personal relationships and home life.

27. SUNDAY. Fortunate. This is a day to be practical-minded in everything you do. Figure out the bottom line before beginning a project. If costs seem excessive, forgo participating for a while. A love of animals can be the focal point of the day. You may want to groom a pet or teach a dog a new trick. Adopting a stray can liven up your home and put a smile on everyone's face. There is a strong element of luck accompanying your actions. A money windfall is not foreseen, but you can be lucky in giving and receiving love. Children can be especially pleasant companions. You will appreciate their openness, and may learn something from them. Life through their eyes has a special sparkle that they can transfer to you without even being aware of it.

28. MONDAY. Ordinary. Stick to usual workaday routine. Home and family matters should be put out of mind while you are on the job. Do not allow a burst of enthusiasm to cause you to overlook careful planning. Whatever is worthwhile is worth doing well. There can be an unfortunate consequence if you are too trusting. An honest difference of opinion must not be allowed to escalate into an argument. Agreement can be reached if you are willing to back down in your demands a little. Any letter or other written document should be short and to the point. Rambling on can get you in trouble; your listeners or readers may mistake wordiness for lack of a carefully thought-out plan.

MARCH

1. TUESDAY. Optimistic. Pisces students, or those interested in returning to the classroom, can find scholarship aid close to home. Check through a catalog for the courses that seem most interesting to you. A varied selection gives you a good, well-rounded background. Put off specialization in a particular subject until you have gained some on-the-job experience. It can help to maintain a low profile while keeping your eyes and ears open. Be alert for clues to future actions in the words of a principal or college dean. Ivory-tower types do not have all the answers but do have a lot of worthwhile theory from which you can draw your own conclusions. In this, the Pisces birthday month, you will be making resolutions for change and growth. Good luck accompanies your efforts.

2. WEDNESDAY. Hectic. Focus on what is possible to the exclusion of wishes and hopes. There is plenty to do without looking around for any more projects. Teamwork is favored, although you may have to carry more than your fair share of the burden. Pitch in without worrying about the percentage being done by anyone else. Rules should not be bent or broken. If you make an exception for one person, you may be expected to do so again or to provide the same favors for someone else. You can make a really favorable impression on an important higher-up. Prove that you understand their orders and are able to carry them out without having to be monitored every step of the way.

3. THURSDAY. Variable. Others are providing the leadership now while you follow along. Do not make any special demands or take any action that would cause you to stand apart. Local trips can be combined in order to gain the most from your effort. Take along a list and stick to it. Communicate by letter or phone if you need to confer with someone at a distance; traveling to meet in person is not necessary. Through business activity you can form a new friendship; romance, too, can start on the job. Keep a secret no matter how provoked you may be. Patience will lead to justifying a recent action that may seem odd to those who are not aware of its impact.

4. FRIDAY. Mixed. Matters are beginning to work out in your favor both in business and at home. Plod along without overlooking vital steps that can make all the difference in the end result. Others may be able to get by with shoddy workmanship, but you will never be satisfied unless results are up to your high standards. Being too independent will not be appreciated by those in superior positions. If you stray from the straight and narrow you will be jerked back into line. Keep an open mind to new ideas and proposals. What has worked well in the past is no guarantee of future repetition. Seriously consider an offer to take on new responsibility even if it involves relocating.

5. SATURDAY. Important. The spirit of discovery has you honing in on new opportunity close to your home base. Enlist the cooperation of your mate or another family member. You can secure financial backing from an older relative who appreciates your effort and recognizes your ability. For Pisces who must be on the job, this is a starred day for a breakthrough. The quiet atmosphere gives you time to think and experiment. You can come up with a revised plan to counter problems that have been holding you back. Someone you want to know better is playing hard to get. Make him or her sit up and take notice of you by using a third person to rouse a little jealousy.

6. SUNDAY. Productive. This weekend continues to be useful and productive. Discussing business matters in a social atmosphere could be worthwhile. Someone you know as a neighbor or friend could also be an excellent partner. Use your diplomatic skills in a situation where tempers threaten to flare. Act as a negotiator to bring together divergent views and find the middle ground. Give other people the benefit of the doubt when their motives come into question. There is more than one way to arrive at a desired goal; yours may be best for you but not for everyone else. There is a chance today to be part of a group devoted to humanitarian efforts; give time as well as money.

7. MONDAY. Sensitive. Tact and diplomacy are all-important to successful dealings with people in high positions. Pisces may have to play up to the boss or another superior in a low-key way. Put an emphasis today on positive aspects. You can change someone's mind most easily by making the person believe the idea is their own in the first place. Before accepting an invitation or other offer, weigh the cost in overall financial terms as well as the money you will have to put up front. It might be necessary to decline with regrets. What you hope to achieve and what you are able to do may not be one and the same. Relationships with the people close to you, even neighbors, demand extra consideration now.

8. TUESDAY. Outstanding. Pisces intuition is right on target when it comes to responding to the needs of a family member or co-worker. A specific request might be best met by showing the path ahead but not walking along it. Working in tandem is most beneficial if duties are shared equally. Otherwise you may wind up feeling resentful. Your outgoing personality puts you first on the list of those being considered for promotion. Do not let up now that you are so near a long-term goal. Try something new in a quiet way to test the results. You will enjoy an aura of mystery and secrecy. A relationship is moving from one stage to the next in quick progression. Enjoy it without questioning how or why or if you are deserving.

9. WEDNESDAY. Uncertain. An imaginative idea can be transformed into a money-maker if you are willing to devote the time and effort necessary to heighten your skills. A professional appearance is necessary in product and person. Do not downplay your skills. If you appear uncertain, you could be turned down for a loan or other help. Look for ways to expand your circle of friends and acquaintances. Apply for membership in a society or club that piques your interest. Delving into history or the occult is likely to appeal to the Pisces personality. Answers to your hardest questions are not easy to get. You may only receive clues and have to make an educated guess from there.

10. THURSDAY. Mixed. Whatever is being done in secret can be hurried along if you apply advanced techniques. Be careful, however, that you do not go overboard with the newest and most modern. There is some special benefit in a slower pace that allows you to stay in complete control. Property or a certain possession may be in dispute. You could require the services of an attorney if unable to straighten out the problem on your own. Do not give in to avoid an argument; your resentment will make you miserable. It can pay to join forces with a person whose interests are the same as your own. Together you can halve the work and go far toward doubling the results. Both the Moon and Sun in Pisces now give you good luck.

11. FRIDAY. Routine. Stick with everyday routine although you would prefer to take the day off and get away. Sound out the boss or another in-charge type before deviating from usual routine. Headway will be slow but sure. There is the possibility that you lack necessary skill or perhaps tools for a job that has been assigned to you. If so, get some help before proceeding. False starts are indicated if you believe you can make a go of it totally on your own. By joining forces with others you can achieve common goals. A phone call saves you the time and expense of long-distance travel. If you sense an argument brewing, back down and wait to fight it out at some other time.

12. SATURDAY. Variable. Pisces are happier today acting independently and avoiding any type of team effort. In a group you may feel that you are losing your special identity. Research can be beneficial; spend some time conferring by phone or by FAX messages. Consider all current communications that seem to be converging on a particular project. You can make things happen if aware of what can go wrong. Pisces parents can learn a lot from the actions of their offspring. You and your mate need to join forces in enforcing rules and regulations around the house. Children naturally try to divide and conquer; prove to them that you are smarter than they think.

13. SUNDAY. Good. Entertaining on tap today could be not only fun but a way to advance your job prospects. Get to know people on the top rung of that elusive ladder. Who you associate with can rub off on you in many ways. Try to remember the people to whom you are introduced and some personal tidbit about them or their family. Pisces involved in any type of sports, whether as a player, coach or referee, will enjoy the competition. Win or lose, you rid yourself of tension and stress by being part of a team. Evening hours favor studying or reading rather than wasting time in front of the television screen. The biography of a famous person offers worthwhile ways to get ahead.

14. MONDAY. Hectic. The Moon in Aries promises excellent results as the reward for your extra effort today. Do not sit back and wait for someone else to run with the ball. Grab it and head for the winner's circle. You can make things happen through independent action. The boss or another superior is not available to hold you by the hand and take you step-by-step through a project. Make less important decisions on your own; confer only about major policy. People are willing to bend rules on your behalf, but do not ask for too much. Imagination can bridge a gap in hard facts. Rely on your good Pisces intuition when there is nothing else to go on.

15. TUESDAY. Pleasant. The pressure is off today, making this a pleasant time as well as a sociable one. Get to know a co-worker personally. Listen to the boss as a human being instead of a superman with all the answers. Pisces are in a giving mood today. It will please you to help someone less experienced or less fortunate than you, and probably anonymously. The only thanks you need will be your own self-satisfaction at being able to lend a hand. Follow your naturally good instincts in deciding which charitable organization is most worthy based on your own experience. Be prepared to meet a friend or family member at least halfway. You have time to be generous now.

16. WEDNESDAY. Misleading. Heed warning signs that others may be missing. Do not allow people to brush off your concerns with a pat on the head. Misleading information could be broadcast as the gospel truth. Nothing is quite as it seems. Your Pisces judgment can spot a bluff and cut it to shreds. Proceed in a cool, calm manner. Do not expect anyone to go out of his or her way on your behalf. Differences that exist with your mate or partner are not going to be cleared away overnight. If you can get people to talk about a problem you have made good progress. A frank discussion can bring out hidden grievances that have been stalling a project since early in the year.

17. THURSDAY. Excellent. A friend comes to your aid just when you are wondering where to go for help. You can also get your way with someone in a high position if you state reasons and rationale logically. Pisces spirits are soaring. There is no stopping you once you know what you want. A new idea can be nurtured to success if you are patient. By analyzing past mistakes you know what to avoid now. Find a way to utilize a talent that you have been developing as a hobby. The more you are able to do in a competitive situation, the more you will be in demand and able to command a higher rate of pay. Loved ones make you realize how appreciated you are.

18. FRIDAY. Tricky. Tension and stress affect your mood and could cause you to fly off the handle at a real or imagined slight. Think about what you intend to say before uttering a word. There is a trick to getting along: you have to treat other people as you find them, not as you want them to be. If health is a problem, discuss available remedies with an older family member or friend. Consult a doctor next week if the condition has not cleared up by then. This is not the time to loan or borrow anything of value.

Being in debt can lead to a broken relationship due to the pressure of having to repay. If repair work is necessary around the house, obtain a few estimates first.

19. SATURDAY. Mixed. Changeable conditions can land you in all sorts of trouble. Keep your distance from neighbors and others who are known to start as well as spread gossip. Someone who attracts you on first meeting may seem less appealing as you get to know them better. Guard against making a commitment either to them or to yourself too soon in a relationship. Pisces are likely to be blinded by physical appearance and overlook mental incompatibility. You cannot be happy for long with a person who does not operate on the same wavelength as you. Try to get some time alone for contemplation of all the issues. You may discover that the answer to a problem is not difficult.

20. SUNDAY. Buoyant. Do not wait for family members or friends to come up with suggestions for the day. Check the newspaper for entertainment ideas, pick one or two, and make your plans accordingly. There is a strong element of good fortune playing into your hands. A sold-out concert or other performance may have just a few tickets when you happen to call for them. Traveling out of town should not be a problem. In fact, you will enjoy the companionship of your mate or steady date without interference from hangers-on. Ask a question that you have been pondering; luck today allows a direct response that is sure to be to your liking. Give free rein to romantic impulses. The Pisces birthday period for this year ends tonight on a happy note.

21. MONDAY. Useful. It is important today to appear in charge even if you are harboring some secret doubts. The person in control has an extra degree of power. Useful work can be done under the leadership of Pisces; you do not actually have to pitch in or get your hands dirty in the process. You can gain clearer insight into a matter that has been puzzling you. The pieces are beginning to come together. Your partner or another important person in your life has a suggestion that should not be ignored. Speculating or gambling is not recommended. Judgment in financial affairs could be poor; you cannot bank on a hot tip. Join with friends for low-key evening entertainment.

22. TUESDAY. Rewarding. You should have no trouble selling yourself and your ideas. If you believe you deserve a raise or a promotion, talk to the boss in private. This is also a fine time to present a proposal that could lead to advancement if you are able to pull it off as you expect. Do not take no for an answer; it could be necessary, however, to settle for maybe. Even if you do not feel fully prepared for a new start, make a tentative foray into an area that is not usual for you. What is occurring overseas could lead to special rewards if you keep on top of the situation. Tune in to an all-news station so that you do not miss late-breaking developments having a bearing.

23. WEDNESDAY. Disconcerting. A situation that has been causing some trouble is growing more intense. Take action as soon as possible or you may have to watch a good idea go up in flames. There is power in numbers. Join with a group of people who share your goals and idealism. Working alone can be disconcerting. It will be difficult to judge who is on your side and who is only pretending to be. Make do with supplies already on hand. There is not enough money coming in to buy new equipment now. Only after the first blush of success can you afford to splurge. You have no choice but to pay off bills before incurring any new debt. An evening workout can help alleviate stress.

24. THURSDAY. Easygoing. Take it slow and easy today. Let others set the tone and the pace. Pisces-born followers have a definite advantage now. You will get credit for what you do and will not have to take the blame for a project if it should go wrong. Get in touch with friends or family members at a distance. Write a long, chatty letter to update them on all that has been happening. You do not need a major event to spur you to write. Tasks requiring concentration may be too much to handle now. Your thoughts are apt to be scattered here and there. Something that usually comes easily may require more concentration than you are able to supply. Give a loved one a treat tonight.

25. FRIDAY. Beneficial. A reversal of yesterday's trends is foreseen. Conditions now put Pisces in power positions. People are listening to you and ready to follow your lead. Fill in a leadership vacuum that no one else seems able or willing to do. Do not let anyone else to make plans on your behalf. Keep your finger on the pulse of all that is going on. Enlist whatever help is available to assist you in furthering ambitious plans. A partnership combining your talents and a co-worker's love of detail can be particularly beneficial. New alignments are foreseen now. Someone who has been a competitor is ready to side with you. Push to finalize a deal right away.

26. SATURDAY. Confusing. Nothing is quite as it seems in your home. A family member is being stubborn about one matter but is probably upset about something entirely different. You may have hurt someone's feelings and not be aware of it. Getting loved ones to open up and talk to you can help resolve the problem situation. Shopping requires extra caution so that you do not accept a substitute for what was advertised at a special price. Demand a rain check if the merchandise you want is not in stock. Some double-dealing is likely; do not fall for lame excuses. You have the determination today to give up a habit you know is a negative health factor. Once your mind is made up, you will achieve your goal.

27. SUNDAY. Outstanding. There is plenty to do, and you will not want to be idle today. Direct your energies toward useful projects around the house and in the neighborhood. When you see something that should be fixed, get right to it. The more you have to do, the better it will suit you. Nervous energy gives you greater stamina than others in the family. Enlist help from more than one person or you are likely to burn them out and have no one to rely upon. Entertaining or being an invited guest is not apt to appeal. Rearranging furniture can give a room an entirely new look at no additional cost. Find a way to display a family heirloom where it will be a focal point.

28. MONDAY. Fortunate. Pisces are apt to be in particular favor with the home office. Higher-ups are aware of what you have been doing; co-workers, too, know that you are a bright light worth following. An inquiry about your future prospects gives you valid reasons to be confident about a pay raise or promotion. Learn a new technique that makes you even more valuable both to your current employer and to competitors. It cannot hurt to be in a bargaining situation where your services are in demand by companies willing to pay a premium. Someone you love is ready to make a fuss over you. This evening you will feel warm and loved more so than usual.

29. TUESDAY. Fair. Deal directly with those who are doing work on your behalf. If you can avoid the middleman you can save a lot and also get exactly what you want. Details are especially important now and are likely to occupy much of your time. Avoid delegating work that is based primarily on an idea in your mind. There is opportunity today to present a plan to a higher-up or to the general public. Even if you have received prior rejection, try again to win the go-ahead that you need. A partnership problem could slow you down. Money in a joint account cannot be withdrawn without the approval of the other person authorized to write checks.

30. WEDNESDAY. Exciting. What is least expected may be most rewarding. Pisces are ready to respond to the smallest opening with a burst of enthusiasm. Your excitement is contagious. Whatever you decide will meet with approval from those with whom you have cooperated in the past. A newcomer, however, may take a little more persuading to join your team. Intuition plays a major role in your progress. Act on a hunch even if it seems to go against prevailing opinion. A financial statement is close to being finalized. When you have money in the bank you can relax and give free rein to your creativity. Listen to the advice of a person who knows how to live as well as work.

31. THURSDAY. Lucky. Travel can put you where the action is. Book reservations early in the day for a flight before nightfall. Do not wait to make precise arrangements; you can get a hotel room or rent a car when you arrive at your destination. The action is far from your normal base of operations. If you are present on the scene you can help make things go your way. Otherwise you are at the mercy of those making the decisions without your direct input. Pisces able to speak a second language have special advantages. Luck is riding at your side. Someone you once helped in the past is now in a position to return the favor. This could be the breakthrough you have been seeking.

APRIL

1. FRIDAY. Productive. Be on the job a little earlier this morning so that you have a better chance to finish necessary work and leave ahead of other workers. Decisions have to be made in rapid-fire order by Pisces in charge. You can count on obtaining cooperation whether projects are shared or are basically your own domain. As a result, work will be easier and results more satisfactory. Morning is best for writing and planning; later in the day your energy falters and mental processes slow down. There is more going on at home than on the job. On the way home pick up a few extra snacks to have on hand for drop-in visitors this weekend. Buy food that will not perish quickly.

2. SATURDAY. Excellent. The harder you focus on a situation, the more possibilities will become apparent. Do not wait for a brainstorm; make it happen through direct attention that helps you winnow out the most likely answers. Family members are agreeable to anything you suggest. Frank, open communication is the key. Avoid casting blame on any one person; instead, let everyone be part of the solution. You have many opportunities today to carry out personal plans. Put the house in tip-top shape, including polishing crystal and washing windows. Insist that pets stay off the furniture so that your family's clothing is not full of stray hairs. Your mate wants to please you in every way, which helps to release some of your inhibitions.

3. SUNDAY. Disquieting. Despite your well-laid plans nothing will go exactly as you had envisioned today. A morning arrangement may be put on hold due to weather or the illness of a family member. Or you may arrive at your destination only to discover that there is no place to park or a full house with standing room only. You have little choice but to make the best of a disquieting situation. Later in the day drop in on a friend or family member who needs to be cheered up. Your positive outlook can be good therapy for them. Travel is favored providing you allow ample time; rushing is especially stressful on youngsters and is likely to make them irritable. Take precautions on the sports field.

4. MONDAY. Variable. If you can get off work today you will be happier for it. If not, concentrate only on what cannot be postponed. Higher-ups are apt to turn the other way if you are not as busy as usual. The only pressure is being applied by the Pisces personally. Avoid any confrontation with co-worker or neighbor. Walk away rather than continue a conversation that seems to be turning into an argument. You may have to make up an excuse to get out of a social invitation or to cover your failure to show up at a get-together held over the weekend just past. That special person in your life will come to your aid to back up whatever you say. A friendship shows signs of developing into romantic love.

5. TUESDAY. Outstanding. Conditions are settling back to the normal hustle and bustle that you thrive on. You should feel a lot more optimistic. Plans can be expedited by seeking help from those closest to you. Travel arrangements need to be made early in the day for a trip later this month. Do not wait or you might have to take a red-eye trip in the dead of the night in order to arrive for a meeting. Consider alternative arrangements as a backup plan. Cooperation is yours for the asking today. Pisces determination is a great drawing card in obtaining help; everyone loves a winner, and you are definitely on the winning track. Do not show surprise if the boss or another higher-up comes to you for off-the-record advice. Your reputation for keeping a secret is earned.

6. WEDNESDAY. Changeable. Circumstances do not favor new starts. Anything out of the ordinary requires more time to convince those around you that it is in their best interest as well as yours to join forces. A new idea is unlikely to get the approval of a licensing agency or other government bureau that must pass judgment on your plan. Lack of money could thwart your effort as well. The promise of a loan is not enough security to go out and buy new equipment and supplies. Have the money in hand before spending any of it. Do not overload yourself with extra duties and responsibilities. The Pisces vitality is slowly returning to pre-holiday levels but is not yet there. With the Moon in your sign today, energy will slowly rise.

7. THURSDAY. Useful. Stay close to your usual base of operations this morning. People at and from a distance will only confuse you. Stick to what you know you can handle well. By midday confidence is on the upswing and you can take a well-calculated risk with good indications of success. That is the best time to turn on your persuasive charm in dealing with the boss or another prominent person. Filling out forms could occupy a chunk of time. Be as complete and thorough as possible. Resuming negotiations that broke off earlier could be worthwhile if you have a new offer to put on the table. Ask for a little more than you might actually be willing to accept in a signed deal.

8. FRIDAY. Easygoing. Pisces have a chance to catch up and take a deep breath today. There will be plenty of time to review developments of the past week and concoct a revised plan if necessary. Someone you thought you could trust may be causing you to wonder if your judgment was on target. Be more observant of this person's actions. Study and self-improvement courses are helpful in advancing your career. A good how-to book can bring you up to speed in a new technological advance that has other people buzzing. Consult with an attorney or other professional if you need hard facts and advice. By evening you are ready for socializing with those who like you just the way you are.

9. SATURDAY. Happy. Good luck is coming your way via a friend or neighbor. Be ready to drop plans that can be postponed without disappointing someone else. Some important changes are occurring in your own backyard. What is drab and commonplace is being transformed into a feast for the eyes. Enjoy the companionship of a child. Through them you can see things that have always been there but are rarely noticed. Creative hobbies hold special appeal. Put more of yourself into a project designated as a gift for someone close to you. Make it as personal as possible by including an inscription or dedication. Enjoy being part of a partying group tonight, but act as a responsible adult at all times.

10. SUNDAY. Pleasant. You may not feel like doing much except staying at home and puttering around. Plans are not necessary in order to enjoy yourself today. Flit from one activity to the next without feeling compelled to finish anything. Ideas are flowing fast and furiously. Testing them out is one of the joys of life even if you know of no practical application at this time. You will get a great measure of satisfaction from putting personal affairs in apple-pie order. Pay bills and write a long letter. File away important papers and throw out the rest. Pisces operate best in an uncluttered environment where everything has a special niche and can be found easily. Then you can move ahead freely.

11. MONDAY. Stimulating. Alter your routine for the day and all of your senses will be stimulated. Shake things up just for the excitement of it. Plan on having lunch with someone you want to get to know better, or make arrangements to meet this evening. There are some ongoing problems over which you can exercise no control at this time. Put them in the back of your mind to worry about later; pondering them now does no good at all. You do not have to spend a lot in order to make this day a success. Clothes now in your closet are fine for whatever social engagements are on your schedule. You may want to get a haircut or have your hair colored, however. Focus only on the present.

12. TUESDAY. Demanding.   Avoid actions or decisions made in haste. Take your time with any and all requests. If an immediate answer is demanded, you would be wise to say no. This is not the day to sign a contract or any other legally binding document. Keep money where you know it is safe even if the return you are receiving is not as good as it might be in a more risky venture. Financial activity is too complicated for rash action. Look into opinions being offered by those who are paid to analyze and make suggestions. Do not let a favorite possession deteriorate due to weather damage or overuse. Treat everything you own as though it were irreplaceable. Do not let children shirk responsibilities.

13. WEDNESDAY. Lucky.   Impatient Pisces have a strong element of luck that can take you in a hop, skip and jump from the start to the finish of a project. All the help you need is available. Cooperation is yours for the asking. Creative work, or anything that depends on imagination, is especially favored. Your mind is roaring along at warp speed, coming up with alternatives whenever you seem to hit a dead end. You will find it easier to influence the people who are important to your progress. The boss is basking in the reflected glow of work that you have done. Seize a chance to talk to a newcomer about developments at distance that could signal the start of a new trend.

14. THURSDAY. Outstanding.   Any remaining obstacle that has been holding you back can now be overcome. You have free sailing to proceed as you see fit. Do not be impeded by a family member or co-worker who needs constant reassurance every step of the way. You know what your long-term goals are and how you intend to achieve them. The Moon entering Gemini today gives you added incentive and drive. Teamwork makes it possible to meet an important deadline with time to spare. Be sure to share kudos and congratulations with everyone involved. Loved ones will be delighted if you come up with a plan for evening entertainment that takes everyone out of the house for a few hours.

15. FRIDAY. Harmonious. Personal relationships, and particularly a love affair, are in perfect harmony with other aspects of life. There should be no stress between what you want as an individual and the expectations put on you as part of a working team. The news is positive, putting you in a continuing optimistic frame of mind. That special person in your life will be delighted if you propose a trip together. You will not have to convince anyone to go along with your plans; mention them and you should receive immediate agreement. There are strong indications of extra money coming through a prize or other reward for work that was recently finished. You could be in line for a bonus or a promotion in recognition of your diligence.

16. SATURDAY. Sensitive. Look into a situation in your own community that is bothering a lot of your neighbors. Be willing to sign a petition, donate time or provide other help to the side you support. If you take a hands-off attitude you will have to live with whatever happens and have no basis for complaining about it. Your strong principles could drive you to be in on the organizing of change that seems necessary. A chance encounter gives you good opportunity to make a point with an elected official. Do not fret about a hobby or educational project that is not working out to your expectations. Put it aside for a while and go on to something more satisfying. Encourage children to learn a new skill.

17. SUNDAY. Fortunate. Bonds of affection are growing stronger for both married and single Pisces. That special person wants to please you. A new addition will be welcomed into the family circle. You will be relaxed and happy in a group of people you know well. There is no reason to put on airs or pretend to be someone you are not. Cast out feelings of jealousy about the recent promotion of a friend or a new acquisition. You have all that you need and then some. You can expect fortunate results if raising money or seeking volunteers for a cause you believe in wholeheartedly. Champion the underdog who is unable to stand up for rights that are being denied him or her.

18. MONDAY. Important. A long-anticipated wish is close to your grasp. This day is important because of the people with whom you are associating. Do not hesitate to ask for a favor; you will not be refused. Arrange to be where the action is. If you have not been invited to a closed-door meeting, try to wrangle an invitation or to go in place of someone unable to attend. Be flexible in thinking about the future. What seems the surest path to success may not be right for you. There are detours that can make you more valuable and enhance your reputation. Your track record to date speaks for itself; no one underestimates your abilities and determination. The shy Pisces might be helped by taking speech or drama lessons.

19. TUESDAY. Manageable.   Budget your time and energy so that you have enough to go around. You are being pulled in a number of directions, and all deserve a fair amount of attention. Be aware of your own limitations; delegate work that others can handle as well as you could. A current project holds great promise for the future. Double-check as you proceed so that no initial error is repeated at later times. Even small variations in measurements or wording can throw off final results. Be sure to encourage a co-worker or family member who is trying as hard as you but not yet achieving the same level of results. Later in the year you will get a needed lift when they return the favor.

20. WEDNESDAY. Useful.   Nothing comes easily today, but there are definite rewards as you diligently plug away toward a goal. Be willing to redo certain parts of a project that are not up to your high standards. What is satisfactory for other people may be less so for you. Do not make this into a major cause for upset. You can quietly make changes that you are authorized to do without having to cast blame or find fault. A higher-up is evaluating your persistence and determination. If you are in a mutual enterprise, be sure to consult your partner, particularly if you seem to be going over budget. Renegotiating a contract could be the answer if costs are exceeding expectations.

21. THURSDAY. Stimulating.   Your mate or partner has some excellent ideas, but it is up to you to step in and help implement them. Even the best idea is worthless if not put into operation. Stimulating people enhance your creativity. Join a group of like-minded enthusiasts who share your abiding interests. There is something to be learned by even the most expert Pisces. Today favors taking advantage of opportunity before someone shoves you out of the way. You do not have to be a bully to get ahead, but you will benefit from being assertive. Anything important that is mailed today should be insured for full value. It is better to be safe than sorry even if it costs you extra.

22. FRIDAY. Optimistic.   Curiosity can lead to a breakthrough that will earn you more money and enhance your reputation. Follow through with an idea that other people downgrade. You do not have to obtain permission in order to work during your off hours. Maintain a degree of secrecy in initial stages. Aim to please yourself in methods and procedures. What has been a hobby can become a money-maker if you are able to buy supplies wholesale and find a sales outlet. Romance is a shining beacon throughout the day. That special person is waiting for you at the end of your work and will not let you think about anything else except your life together. You will, however, share ideas about health and fitness.

23. SATURDAY. Uncertain.   Guard against giving orders to family members as though they were in your employ. Make requests instead of barking commands. Conditions are uncertain at home. There is a chance to make a profit through property transactions, but a co-owner with you may not be willing to sell. Buying a new home or a recreational vehicle is favored only if the price is right. Being part of a crowd does not appeal. You will be happiest as a twosome or even on your own for most of the day. Check in with a friend who has not been feeling well. Offer to run some errands or to prepare a meal. Your own health could force you to go to bed early tonight with a heating pad.

24. SUNDAY. Good.   Finding ways to save money keeps you from having to earn more. Shop around for a bargain in what you must have; skip the nonnecessities. An advertised sale could be a bargain bonanza if you arrive just when the store doors open. You may even want to stock up on gift ideas for later in the year. Family members are surprisingly agreeable. Whatever you suggest will be all right with them. It is not too early to begin considering vacation locales. Determine whether you want a water-oriented resort or a more relaxed atmosphere where your every whim is catered to and you do not have to lift a finger. The Sunday newspaper may have good values for vacationers able to book reservations well in advance.

25. MONDAY. Slow.   You can afford to give extra time and attention today to matters of a personal nature. There should be little pressure to produce. The boss or another higher-up is satisfied to know you are available on an as-needed basis. Plan a party or other get-together for a weekend in the future. A family reunion could also be an option, but it takes someone to stir up interest and then make the arrangements. Pisces parents may need to check in with their child's teacher to find out if any extra help is needed at home as the school year winds down. This is not the time to incur any additional debt, especially if your tax burden is higher than you expected. Make do with supplies already on hand.

26. TUESDAY. Pleasant. This is another day free of pressure except that which you exert on yourself. Look for a way to help a friend or co-worker who is too proud to request assistance. Be sure to keep a secret that has been entrusted to you. Any rumors that are spreading around should be examined under a microscope before you continue to pass the word. A person's reputation can be damaged by a coincidence that is totally innocent. It is a favorable day for Pisces to indulge in pleasures of the senses. Choose companions with care so that no one gets in trouble. Romance is sure to benefit from the extra attention that your feelings are generating.

27. WEDNESDAY. Productive. You cannot escape the pressure to produce today. Work is being passed along to you for review or input. Be more thorough than expected. You can impress the boss by doing a little extra without expecting a reward or individual notice. Something you have been hoping would occur is apt to take you by surprise. Your spirits will soar when an important person singles you out in a crowd. The day is starred for presenting forward-looking ideas with a well-detailed plan of attack. You may lack some particular skills, but you know where to find the help that is required to achieve your aims. Leave details to others while you operate on a higher plane.

28. THURSDAY. Challenging. A new approach may be necessary in order to avoid mistakes made in the past. Do not cling to the old ways out of fear of learning something new. You can catch on quickly, although it might take you longer than a newcomer fresh from training. Do not give up; persevere until you are satisfied that you know what is necessary. Conditions improve as the day progresses. The boss's morning announcement may be rescinded later in the day. Nothing is written in permanent ink now. Be noncommittal if asked to make a decision affecting a group to which you belong; you are only one member and cannot speak for everyone. Shun any form of speculation or gambling, especially games of chance that require big money wagers.

29. FRIDAY. Quiet.   The end of the workweek for most Pisces will be a surprisingly quiet day. A deadline that you have been working to achieve may be postponed; you will not know whether to be glad or mad after the pressure you have applied on yourself. With less pressure, you have the quiet time to compose a letter, report or other written document. Once you decide what you want to say, the words should flow smoothly. Be sure to include your dream for the future as a means of influencing those who are beginning to lose hope. Make an appointment for a medical or dental checkup to ease your mind of any health concerns. Evening favors staying home in the arms of your loved one.

30. SATURDAY. Mixed.   It is up to you to find a compromise that will bowl over a stalemated situation. Do not expect others to give in until you show that you are ready to do so as well. Intuition could be leading you down the wrong track; act on hard information that can be verified. Finances are adding strain at home. Pore over the budget and come up with a more realistic one for next month. Interest charges could be taking more and more of your pay. Look for ways to pay off outstanding debt before buying anything else on time. Have a quiet dinner tonight with friends, either as a guest in their home or as the host for the get-together. Romance takes a backseat if Pisces focuses on friendships.

MAY

1. SUNDAY. Rewarding. Pisces can find plenty to do as this merry month gets under way. Family members are depending on you to come up with a plan and then help carry it out. Work around the house should not be put off. If you cannot tackle it all yourself, scout out a reliable professional for the more difficult jobs. Gardening appeals, although you may not have the greenest thumb. A nursery can help you select the right plants or seeds that will brighten your landscape. Be wary of tackling jobs that are strenuous; let a more physically fit family member do the lifting, loading and digging. If you are seeing stars before your eyes, it may be that love has stunned you. Do not be blind to the risks.

2. MONDAY. Variable. People are drawn by your aura of self-assurance, but it is up to you to enlist their cooperation and maintain their interest. Assign jobs that are important; you cannot handle everything personally even though you might like to do so. Education never stops; Pisces should look into courses being taught at a nearby university to upgrade skills that only a short time ago were sufficient for the job but now are becoming outdated. Creativity cannot cover for lack of knowledge after a certain point. Do not allow a worry to bring your actions to a standstill; move to counterattack. The best defense is often a strong offense. Confiding in a trusted friend could alter your perspective.

3. TUESDAY. Outstanding. People have to work hard to keep pace with Pisces today. You are apt to move ahead at a fast clip, outdistancing competitors and helpers alike. Take charge of ongoing operations. Step in without waiting for a formal summons to action. Your judgment helps you to take chances that others deem too risky. You know better having worked out the details mentally before you ever begin. A friend or older family member needs a lift to continue a struggle that is almost becoming too much for them. Your confidence in their ability is just what the doctor ordered. Be generous in sharing time even though you have to steal it from a personal project.

4. WEDNESDAY. Pleasant. A book can provide the inspiration you need to move closer to a long-term dream. Or it may be that you are inspired to write about your own experiences as a guide for others to follow. This is a starred day to begin a new project. You have the patience to follow through without definite indications of success. Catch up on the latest news in the neighborhood. A chat with the person who lives next door can be an eye-opener. You may have good reason to buy a special present for an upcoming event that you learn about today. A ho-hum love affair can be given a boost if you are able to forget a real or perceived transgression. The Moon in Pisces today enables you to express deep feelings without fear of the consequences.

5. THURSDAY. Enjoyable. Personal relationships are back on track and should provide the happiness that you had come to expect. Good news from someone out of town could prompt you to plan a trip before the end of the month. Consider sharing vacation accommodations with someone you have known since school days. Take people at their word; it does not pay to look for hidden meaning. Trust your good instincts when it comes to judging character. The initial success that you are enjoying now is likely to bring a wealth of new offers. You can pick and choose like a squirrel in a forest of oak trees. There is strong indication of new friendship or love. Take advantage of the Moon in your sign now to open a meaningful dialogue with an important person.

6. FRIDAY. Good. A stubborn streak that is not too often on display in Pisces is coming to the surface now. Do not back down from what you believe is right unless shown indisputable evidence. Your judgment is not always right, but your reasoning is excellent. The day favors trying to secure a pay raise or promotion by talking with the person in charge. Let it be known that you believe you deserve to get ahead. If you wait for someone to notice you the snow may be on the ground. Release a sense of urgency by getting some physical exercise. Consider joining a sports team or athletic league for the fun of it as well as the activity. Win or lose you will get more for the camaraderie than you bargained for.

7. SATURDAY. Sensitive. You are likely to brood while others are only interested in having fun. Go your own way and everyone will be happy, at least during daytime hours. Later you may want to get together to enjoy a movie or play with a message. Manual work, providing it is not too strenuous, could be useful. Get out the hammer and saw and do some repair jobs that for safety's sake should not be put off. You can learn all you need to know from a good how-to manual. Be careful about accepting an offer that ties you down to one person. Keep your options open. Friends are pressing for an answer to a proposal they hope you will accept. Put them off a little longer.

8. SUNDAY. Disappointing. After yesterday's frustrations, today's disappointment will not come as a major surprise. Be prepared to apologize even if you do not know exactly why. You may have offended a friend or family member because you were not paying close enough attention to their needs. Associating with a stranger can be a welcome relief; expectations will be negligible and you can act naturally. Money matters are upsetting. You may think you have lost a sum of cash when actually it went for numerous small purchases that add up to a significant amount. Keeping track of your expenditures for the week ahead helps cut down on unnecessary costs.

9. MONDAY. Difficult. Do not believe even half of what you are told and less of what you read. Rumors are rampant. You could put a relationship in danger if you seem to trust one person's word in speaking out against a co-worker or friend. Be cautious in dealing with business associates. Someone is being two-faced, telling you what you want to hear but then turning around and doing the opposite. Separating truth from fantasy takes time and patience. Verify information with independent sources. This is not a time to make any major purchase; competing claims are too confusing and difficult to sort out. Try to anticipate trouble in order to ward it off. A firm hand on youngsters is required both at home and at school in order to teach them responsibilities.

10. TUESDAY. Manageable. After the past few difficult days you are ready to come up for air and take a deep breath. Working on your own is favored, particularly if a deadline is looming. You can manage your private affairs if not burdened with the problems of other people as well. You do not have to turn a deaf ear to them; merely postpone action as they have done when you asked for help. Be wary of crossing the invisible boundary between friendship and romance. You can damage a relationship if you move too fast. Wait to be sure not only of the other person's feelings but also of your own. Infatuation comes in many disguises, including the true love that is worth waiting patiently for.

11. WEDNESDAY. Variable. It may be necessary to rearrange your schedule or cancel an appointment because of a health problem. You have to be good to yourself before you can be useful to anyone else. Get a professional opinion and treatment recommendations. If pills are prescribed, check to be sure they are compatible with what you already take. A soak in a hot tub or a massage can relieve muscle pain. Consider obtaining advice about nutrition and diet from someone with training in that area. It is not smart to go on a stringent diet without first getting a medical okay. Do not attempt to make major changes on your own. Many people have your best interests at heart and are perfectly willing to help if asked. A parents' support group can give you a fresh perspective.

12. THURSDAY. Stressful. Pressure is building to a crescendo. There is no time to waste today. Get an early start and keep up the pace. You can ask for favors, but do not assume they are going to be granted. The one favor you are most unlikely to be given is a deadline extension. Finish a project as best you can; if it is not up to your high standards, it nevertheless is likely to satisfy the boss. Be wary if offered a bribe or inside information. You may be put to the test to see how you will react. Anything underhanded is likely to have serious repercussions in the future. In addition, your Pisces conscience would be in turmoil. Love life takes a backseat to a child's problem; try to get a good night's sleep tonight.

13. FRIDAY. Disquieting. For superstitious Pisces, this Friday the 13th is apt to come as no surprise. Activities are going on behind a closed door and you are deliberately being kept from knowing. A friend or family member craves more independence; only later will this person realize that your advice was right on target. You cannot run anyone else's life; concentrate on your own affairs. Attempt to build bridges instead of burn them behind you. If you must quit a job or an assignment, strive to leave on good terms with everyone involved. A threat may only be an illusion, but to you it is very real. You can be your own worst enemy if you are too trusting. Continue to monitor a teenager's activities.

14. SATURDAY. Mixed. Stand up for yourself and you can push through changes you want. Do not back down in the face of opposition. No one is going to give in readily, but they can be convinced with a combination of reason and pressure. Go after what you want with determination. A love affair that seemed to be ending could be renewed if you try a new tactic. Reverse roles and let it be known who is boss. Insist on an answer rather than merely requesting a reply. Be tactful but firm. You can afford to make a special purchase that will enhance your appearance and give you added self-confidence. When you know you look good you do not shy away from confrontation.

15. SUNDAY. Sensitive. Little things are apt to irk you throughout the day. You may take affront at a remark made only in jest. Be wary of reading more into what someone says than what was intended. A newcomer is attempting to establish a footing on which to operate, and in doing so could be stepping on your toes. You can afford to retreat but not to give in totally. It is important to stand up for yourself rather than waiting for another person to take your side and state your case. Check that you have adequate insurance on home and property. It could pay to have a video of your possessions in case a question should arise in the future. Travel can highlight the day, although Pisces should not be driving on deserted streets after dark.

16. MONDAY. Ordinary. Colleagues can be influenced if you are working as part of a team. On your own, however, you will not make much of an impact. It will be difficult to arrange cooperation unless you give in more than you may now be willing to do. When it comes to the bottom line Pisces do what is necessary. Try to stay out of a dispute that is none of your concern. Do not champion the cause of a person who recently turned his back on you when you needed help. Be prepared to hold out longer than they and you will win. Higher-ups are watching with interest. You can enhance your reputation by proving that you can control your temper. A health problem should not be ignored.

17. TUESDAY. Harmonious. You have come through a hailstorm of criticism and made it this far; the rest of the week should be smooth going for you. An activity that you have been involved with from beginning to end is giving you great satisfaction. No one understands how much you have devoted to achieving a goal that seemed only a dream earlier in the year. But the boss is keeping tabs on your effort and will not forget. Emphasize the positive in all relationships. Take special note of ideas being propounded by someone who works with or for you. Socializing with a potential partner can be good for business. Harmony reigns when Pisces are at ease and freely expressing their enormous creativity.

18. WEDNESDAY. Changeable. Much can be achieved if you put your mind to it. People are looking to you for ideas and leadership; do not let them down. Be prepared to bend with the prevailing wind, but do not break. You may have to find a way around an obstinate person or a government regulation; do not expect to change it to your liking. Take time to think things through to their logical conclusion. The frustration that has been evident is quickly evaporating. You are seeing matters in a clearer light and realize that you were at least partly to blame for an impasse only recently broken. Move on without looking back; there is too much to be done to waste time on regrets.

19. THURSDAY. Fair. Challenges involved in branching out into a new area may seem major, but if you take them one at a time you can cut them down to size. Do not jump into anything body and soul. Instead, wade slowly as though the water is very cold but you are determined to get wet. You have to overcome your own personal objections before you can meet the challenge from an outsider. Self-confidence is on the upswing. A partner can be brought in to share a burden with you. Travel with definite goals in mind should be worthwhile. Get to see the person at the top by making an appointment beforehand. It is also a favorable time to plan your family vacation.

20. FRIDAY. Satisfactory. Straight talk from a family member or co-worker lets you know where you stand. From there it is only a matter of coming up with reasons that will be convincing to them. It is what you do not know that can hurt you most. Excuses are not going to be accepted for a botched job. If you do not get it right the first time, keep trying until results satisfy you. You can argue all you want while a decision is being made. Once it is announced, however, you are obliged to accept it and live with it. Someone who has attracted your attention is the shy, retiring type. It is up to you to make the first move if you want to become better acquainted. Take advantage of the good vibes on communications.

21. SATURDAY. Variable. Leave room to maneuver instead of trying to make everything cut-and-dried. Social arrangements should be general. Plan on getting together with friends later in the day, but wait to see how you feel when you are with them before deciding if you will go out or stay home. Creativity is a special Pisces attribute that can be turned to practical purposes or used primarily for self-expression. Taking a class in a new technique opens up possibilities for you. You may also have the talent and experience to write an article or a book for a special audience. Set your sights higher than normal. You can surpass even your own expectations if you have the courage to go against the general consensus. Influences favor taking steps toward independence.

22. SUNDAY. Buoyant. This is one of those days when you should be able to do anything you please without encountering opposition. Family members are ready to cooperate if you need help or vanish if you want some time alone. Ideas are flowing faster than you can possibly use them. Jot notes to yourself for future reference so that no brainstorm is wasted. New places and people interest you. Joining an organization can open doors and put you in the midst of a new crowd. Pisces in love may be traveling for a quick rendezvous in an out-of-the-way locale. Romance that has to be kept a secret for good reason is especially exciting. Be careful or the sparkle in your eyes will give you away.

23. MONDAY. Demanding. It is not easy refusing a co-worker's request or saying no to a family member who asks a special favor. But the day's schedule has been set for you and there is no backing out of commitments. Morning hours are best for meetings and negotiating sessions. You will be sharp-witted and can turn a small opening into a major breakthrough. Finances must be carefully handled. Do not loan money or anything of value. If you are borrowing, shop around for the lowest interest rate. Even a small percentage difference can add up to a considerable sum over the life of a loan. Pisces awaiting payment for work done earlier should send a reminder without delay.

24. TUESDAY. Optimistic. Optimism is soaring as you begin to see the light at the end of the tunnel. Hold to a plan that has been worked out with your mate or partner. If you deviate and things do not work out as expected you could be held accountable. You are in the fortunate position of having people come to you for favors. Dole them out thoughtfully. Some unexpected income is foreseen as the result of a prize or other special award. This is a good day to enter a contest based on skill rather than luck. You can hold your own with the best in the field. It should be possible to get home earlier than usual; your mate or date will enjoy an unexpected night on the town.

25. WEDNESDAY. Changeable. Whatever you put your mind to today can be handled to your satisfaction. The trick is knowing what is most important to long-term success. Someone is urging you to take one course of action while an equally important person tugs at you in a different direction. Make up your own mind; it is more important to please yourself than to try to satisfy divergent views. Conditions are not static. What has worked in the past is unlikely to continue to be as effective. The element of surprise is a definite help. You have nothing to gain by acting the role of a martyr. Be a realist in all of your actions. Travel for a romantic rendezvous is indicated. Pisces will bask in love tonight.

26. THURSDAY. Mixed. If you fear making a mistake you will never take the chances necessary to get ahead. Obtain as much information as possible about a choice you are being asked to make. Do not allow anyone else to persuade you one way or the other. Normal activity is slowing down, giving you a peaceful period for deep thinking. Spend some time behind a closed door, or hide out in the library alone with your thoughts. Your ideas are beginning to jell into a cohesive plan. One step leads to the next in logical progression. If an idea does not fall into place, it probably should be shelved until conditions are more favorable. Heed your body's messages and go to bed early for good health.

27. FRIDAY. Confusing. You may have to ask for a second chance because conditions have changed. Do not be so bull-headed that you lock yourself into a corner and have no room to maneuver. No one expects you to be perfect, although you may fancy yourself close to that exalted goal. There is enough confusion to confound the best of plans. Appearances are apt to be deceiving. This is not a good time to hire a new worker or to interview for a job that has been advertised. What you see is not what you are going to get. A project that has grown stale can be revitalized by breaking with tradition in new and innovative ways. Give your mate or date the benefit of the doubt tonight.

28. SATURDAY. Sensitive. Be sensitive to the needs of a family member who is trying to act tough or uncaring. Offer help without making it apparent that you know they need it. Your activities today may bring you into contact with an important person, perhaps an elected official. Be ready to listen with an open mind to them. Nostalgic thoughts could make you wish for the good old days, even if these were not that long ago. Try to let go of the past and look ahead confidently. A new planetary cycle emphasizing the sign of Cancer, which is most compatible with Pisces, is beginning tomorrow. Find an activity to distract your attention for a while. Music, whether you are listening or playing, can be soothing. Find an upbeat movie to enjoy with mate or date.

29. SUNDAY. Variable. The new cycle begins with special promise. Someone you have not seen in a while is making plans for a visit, perhaps by invitation or by surprise. Be sure to have extra food on hand so that you can extend the hospitality of your home to drop-in guests. There is opportunity today to pay back a favor. Place more responsibility in the hands of those who have worked hard to earn it. A family member may seem like a child to you, but their talents have taken them far. You can learn a lot from a book of poems or short stories. By reading into them your own experiences you get a broader view. A certain matter affecting an in-law or other distant family friend should be left in limbo for now.

30. MONDAY. Slow. There will be a lot of talk but not much action today. Take it slow and easy; do not force the pace in any activity. Anything done under a threat is likely to backfire. You do not have the patience to see a project through to its logical conclusion. Plans already formulated may have to be scaled back because there is not enough money or time to fulfill them as first envisioned. If everyday routine is beginning to wear on your nerves, break out of the usual pattern. Get in touch with someone at a distance who wrote you a letter earlier in the year. Share what has been going on, with an emphasis on the good times. You may want to send a few photos for their enjoyment as well.

31. TUESDAY. Pleasant. Working relationships are especially pleasant. You can build a good team to accomplish common ends. Seriously consider advice that you previously rejected. It is never too late to change your mind. A person with less training or experience than you has some insight that you can use. A project growing stale from repetition will benefit from an infusion of creativity. Turn boring routine into a race against the clock. Devote extra attention to details that are your sole responsibility. Be sure to dress appropriately for the day's activities. You may also need to shop for clothes that will be appropriate for a formal affair you will be attending next month. With the Moon rising in your sign of Pisces today, you are filled with hope for the future.

JUNE

1. WEDNESDAY. Good. Conditions at your place of work and at home are upbeat and pleasant. You know there is support available if needed. Review plans that were concocted earlier in the year. This is the time to find ways to launch projects without having to be personally involved at all times. Delegate as much as possible to people you know and trust. What is simmering may not be quite ready to come to a boil, but those necessary arrangements can be made and put in place now. Interesting contacts can be met through an organization that meets on a regular basis for lunch or dinner. Join for the social aspects; if more comes of it you are ahead of the game. The Moon in Pisces today makes you persuasive and attractive, drawing new people to your cause.

2. THURSDAY. Promising. There should be no cause for complaint today. Concentrate some attention on your personal health and well-being. Making an appointment for a physical checkup is a good first step. Take your doctor's recommendations to heart. If you are advised to give up an unhealthy habit or to lose weight, seek a support group for added incentive. This is also the best time of the year to make a commitment to exercise regularly by joining a sports team or a health club. Personal magnetism is bringing new people into your sphere. Someone from the past may also crop up once again, ready to resume a partnership that was once very successful. Eat lightly and nutritiously tonight.

3. FRIDAY. Demanding. Patience and understanding are vital to avoid conflicts on the job. People will demand much from you but be willing to offer little in return. The scales are not balanced in your favor today. Make the best of a difficult situation. Rely on your own intuition and past experience instead of seeking advice. Do not let anyone see that you are unsure of yourself. Take a long, hard look at your career prospects. Some changes could be useful to long-term progress. Returning to school as an evening student or studying with a home tutorial can bring you up to speed on the latest technology. The more skills you have, the more valuable you are to an employer. Knowledge for itself is also your goal.

4. SATURDAY. Fair. Guard against allowing jealous reactions to sour a relationship that is beginning to develop. Be appreciative of what you have. Friendship and love are much more important than any possession. Too much togetherness today can put a damper on creativity. Spend some time with your own thoughts. Take a plan a step further before seeking help in implementing it. The more people who become involved, the more diluted your original ideas are likely to become. You can offer advice and constructive criticism to a family member; whether they accept it is not up to you. If you talk too much you can raise more questions than you answer. Be willing to compromise.

5. SUNDAY. Mixed. You will not want to sit around idly today. Direct your energies toward getting to know neighbors and building strong community bonds. Take part in a local charity drive or sports event. If you cannot be an active participant, offer help in writing publicity or collecting funds. The more you have on your schedule the better it will suit you. A lazy day is not your cup of tea. Pisces parents may be busy straightening out a problem involving their child and another person of the same age. Stand up for your own family, but not to such an extent that you are blinded to their flaws. Inject humor in a potentially troubling situation, but do not back down and thereby compromise your principles.

6. MONDAY. Satisfactory. Program yourself to work surely and steadily on what is most important. Put out of mind those nagging doubts that can bring work to a standstill. If you do not try you will never know what could have been done. There is help available, although you may have to pay for it. Details must not be overlooked. The Moon in Taurus warns about taking anyone or anything for granted as you finalize plans. Get promises in writing if possible; otherwise follow up a conversation where a commitment was made with a letter that serves as a reminder. Do not let up in your program of exercise and diet. Be good to yourself and you will have more energy to help others.

7. TUESDAY. Manageable. Dress for success and you are more likely to attract favorable attention. Work is manageable if you take it in small doses. Do not think too far ahead or you may lose confidence worrying about all you have to do. Your positive outlook is attracting interest in the right places. Someone in a position to hire and promote knows of your achievements and current goals. When you feel strongly, stand up and add your voice to a debate. Individually you can accomplish less than if you are part of an organized effort. A friend's suggestion to form a new partnership is serious; give it some thought and possibly even make a commitment right now, or you could wind up regretting a lost opportunity.

8. WEDNESDAY. Changeable. The pace is slowing, which can make you impatient as you wait for a higher-up to give the green light to proceed. You are not operating in a vacuum. What you want must coincide with the goals of other people in order to have a chance for success. Morning hours are good for interacting with the public through sales or other direct methods. By afternoon, however, you will want more private time. It is not smart to volunteer for anything. Changing conditions are unclear; you could wind up on the losing side with no way out. Travel can be useful if you get to see the person in charge. Do not settle for a meeting with someone unable to make decisions.

9. THURSDAY. Fortunate. Find out what is going on behind the scenes. Ask enough people and you should be able to piece together a valid scenario. Financial affairs are especially promising. Pisces can earn extra money through writing or a speaking engagement. Those who are sports-inclined may be able to secure a paying position as a coach or referee. You do not have to be directly involved in an activity in order to be part of it. Stagehands are as important as performers. Seek the cooperation of your mate or partner in balancing your personal budget. You can cut expenses by giving up one small luxury such as eating out on a regular basis or making long-distance calls when a letter would be equally useful.

10. FRIDAY. Profitable. Money continues to be the prime focus of Pisces activities. Check that bills have been paid. A new offering could become profitable if you stay involved for a while. Investment is much more important than speculation. As a gambler you can go broke. Writers and artists may make a major sale now. Free time can be used for earning part-time income in an enjoyable way. Your creativity is in demand if you are able to package it for a specific audience. Put the best possible face on a situation that is not to your liking. Withholding criticism is as important as offering an endorsement that is only lukewarm. Friends will transport you to a dream world tonight.

11. SATURDAY. Fair. An argument may arise at home that forces you to sit down and have a serious discussion. When you thrash out the problem you will be closer personally. You can make a fresh start if you and your partner are both willing to try.

Be sure to listen more than you talk. With an open mind you can understand the emotion that has been stirred up. A romance that seemed to be turning sour can be sweetened with the right sugar-coated words that come from the heart. Do not be shy about saying those three magical words: I love you. Friends may be too busy to give you the help you need. Put off a project rather than do a halfhearted job that is not satisfying.

12. SUNDAY. Pleasant.   Enjoy the day despite some lingering problems. Relax in the company of loved ones. Family members who do not live with you would welcome a phone call or a visit. You will get along especially well with the older generation. Advice from a grandparent should not be ignored. Bring along a camera if going on an outing. Take pictures to highlight the fun of the day. For some Pisces, photography could become a source of secondary income as well as pleasure. Leave your watch at home so that you are not bound by any time restrictions. Activities on the spur of the moment are likely to be most enjoyable. Include a newcomer in your plans.

13. MONDAY. Variable.   An idea may not be as simple and straightforward as you at first thought. Look into all the angles and then reconsider. Postpone an ambitious project until you are fully into the swing of work. It will take some time this morning to shake off the weekend. By afternoon you are back on track and will know just what to say when the boss or another superior comes to you with a personal request. If asked for advice, state your opinions truthfully. No one wants to be surrounded by yes-men who only say what they think the questioner wishes to hear. Do not let go of a plan that seems worthwhile. When the time is right, you can be the first to act.

14. TUESDAY. Disconcerting.   Someone you have come to rely upon may be leaving for a vacation trip or relocating permanently. It will take a while to fill the emptiness that you feel. Focus on a reunion that you have planned for later in the month. Being without a supporting person for a while gives you added insight about your own strengths. You can stand straight and tall on your own two feet when the need arises. The promise of a check in the mail may prove false. It could be worthwhile to make a trip to collect money owed to you. Do not chance your luck in any way. There are no shortcuts to fame and riches although advertisements would have you think so. It is a good time to begin a new health regimen, as the Moon now in Virgo promises quick results.

15. WEDNESDAY. Pleasant. All means of communication will be helpful in your search for answers. Begin to correspond with a person whose writings or television appearances are important to you. A half-finished job can be rushed through to completion by enlisting the help of co-workers or family members. It is vital to meet a deadline. A new contact gives you a fresh slant on a project that has grown stale. Shake off boredom by trying a different approach. Your ambition is combining well with the opportunities that are opening up. Jump at a chance to get in on the ground floor of a project just getting under way. A new alignment of teammates keeps you from becoming complacent.

16. THURSDAY. Important. Nervousness can be the result of expecting too much or asking too little. Personal relationships can be restored to their former luster now if you give without waiting to get. Also be willing to accept a favor, friendship or love without wondering why it has come to you so easily. With Venus, the love planet, going into generous Leo, a new cycle of affection in all relationships begins. The sky is the limit for Pisces people today. Whatever you want is within your grasp if you are willing to work and wait. Family members are especially cooperative. You can learn a lot from a youngster who is wondering. New partnership is highly favored. Be thorough in interviewing someone you hope to work with for a long time to come.

17. FRIDAY. Productive. Rush to finish up all those small jobs you have been putting off. Combine trips so that you are not out too long. Try to organize your life so that there is a time and place for everything. Keeping a running list of what is to be done can help. Follow through with an urge to give your time to a worthwhile cause. Volunteer without waiting to be asked. Teamwork is highly favored in all activities. Much can be accomplished as part of a group. Co-workers and friends know that they can count on you, and you should be coming to the same understanding with them. If you attempt to be too self-reliant you lose out. Romance is happy providing you are not expecting too much.

18. SATURDAY. Enjoyable. Socializing can be the highlight of the day providing you relax and have a good time with your guests. Invite friends or neighbors to come over for an outdoor barbecue or a pot-luck meal where everyone brings food to share. There is no need to plan a formal affair; paper plates and plastic utensils are fine. Your powers of creativity are surging. Do not work from a kit of assembled materials. Put together your own individual combinations of color and texture. Make up a pattern as you go. Rules are a good starting point, but with experience you gain knowledge of when to break or bend them for a certain effect. Do not be pressured into selling what you create.

19. SUNDAY. Stressful. Family needs are apt to conflict with today's schedule. You will have to fit in more than anticipated so that no one becomes angry. Give children special time and attention. Get down to their level and share an activity with them. Some friendly competition can encourage you to try a new sport or skill. People want to be part of your team and are expecting a lot from you. If the stress gets greater than you are willing to bear, sit on the sidelines for a while and let someone else take over. It is a good day for browsing through a catalog of furniture or jewelry. Make up a pretend shopping list in case you become an overnight millionaire. If you are determined enough, a dream can come true.

20. MONDAY. Satisfactory. Someone is hoping you will write or call, but pride could be standing in your way as well as theirs. Be the first to make a move that should restore a relationship you want back on track. Go out of your way to make a newcomer feel at ease. Pairing up with someone who lacks your skill and experience can be the best teaching method. Be sure to put into practice what you preach. Pisces who control money belonging to other people must maintain detailed records. Account for everything that you spend. Your cheerfulness makes work go smoothly. Take on a task that someone else started but dropped. With new enthusiasm you can make it a success.

21. TUESDAY. Rewarding. Look for ways to cut costs at home or on the job. You may be able to reduce insurance premiums by making the deductible amount higher. Or you can reduce transportation expense by arranging to carpool or use public transportation. Traveling some distance to a mall offering deep discounts can save you a lot. Repairs, too, can be done with the help of a good manual that explains procedures step by step. Someone who is seeking advice will benefit from the creative approach that you take. Guard against passing judgment on anyone; just give them help in the way they want. The evening's plans may not work out if you have to put in some overtime hours.

22. WEDNESDAY. Hectic. Your Pisces popularity makes you in demand. You can set the tone and pace at home or on the job. Timing is all important. What is practical today could be all wrong tomorrow. Stick to a schedule as closely as possible so that you do not disappoint anyone. A few phone calls can eliminate the necessity of traveling to meet in person. You will prefer the company of people who are as dedicated as you. Someone with a so-what attitude is likely to grate on your nerves. Mental tasks can be completed in record time, for your mind is active and agile. Make a plan and put it into immediate operation. Identifying goals is half the battle. This is an excellent period for studies and education in general. The determined Pisces may decide to go to summer school.

23. THURSDAY. Useful. Complaining is not likely to accomplish anything useful. Instead, find a way around objections and obstacles. The pressure to produce has been intensified. The boss is not going to accept even the most valid excuse. There is money to be made by turning a hobby into a profitable sideline. Look for ways to sell what you make at competitive prices. Do not undersell or overcharge. Keep savings where you can withdraw the money if necessary. Tying up your cash reserves in stocks or property can put you at a disadvantage later in the year. Something that has been perplexing you is becoming much clearer. It may be that a person has blocked your view of the true facts.

24. FRIDAY. Manageable. There is no need to draw up elaborate plans to handle everyday routine. Stick to ways and means that are comfortable for you. The newest in technology is useless if you spend hours trying to get it to work. A new alliance can be worthwhile. Teaming up with a former competitor gives you an added advantage. But guard against taking cooperation for granted. If one person on a team is not doing their fair share, everyone suffers as a result. It is a starred day for gathering information from a variety of sources. Weed out what seems possible and concentrate on that for a start. Evening hours are starred for an intimate rendezvous with the one you love.

25. SATURDAY. Happy. You are tuned into the same wavelength as family members. Discord at home should be minimal. Even teenagers who tend to have something to say about everything are looking forward to a joint family activity. It is a fine time for a trip leading to a destination that is a mystery. Consider a day at an amusement park as a surprise treat. Romance is in the air for both married and single Pisces. Your desires will not be denied. Pop that all-important question with certainty that the answer is what you want to hear. An announcement will be greeted with good wishes and congratulations. A chance meeting may actually have been carefully planned, but you will be delighted by it.

26. SUNDAY. Easygoing. Companionship gives added pleasure to the day's events. If a family member is preoccupied, call a friend who enjoys the same activities that interest you. Older relatives, too, would welcome a chance to spend some time alone with you. Accept whatever invitation comes your way. You do not have to dress to impress anyone now; merely please yourself. A business deal can be discussed in a social setting with good results. An unconventional idea is strangely attractive. Check into it before deciding if it is right for you. Loved ones will not stand in your way. Be open to all sorts of possibilities. Tradition should only be a guide, not a hard-and-fast rule, so dare to experiment.

27. MONDAY. Productive. Arriving at work early gives you the edge on those who would like to challenge you. Calculate the odds of getting your way. If they are slim, come up with a new plan that will be more acceptable. Express yourself openly and generously. You do not like to be ignored or overlooked. Extra attention gives you added impetus to try harder. Challenge yourself to complete a current project before going on to something new and more exciting. Attention to detail is crucial. Your good Pisces reputation hinges on keeping a promise even if those involved have forgotten all about it. Make it clear that your word is your bond in all matters. The Moon in your sign today and for the next two days surrounds you with good luck.

28. TUESDAY. Sensitive. Do not allow personal feelings to divert your attention from the job you are paid to do. Getting along with a variety of people is essential. Those who grate on your nerves deserve the same respect as your best friend. If a newcomer seems to know more than you about a subject you find important, consider taking a refresher course or learning on the job. You may be taking too much for granted. Some learning is possible through osmosis, but hard study is also necessary. A biography of a famous person can be inspirational as you contemplate changing directions. What a family member is proposing could have a significant impact on your future plans.

29. WEDNESDAY. Rewarding. Lady Luck will not stray from your side throughout the day. Whatever you touch can turn into a money-maker. There is a golden opportunity right around the corner. Follow your natural instincts when it comes to joining an established team or forming your own. Pisces judgment will not falter even in the face of stiff opposition. A deal is likely to go through because you pretend not to care too much. Negotiate from a position of strength. A friend needs to talk about a problem that does not directly involve you. Give your undivided attention and your best advice. Helping others provides you with the highest sense of gratification.

30. THURSDAY. Productive. Assert yourself in a positive way. Be willing to offer a carrot instead of threatening with a stick. Cooperation that is freely given is more useful than anything that you have to buy or coerce. You can convince your mate or partner to withdraw joint funds for a new venture if you offer to give them equal billing and an equal return although you are doing most of the work. Do not confide too freely in a person you have known only a short time. Keep a secret that you have sworn not to reveal. The past should be laid to rest as you look ahead expectantly to the future. Your Pisces determination helps you get through the rough times with your reputation intact and your ambition on the rise.

JULY

1. FRIDAY. Lucky. A dream gives you a clue to future action. Luck is going hand in hand with your Pisces intuition. Do not hesitate to make a change that seems right although you might have trouble convincing your mate or partner why you think so. Carefully consider a new opportunity that would divert your attention from an ongoing project. Your energy and efficiency enable you to do more than you think but less than you might like. Now is the time to set your sights firmly on moving up the ladder of promotion. Be ready not only for additional responsibility but for playing the get-ahead game socially. An unexpected move puts you far ahead of the competition.

2. SATURDAY. Confusing. Unannounced visitors have to be melded into your plans for the day rather than dropping everything on their behalf. Invite them to help with outdoor work before partying or picnicking. You may want to go on an excursion to buy farm-fresh vegetables or just-caught seafood fresh off a boat. If an argument heats up, find a way to defuse the situation with humor and goodwill. A frank discussion helps to iron out trouble before it escalates. Be sure family members understand what you expect of them; you, too, need to know what they want from you. Romance is highlighted if you get a chance to be alone with your date. Opposition from an older family member can put a damper on a relationship just beginning to emerge.

3. SUNDAY. Rewarding. Reconciliation with a friend, lover or mate following a period of separation makes this an especially rewarding day. Be ready to forgive wholeheartedly, although it will take longer to forget. You gain greater appreciation of family members as they stand by you in difficult times and are ready to cheer loudly when things are going well. Flow with today's tide of events. If you are driving any distance, plan a route that is away from the main traffic arteries. On a back road you can enjoy the scenery and stop to browse at an outdoor sale. Look for a place to eat in a garden setting to celebrate early the spirit of tomorrow's holiday. There is no holding back romance tonight.

4. MONDAY. Sensitive. Be careful what you say, and to whom. Emotions are at a high pitch today among family members. You can hurt someone's feelings and not even know you have done so. Be willing to go along with plans proposed by others, and to be enthusiastic about it. Your mood rubs off on those who love and admire you. A decision is being made that will affect you and your family. Be alert for clues so that you can add your own opinions before it is all decided. Be as considerate of loved ones as you are of friends and casual acquaintances. Curtail criticism as much as possible. What is right for you is not necessarily best for someone else. Respect people's differences.

5. TUESDAY. Pleasant. Find an outlet for your humanitarian desires so that you know your time or money is going to the cause which you intend it to help. It could be useful to check with an agency to find out how much a charity spends on fund raising and how much is actually used for the cause. This is a good day to donate services or specific items to a charity auction or other moneymaking effort. Pisces artists and performers have a chance to enhance their own reputation while doing a good deed. A new idea is too good to pass up. Get in on the ground floor of opportunity. Money invested can now earn a good rate of return if you are patient. Consider returning to school for refresher courses.

6. WEDNESDAY. Mixed. Teamwork is the best bet. When you work as part of a group your ideas become fine-tuned and refined by mingling with other plans. Pisces tend to be high-minded but not always practical. Consider costs before launching any plan. Terms being offered are the best you can expect; sign on the dotted line without delay. If you postpone action the competition is going to catch on to what you intend to do. Advice from an attorney or other professional can help, but it is vital to steer clear of court action. You should be able to get by on less sleep than usual. Late-night brainstorming helps come up with a better way to handle a touchy situation.

7. THURSDAY. Difficult. This is one of those days when practically nothing will proceed as you had envisioned. A person who promised help is apt to back out. Financing that seemed assured may be withheld. Whatever is accomplished has to be done on your own and in your own way. Do not depend on past success as a guideline to future action. Conditions are too dissimilar to even draw comparisons, although on the surface they may seem the same. A last-minute phone call could force you to cover for an absent family member or co-worker. Try not to let anyone know what is troubling you. When the air clears, you want to be able to say you knew it would all along.

8. FRIDAY. Variable. Avoid anything underhanded or even mildly suspicious. Be totally honest and aboveboard in all of your dealings. You cannot expect people to do as you say, then turn around and pursue an opposite course yourself. It is up to Pisces to stand tall on a pedestal as an example for others to follow. By doing your best you can avoid losing face or money. This is a favorable day to make some personal changes. You have the willpower to give up a habit you know is unhealthy or to adopt a healthier lifestyle through better diet and more exercise. If a friend or neighbor drops by, do not allow talk to go beyond the time you have available. Find a way to ease him or her along without making anyone feel unimportant or unwanted.

9. SATURDAY. Changeable. Tear up your preconceived ideas for today and start over with a clean slate. A child's request, or an idea suggested by another family member, should be given precedence. There is nothing so vital that you cannot take time out for a swim, boating or a walk through a park. Shopping can be worthwhile, especially if you are considering a major purchase. You could come up with a winner at a yard sale or other secondhand outlet. Do not allow thoughts of work or personal concerns to intrude on your activities today. A problem that has been hanging around since the start of July will not benefit from more worry. Conditions are changing, and a new planetary cycle beginning on Monday will take care of the problem in a natural way.

10. SUNDAY. Excellent. Pisces are able to exert considerable power and influence in any group. Pick a target and go after it without holding anything back. It is a starred day for efforts to improve your community with your own effort and sweat. Your dedication is a draw to other concerned residents. Turn your charm on a local government official or other higher-up you happen to encounter during the day. Press for changes that you believe are necessary. Be sure to make it clear that you are speaking not only as an individual but as a representative of an organization or informal group that wields power at the polls. Romance is the high point of the day. Relax in the arms of that special person.

11. MONDAY. Harmonious. Willpower will not let you down. Whatever is most important should be tackled first thing this morning. Make a few phone calls to set up appointments for later in the week. Your Pisces ability to get along with people from all walks of life sets you apart and gives you special access. Show compassion to a friend or co-worker going through a difficult period. Be ready to listen and encourage. Offer forward-looking advice rather than focusing on the past. What you lack in imagination you can make up by your dogged determination. Once you get hold of an idea you do not let go until satisfied with the results you have achieved. Mercury now in Cancer deepens your thinking.

12. TUESDAY. Variable. The absence of a relative or co-worker may force you to take on additional work on top of your own load. Find a way to speed through what usually takes the better part of the day. You may have to sacrifice some perfection in order to finish on schedule. If someone at a distance is ill, be sure to send flowers or a get-well card. Make time, too, to stop by to visit a hospitalized or homebound friend. It is an outstanding day to volunteer at a hospital or nursing home. Your positive outlook is good medicine for those who are healing. Do not rely solely on memory for names and facts. Check with a trustworthy source if you have any doubts.

13. WEDNESDAY. Profitable. Change your routine so that you do not settle into any sort of rut. This is a good time to find a new route to work or a new store offering more of what you want. Business and career affairs are on the move. You can earn more by taking on additional responsibility. Prove what you are capable of doing when given the opportunity. The boss or another superior is keeping tabs on your progress. Loyalty to the company that pays you a salary, or to the customers that buy what you sell, is a prime asset. A goal that you have been working to achieve can be hastened along with more attention directed to it. If you spread yourself too thin results will be slow coming in.

14. THURSDAY. Stimulating.   Follow through with an urge to donate your time, money or services. Do not put a price on what is too precious to ever sell. Discuss a new idea with someone close to you who understands your basic drive. Their input can help put your brainstorm into operation. Extra energy is yours to enjoy and use wisely. You can step into a leadership role and no one will mind. In fact, you will be welcomed by a group that has been floundering. Be original when prior solutions have not worked out as expected. A new twist to an old idea makes it uniquely your own. You are ready to proceed with a new start. Venus in Virgo, your zodiacal partner sign, accents Pisces creativity and communication skills for the rest of the month.

15. FRIDAY. Slow.   Success depends on making the most of what you have, not wishing for more. Conditions are slow and lethargic. It will be difficult to arouse cooperation, and on your own you are limited by insufficient time and money. But you can make progress in thinking and planning. Ideas are flowing fast and furious. Keep a file for future reference when the well seems to run dry. Seeking advice from more experienced people can be useful, but you need to be the ultimate judge of what is best for you and your family. A romantic relationship that has not been living up to your expectations needs an injection of fun and excitement. Make plans for the weekend ahead.

16. SATURDAY. Mixed.   Do not back away from a person and then expect to be chased. Consistency is important to maintain a relationship and help it grow. Prove by deeds as well as words how you feel and what you want. Keeping a problem to yourself lessens the chance of resolving it. Bring it out in the open and discuss it fully with those who are most involved. Together you can find a solution, or at least agree amicably to disagree. Children demand special attention today. Go out of your way to take part in their activities by coaching a team or playing the role of tour guide to a zoo or amusement park. You may not be in total control, but you are setting the tone.

17. SUNDAY. Easygoing.   Rest and relaxation are the prime activities today. Do nothing that is likely to cause you to sweat. If you show off a little no one is going to mind. Put your special talent on display for all to see and enjoy. Be equally appreciative of the antics of family members and friends. Getting together with neighbors can be enjoyable. There is no reason to issue formal invitations or to go to great lengths to prepare food. A casual party will be fun for all. Some friendly competition can encourage you to try something new and different. It would not be smart to bet money on the outcome, however. Pisces are capable of inventive schemes, especially now with the Scorpio Moon impacting your creativity in a powerful way.

18. MONDAY. Sensitive. Do not allow optimism to cause you to overextend yourself or your resources. Keep plans as practical as possible. Know what you want before you try to get it. Concentrate on what is most important to the boss or another higher-up, although this may not be what you would prefer to be doing. By getting organized early in the day you accomplish more than if you drift from one project to the next. Make a list for yourself, then cross out accomplishments as they are completed. Try to leave nothing important undone. If you stop in the middle of a project you may never be able to gain momentum in that area again. Influences still warn against recklessness with money; avoid any form of gambling.

19. TUESDAY. Happy. A letter or phone call from someone at a distance gives you good reason to be happy. You may be invited to a party or asked to take part in a ceremony now being planned. There is no reason not to accept additional responsibility if you can fit it into your existing schedule. Your high energy level allows extra room for what you want to do. Figure out where the power lies, then get as close as you can to it. Who you know is as important as what you are able to accomplish. You will be persuasive speaking to a group once you overcome initial stage fright. Practice in front of a mirror so that you gain self-confidence. Today's vibes favor travel, communications and study.

20. WEDNESDAY. Satisfactory. Teamwork creates a special bond that brings out the best in you as well as in your cohorts. There is definite power in organizing for a cause. Make it clear that you are willing to take a stand and stick to it. Accept some responsibility normally handled by a person who works for you. There are favorable auspices for launching a new project or branching out in a new direction. Nothing is holding you back but a certain unease about the unknown. Once you get your foot wet you are ready to jump in totally. Affairs occurring at a distance are having an impact on your options. A trip to meet personally with someone operating far from your base can be worthwhile.

21. THURSDAY. Optimistic. Putting business matters before personal life helps to keep you in balance. It is all too easy to push aside work when pleasure calls, but you will have some pangs of conscience if you do so. Your optimistic Pisces spirit gives you clear sailing with a new project for which you are totally or primarily responsible. Call in a few favors if you need some specific help. Whatever you can do on your own will be that much better with input from a variety of people. You know what needs to be done but could use some assistance in deciding how best to handle it. A travel agent can provide interesting ideas about a faraway vacation paradise.

22. FRIDAY. Cautious. The secretive side of your nature deserves to be in command now. Do not reveal your intentions to anyone outside your immediate family. Someone who seems to be on your side could actually be considering making a break and going over to a competitor. If you reveal a secret to someone you think you can trust, you may soon discover that you were wrong. Take care of yourself by monitoring your diet and exercise. Overdoing in any area can be upsetting. Get back in harness if you have strayed from a New Year's resolution. You deserve a pat on the back for trying. Your instincts are excellent when it comes to romancing your mate or date.

23. SATURDAY. Variable. Guard against doing anything that you know will get a family member riled up. Take your clues from their actions today. Follow through on a promise made earlier in the month. Children, in particular, should not be disappointed unless you have a very good reason. A trip today promises pleasure as well as worthwhile results. Shopping can lead to a special bargain in collectibles or something for your home. You can recognize value that other people overlook due to a top coat of paint or a covering of rust. It is not the time to buy such major property as land or houses, however. Wait until prices go down at the end of the season. If you are trying to sell, consider giving an extra incentive to buyer or agent.

24. SUNDAY. Pleasant. If you enjoy some fantasy thoughts they might come true. Let your imagination soar. Imagine what might be if only certain conditions did not exist. For the Pisces in love, this is a day of excellent opportunity to find out what your mate or date is thinking. Time together helps conversation flow naturally. You will be more relaxed as a twosome rather than part of a group. An unusual series of events can put a luster on a relationship that is beginning to pale. Together you can get involved in an activity that brings you closer than you have been for a long time. Be agreeable without actually giving in. The Moon now in your sign, compatible with Mercury in Cancer and Venus in Virgo, is ideal for love matches.

25. MONDAY. Misleading. Nothing is quite as it seems to be at first glance. Take a long, hard look at all that is going on. You may discover that you have been left out of an important gathering or not invited to a party that all of your friends seem to be planning to attend. Try to learn why; it could be that mail has been lost or you were not home to answer a phone call. Some choices have to be made soon about home and career. Decide how much you are willing to give up in order to be satisfied personally and profession-ally. Advertisements may claim you can have it all, but in real life you know you must make sacrifices in one area or another. Always think of long-range contentment, not short-term gain.

26. TUESDAY. Ordinary. Put your Pisces creativity to good use. Break away from the usual into what is out of the ordinary, at least for you. There is little excitement outside your own imagina-tion. A project may grind to a halt due to lack of money or interest from people who are in charge. Management change could be affecting your career potential. This is a starred day to begin considering switching jobs or making a major change in career direction. The Moon in Pisces increases your creative and learning capacity. Returning to school for additional training is one option to consider. Try not to make any immediate demands on yourself or on other people. A hands-off approach is favored now.

27. WEDNESDAY. Productive. A stubborn streak that is of-ten hidden in Pisces is coming to the surface now. Much can be accomplished because you care enough to see a project through from start to finish. Help is available if you do some prodding; otherwise people are inclined to watch but not pitch in. Speak up and ask for a raise or promotion if you deserve one. Your good humor puts people at ease and brings out the best in them. Offer encouragement readily; hold back criticism. A new partnership is favored in business or your personal life. Pair up with a person whose tastes and talents complement your own but do not mimic them precisely.

28. THURSDAY. Frustrating. Patience is mandatory to get through the frustrations of the day. Nothing major is likely to go wrong, but you will be encountering a few dead ends and a lot of red tape. Plod along with confidence. Your emotions are under control except in a situation where you are directly confronted by someone who is as stubborn as you. That is the moment to think of what you want and how you can get it; worrying about getting even is negative thinking. Avoid casual conversation with strangers. It is smart not to carry too much cash or to wear flashy jewelry. Try to fit in as one of the crowd rather than stand out in any way. If you are driving, proceed at a safe speed and stay alert.

29. FRIDAY. Good.   Keep a secret to yourself for a short while longer. Personal relationships are in full swing. Someone you have been admiring from a distance is likely to make the first move to get to know you better. Play a little hard to get but do not appear disinterested. Your abilities are heightened if you are part of a team. You can rely on a partner to come through for you. A lucky break demands that you take advantage of it before others become aware of the possibilities. Your planning helps to recognize an opening. Pisces abilities are in demand. You can set a higher price and expect to receive it without question. There is still the possibility of mishap if you act carelessly or hastily; slow down.

30. SATURDAY. Disconcerting.   Protect your health and the well-being of family members. Pisces drivers should have their automobile checked by a mechanic. You may also need new tires, or at least more air in them. You will not enjoy being a visitor or a host today. Family is enough company and commotion. Give more leeway to a younger person who yearns for additional freedom. Let go a little at a time to see if they can handle it. Be sure to avoid an I-told-you-so attitude if things do not work out right away. Experience has been a valuable teacher for you and will be for those you love as well. A good book is good company tonight. Pisces always gain from being alone and thinking things through.

31. SUNDAY. Cautious.   You have to play by the same rules as everyone else. Do not expect any exceptions to be made for you. An older family member is likely to ask for advice but may then turn around and do exactly the opposite. Forgive and forget is the best recipe for family happiness. You can be too cautious in personal relationships. Speak up and let your views be known, but do not insist that they be followed. Timing is all important. What was right only a short while ago could be wrong now. Someone from the past is coming back into your sphere with an irresistible offer. Put the past behind you and prepare for a new start next month when planetary cycles shift to different priorities.

AUGUST

1. MONDAY. Manageable. More can be accomplished if you hide out behind a closed door where you are less likely to be disturbed. If you are unable to get away by yourself, turn on soothing music to drown out background noise so that you can concentrate more attentively. Working in a group can be distracting; it will take longer to explain your views and to understand objections and then counter them. Try to let differences of opinion go in one ear and out the other. You are on the right track; stick to the current plan. An activity that you enjoy as a hobby can be transformed into a money-making business on a part-time basis at first. Try not to scatter your energies or change your focus.

2. TUESDAY. Good. This is a starred day to be away from your usual base of operations. Travel that combines work with pleasure is favored. Being accompanied by a family member or work associate heightens your enjoyment. There are romantic overtones in all activities now. Go out of your way to make a newcomer feel welcome and comfortable. Be willing to explain procedures more than once to be certain nothing is unclear. Your popularity makes you a natural leader. Someone who has been questioning your ideas is coming around to your view. Welcome their support without mentioning past differences. Evening favors dinner at an ethnic restaurant.

3. WEDNESDAY. Variable. Confusion in connection with a meeting time or place could find you standing alone when you should be part of a group. Try to check beforehand. If you have to make transportation connections, be prepared to run from the place of arrival to your next place of departure. Someone with whom you share a table or a meal could remind you of a former friend or lover. Be wary of becoming too personal in confiding to this person. You may be stirred by the similarities, but the look-alike will not be aware of your feelings. A person you think of as shy or indifferent may reveal a totally different aspect of their personality when you become friendly.

4. THURSDAY. Difficult. Despite the best of intentions, Pisces can be caught off guard and have to come up with a spontaneous excuse. Conditions are difficult throughout the day, both at work and at home. Demands are being made that you cannot meet, but saying no does not come easily. Work that you delegate to others may not be done to your satisfaction. It is not the day to do any more than is expected. If you volunteer for a job you could be saddled with a burden hard to shake off. You will be more efficient working on your own, although in many areas this will not be allowed. Someone is looking over your shoulder at every detail. It would be wise to supervise children closely when they play.

5. FRIDAY. Positive. Contact someone at a distance who has been in your thoughts or perhaps a player in your dream world. You are on the same wavelength even though not in frequent communication. It may jolt you to discover that the thoughts you have had mimic theirs in many details. Distance cannot break ties that once were very strong. Before the end of the day you may feel a special inner glow. Emphasize the positive and you stand the best chance of getting your way. The boss or another higher-up is willing to listen to a well-reasoned argument. The answer is not going to be immediate, however. Be sure to withdraw some cash from the bank for the weekend.

6. SATURDAY. Productive. Please yourself and your family members rather than trying to make a favorable impression on people you hardly know or may never meet. It is pointless hoping to win the approval of every single person. By acting naturally you are true to yourself and uphold your Pisces ideals. Work around the house and yard should not be put off. Be especially aware of potential hazards that could cause an accident. If you cannot handle repair work personally, call in a professional. An older family member is full of worthwhile advice if you are willing to listen. Extra responsibility is coming your way, like it or not, and it centers around your own children or other young people nearby.

7. SUNDAY. Frustrating. Aspiring to high goals may be unrealistic today. You may be held back by traditions that were instilled in you at a young age. Lack of advanced training is also a stumbling block for some Pisces. On your own you can take a closer look at all that is going on currently and find a way to break into the big leagues. Independent study, tutoring or returning to the classroom can be worthwhile. Travel can open you up to new possibilities as you see how things are done in other countries. Prospects look promising from one angle, but you have a lot of work to do to catch up. Romance requires extra consideration of your mate or lover.

8. MONDAY. Outstanding. Yesterday's worries are replaced by a more optimistic outlook as you see your way ahead. Act on a plan recently concocted. Contact people at a distance who might be able to help with advice, a loan or other assistance. The more people you talk with, the more you will understand about what is going on. It does no good to sweat a situation that is currently beyond your control. Focus on the possible. Identified goals are the first step to achieving success. It is an outstanding day for a job interview or audition providing you do some personal public relations. Put negative thoughts out of your mind and act confidently. It is an excellent time to start on a new health regimen.

9. TUESDAY. Excellent. There is a lot going on today, with Pisces standing tall in the midst of it all. Teamwork is favored, especially with you in a starring role. Your ability to get along with all types of people is a special attribute; make the best use of it. Do not delay setting the date for a meeting or other get-together that requires advance travel arrangements. This is the time to stop dragging your feet and to plunge right into a project that has been firing your imagination. You can pick up needed help or supplies as you proceed. With the help of a lawyer or accountant you can work out a financial arrangement that frees up extra money for you to use on current work.

10. WEDNESDAY. Fair. Shy away from making a decision on behalf of someone else. You have enough to worry about in your own realm without taking on the whole world's problems as though they were your own. You may begin to feel overwhelmed by a friend's constant whining. Limit contact if they are dragging you down more than you are uplifting them. Someone to whom you are currently attracted is not doing your reputation a bit of good. It is important to pick and choose associates with care. Be more discreet than usual. Anything you are trying to keep secret is likely to be noticed and could become the subject of some office or neighborhood gossip.

11. THURSDAY. Changeable. Changing over to a new approach could return handsome dividends. Be willing to experiment with what has been suggested without committing yourself to it. Friends are standing by, ready to lend a hand if you need one. Put aside yesterday's concerns and concentrate on what can be achieved right now. You can make a significant difference by speaking up in a meeting or other group discussion. Do not allow what you consider a bad idea to go unchallenged. Point out your objections plus ways you would amend it. Devote some time this afternoon to plotting future moves. Reaching a goal is similar to playing chess; stay a few moves ahead of the competition and you will come out ahead.

12. FRIDAY. Productive.   Do not take no for an answer. Find a way to overcome obstacles by going around or through them. It is important to give the appearance of knowing exactly what you are doing even if you have some personal doubts. A bluff can pay off now. If a certain situation is dependent on the action of others and you have no control over them, forget about it. You can deplete your mental and physical stamina by worrying needlessly. At the first blush of success, you may have more offers of assistance than you can handle. Everyone loves a winner, and you are on a winning streak. A firm hand on the wheel, together with tight control over your rapidly changing moods, is all that is needed.

13. SATURDAY. Demanding.   Early in the day decide whether you are going to do your own thing or follow the suggestions of other people. You cannot satisfy everyone now. Try to be more observant and learn from the mistakes of others; there is no point in making the same errors yourself. All calculations need to be double-checked for accuracy. First impressions could be way off base. Avoid making any judgments until you have more time to consider. Fun activities with the family could turn into a major production if you are traveling any distance. Let someone else do the packing while you concentrate on the route to take. You will be happier in a group than alone with your mate or date.

14. SUNDAY. Uncertain.   Money matters have to be worked out before you can spend on any nonessentials. Go over the family budget with a fine-tooth comb looking for ways to cut costs in one area so that you have more for another. You can find enjoyable free entertainment to replace a costly idea proposed by a loved one. Your understanding of human nature helps when it comes to figuring out why a certain person is being obstinate. It may be that they feel left out or unappreciated. The down side to a new relationship is that you are taking time away from your own family. If you can meld a newcomer into your home life everyone will be more relaxed.

15. MONDAY. Tedious.   Pisces enjoy being in the thick of things where the action is. Today, however, is slow and plodding. Nothing much can be accomplished no matter how hard you try, so sit back and take it easy. Keep your mind from racing to consider all possibilities. If you wait a day or two your choices become fewer and therefore easier to make. Health could suffer from uncertainty. A headache is probably the result of being left out of a decision-making process. Get your priorities right. You cannot dodge responsibility but must not step in and take over in someone else's area. It is the little things that count most now, and one of them is showing you can handle money wisely. Avoid gambling.

16. TUESDAY. Manageable. Resist an urge to buy an item that is advertised at a sale price unless you actually need it. Work is the surest source of income. You can wish and dream about winning a lottery or other significant sum, but do not figure on that money for everyday expenses. Use your creativity to find new uses for what is already on hand in good supply. Trading services with a friend or neighbor can also help you save a lot. When financial matters are under control you feel more in charge. Take time to balance your checkbook; you may have forgotten an entry and be in danger of overdrawing your account. Put away credit cards to be used only in an emergency situation.

17. WEDNESDAY. Productive. This is a starred day to do a good turn without thinking about what you might get in return. Become more involved in a cause you believe in deeply. Helping people less fortunate than you, especially those in your own area, is important. Donate used clothing, food or money to a charity that you know is directly assisting people. You are able to cope today with anything that comes along. Nothing is escaping your attention. Clues based on the behavior of the boss or another person in charge give you an inkling of a decision they have yet to announce. Churn out work by using an assembly line approach to speed it up. Begin a savings campaign in earnest.

18. THURSDAY. Useful. Avoid taking on an extra responsibility until you finish up current work projects. A new offer appeals but will dilute your energy. If someone wants your talents badly enough they will wait until you are available. This is the start of a string of new opportunities that make all of your prior effort seem worthwhile. The training that you have been receiving is beginning to pay off as your reputation grows by leaps and bounds. Share what you know with those who are struggling to catch up just as you once were. Do not turn your back on those who have helped you to get to your current position on the ladder of success. You are on the receiving end of love and admiration.

19. FRIDAY. Disconcerting. Conditions are tense. Getting along with family and friends is difficult enough today, but you may also have to entertain an out-of-town visitor. Small annoyances are magnified into major problems. Take a long-range view of all that is going on. If you do not think you will even remember the situation a year from now, try not to let it bother you. Pisces have a tendency to want to know everything that is going on. But some matters are outside your control and will be decided by other people. At that point you can make a decision. Trying to second-guess them is a waste of time. A tip from a friend could be based on faulty information.

20. SATURDAY. Mixed. Share household responsibility with other family members. It is a good day to shake up the schedule at home so no one is stuck with the least appealing chores on a regular basis. Once work has been delegated, it is no longer up to you to make sure that it gets done. There are so many options open to you today that picking and choosing is difficult. It may be that you are trying to hang on to a relationship that has run its course. A clean break is merciful to all involved. If you must turn down an invitation from a friend, try to make alternate arrangements for later in the month. Despite all that is going on, family love is the one constant in your life.

21. SUNDAY. Pleasant. Socializing is highlighted today with neighbors and friends. Go out of your way to be cordial to a newcomer. Listen to all that is being said. Casual conversation can steer you in the direction of a new idea that could be a reputation enhancer for you. It is also a starred time to participate as a member of a team. You will excel in a competitive situation as long as it is not personalized. Cheerleading a team that includes a family member or friend is also fun now. Romantic attraction is foreseen for single Pisces. With the Moon rising in your sign now, you are irresistible. Someone you are paired with in a casual setting could soon be your companion for a more formal outing.

22. MONDAY. Variable. Do not allow enthusiasm to take you too fast or too far. Weigh options carefully before taking any action today. Conditions are not quite as they seem. You may be reading more into a person's words than they intend. Hold out a little longer before cashing in a bond or an investment. Patience pays in all financial affairs. Negotiations, too, will benefit from less pressure. If you are able to pretend you do not care you are likely to get more than if you seem anxious. There are matters being discussed behind a closed door that will affect you later in the year. Changes being proposed are not all bad, but you must rely on more than intuition to assess them. Investigate on the sly.

23. TUESDAY. Positive. Look after your health by eating properly and exercising regularly. If you have not had a physical checkup in a while, make an appointment. Ideas being tossed around like confetti at a parade can be winnowed down to a few that seem most promising. Breaking with tradition can be useful if you believe you have a better way. An urge to travel can take you away for a day or overnight. Family members are perfectly capable of being in charge in your absence. This is a propitious time to attend a conference or other gathering of people in your line of work. Or it may be a hobby that draws you to a show or exhibit. Despite all that you are doing, you should feel secure about love.

24. WEDNESDAY. Sensitive. Imagination can be useful, but today you could wind up being too fanciful. Stick to the basics when it comes to making money and getting along on the job. Avoid poking fun at someone who usually is a good sport. Their feelings could be hurt because they are worried about a matter you know nothing about. Keep conversation on the light and bright side with neutral topics that could not possibly offend anyone. What you have to say about the opposite sex can also be misinterpreted by a sensitive person. Be wary of making broad, sweeping generalizations. Body language can be a telling factor in how you are being perceived.

25. THURSDAY. Ordinary. Although there is much that you would like to accomplish, conditions are too stagnant for new starts or rushing a project through to completion. Anything that you do in a haphazard manner will probably have to be redone later. Teamwork should be put on hold for a while. You are in no mood to agree with the majority. Aiming for perfection aggravates some people and only annoys others. But you cannot be satisfied unless you do your best. Handle personal relationships with care. Making too many demands on one individual can lead to that person trying to avoid you in all situations. Do not be misled by current feelings of insecurity; they will pass soon.

26. FRIDAY. Disturbing. Morning hours are more productive than any other time of the day. Whatever is important should be handled then. A minor disagreement during or after lunch could escalate into a full-fledged argument. Friends and co-workers will be taking sides and offering you all kinds of advice. Try to remain cool and in control. Before saying anything, weigh your words and the impact they are apt to have. You could wind up going from the frying pan into the fire if you react in fury. Being too independent is not appreciated by those in charge. Straying away from the straight and narrow path can put you in jeopardy.

27. SATURDAY. Useful. Consider ways and means to safeguard your future and that of your family. Consulting with a banker or financial adviser can be useful even if you do not have a lot of money to invest. An insurance agent can steer you to the best coverage for your current circumstances. You may need to find extra income through a part-time job. Or a family member could be talked into returning to work or entering the job market for the first time. Also consider home protection devices such as alarms or window locks. A big, loud dog can be a good deterrent against crime. Go out tonight with your mate or date and be ready for a surprise.

28. SUNDAY. Cautious. Yesterday's concerns are not going to evaporate overnight even if you have made some decisions. Now it is a matter of convincing your mate or partner to go along with your ideas. Emphasize the positive in all such conversation. It is not the day to do anything but talk; put off action until next week at the earliest. You cannot be too cautious when it comes to watching over youngsters. If swimming or boating, insist that safety requirements be fulfilled to the letter. Everyone will have more fun when no one is worried. A picnic can be pleasant providing food is kept at the proper temperature. Bring along bug spray to fend off hungry insects.

29. MONDAY. Tranquil. Relax and enjoy today's events as though you were merely a spectator. Do not take on anyone's problems as your own. If they seek your advice, give them the benefit of past experience; otherwise stay mum. Concentrate on what is most likely to occur. Have a contingency plan in mind in case your first ideas do not work out as you hope. There is no right or wrong way to handle a situation with a co-worker or friend. You have to trust your good Pisces intuition to the fullest. If handling cash belonging to other people, be certain to keep accurate accounts and to save receipts for every expenditure. Avoid borrowing or loaning money.

30. TUESDAY. Mixed. Even the most routine work offers the chance to learn something new. Find a better way, or at least a different method, so that you do not become robotlike. Let your mind wander to ways of passing on an unwanted task to someone else and making them appreciate it. Pisces enjoy being in charge, but today you may be forced into a secondary role. Playing backup to a person you do not particularly respect can be difficult. Give other people the benefit of the doubt whenever possible. You know someone close to you is trying hard; offer encouragement so that they do not give it up. You can succeed in the role of matchmaker or marriage broker.

31. WEDNESDAY. Profitable.   Combining forces with a friend or co-worker can be profitable. You know where your strengths lie and also what weaknesses you have. Teaming up with someone who is an opposite in most ways should work out well. Check to be sure that your goals are similar before starting. Otherwise you may run into problems partway through a project. There is good reason to accept an invitation from a company dealing in large sums of money. Listen to what they have to say without making any commitment. A major corporation offers more opportunity than a smaller business. At some point you may decide to do some private investigating behind the scenes.

SEPTEMBER

1. THURSDAY. Variable.   Keep for yourself those jobs that you do better than most people, but delegate work not requiring your special touch. Pisces excel today at persuasion and publicity. Do not hide behind a shy smile and expect other people to play up your abilities. A demonstration of some sort can help convince those in charge to give you a chance at more responsibility. Appearance is important. Look the part of the role you want to take on. Your good instincts can be trusted when it comes to deciding who will be true to their word and who is spouting forth hot air. A rumor has a kernel of truth and can be a starting point for you in a new enterprise, be it of love or business.

2. FRIDAY. Stressful.   Emotions are running high as stress increases both on the job and at home. Hold your tongue if you cannot think of anything good to say about a new plan. Someone in charge is in total control now. If you do not agree to go along you could be cut out entirely. Talking about a person behind his or her back can land you in trouble. Whatever you say is likely to filter back to the subject of the conversation, and may be further distorted as well. Guard against taking on extra work unless sure you can fit it in. A time schedule is only an approximation; work is likely to take longer than your best estimate indicates. Travel on this holiday weekend can be troublesome, so start early.

3. SATURDAY. Important.   For Pisces who must be on the job, ambition dominates all other considerations. More can be accomplished now than during the standard workweek when the phone rings constantly and people drop by to chat. Work out details of a plan you hope to put into operation later in the year. Know who you want to fill which positions; in a social setting you may be able to find out if they are interested. Judge for yourself rather than believing what you are told by a third party. Avoid signing a contract today unless it is first reviewed by a legal expert. Your signature is your bond; you do not want to get involved in a lawsuit. Choose traveling companions wisely this weekend.

4. SUNDAY. Disquieting.   Home life is apt to be frantic. Preparations for the coming week may have been postponed a little too long. Or unexpected visitors may throw your schedule out of whack. Fall back to essentials only; put off everything else. Family comes before property. Pisces homeowners may have to let the grass grow a little longer or a dripping faucet keep wasting water until you have the time to take care of these matters. Cater to the wishes of your mate or a younger relative. You may be called upon to act as cook and chief bottle washer if doing any entertaining. Chauffeuring, too, falls to you today and perhaps tomorrow if you will be doing any traveling on the Labor Day holiday.

5. MONDAY. Uncertain.   Events of yesterday have left their mark. Pisces are likely to be more subdued and thoughtful than usual. Try to make no demands. If you keep a low profile you are not apt to be tapped for new responsibility, which could be more than you can handle now. Find a way to put more give-and-take into any relationship that you value. You may appear standoffish when actually you are shy. Romance with someone considerably older or younger is starred for the single Pisces. Whatever the basis for a relationship, an age difference can smooth out potential problems. A delay at the start of a get-together may result in burned food and hot tempers.

6. TUESDAY. Tricky.   Beware of taking on responsibility that has not been specifically delegated to you. You could wind up doing most or all of the work but not getting any credit. Conditions are tricky, especially if you are dealing with more worldly-wise people who have some surprises up their sleeves. If you issue any ultimatum you are likely to be ignored. Better to go along with the crowd and stay in the background. Time devoted to personal plans and private thoughts will not be wasted. If you can free yourself of a major worry you have made some significant progress. Shy away from the subject of finance, especially funds shared with a mate or business partner, or you might have to do some accounting.

7. WEDNESDAY. Harmonious. A cooperative venture gives you the feeling that you are part of an orchestra making beautiful music. Harmony is the hallmark of all group effort now. Much can be accomplished when you combine forces with people whose talents and skills add dimension to your own. Good news from a distant contact lets you know that your ideas are having a wide impact. Stay in touch by phone or letter. There is no holding you back from the success you are able to envision. Be generous in sharing without robbing anyone of their individuality. Give as you would like to receive if roles were reversed. Love is the foundation that sustains all of your effort.

8. THURSDAY. Excellent. Personal relationships continue to be high-flying. People are eager to join forces with you, and you will be equally pleased about their support. This mutual admiration society gives you added impetus to work on more than one major project at once. Pisces may be spared the jobs that are least challenging or most routine. You can practically pick and choose among many options open to you now. Your charm and ability to get along make you a leading candidate for a promotion or pay raise. Research can bring to light facts that have been muddled for a long time. Search until you get to the heart of a problem, then analyze it bit by bit.

9. FRIDAY. Unsettling. While the day will not be a total flop by any standards, there are uncertain undertones that should be viewed as warning signals. Someone you have been closely associated with for only a short time is not totally committed to a current project. If a better offer comes along for this person, you could be left high and dry. Work done by others may not measure up to your high standards. You will either have to risk a confrontation by refusing to accept it or put in a lot of overtime hours to redo it to your liking. A strictly down-to-earth, realistic approach is advised for anything new. Do not get carried away by an idea that seems good in theory but is impractical.

10. SATURDAY. Sensitive. Straight talk can calm a situation at home before it erupts into a shouting match. Be honest in expressing your feelings, then listen to what your mate or another family member has to say. Do not take affront when none is intended. Pisces can be too emotional now. It is not a matter of people either adoring you or shunning you. The majority probably are not even paying any attention to you at all. You can win over a few fence-sitters to your point of view, but do not count on being at the head of a parade. Influential people will relax at an informal get-together that you attend or host. Go off in a corner to talk shop and perhaps swap a few trade secrets. Information is power.

11. SUNDAY. Uncertain. Do not jump to hasty conclusions on the basis of rumor or gossip. There is little chance that the information you now have is totally or even mostly correct. Secondhand reports are apt to be way off base. You will probably continue to receive conflicting versions of the same story from different sources. Carefully analyze what you know to be true and build from there. Someone you know and trust can help you weed out untruths and exaggerations. This is not a positive time to seek a loan from a relative or a friend. Make do with your own income. If you must make a major purchase, shop around for a used item that will last long enough to save for what you really want.

12. MONDAY. Mixed. Figure out what has gone wrong, and why. Emotions are running high, with Pisces being caught in the middle of a power struggle or other battleground. First find some safe harbor for yourself so that you can get your thoughts together. Only then can you begin to find a way out. People to whom you look for help and support may be far from welcoming or cooperative. Those same associates who recently were panting to do what they could are now busy elsewhere. You are apt to be given the cold shoulder, although it should not be taken personally. You are fixated on a certain goal while other people have moved on to new challenges. Try to be more flexible now.

13. TUESDAY. Fortunate. Conditions are doing an about-face today, much to your relief. Someone who was argumentative and unhelpful yesterday is now back at your side. You can be successful working as a pair; a large group is not necessary. A loved one has special insight to offer if you are willing to listen. It does not take a rocket scientist to repair a damaged relationship and get it flying once again. It is up to you to make a phone call or write a letter that breaks the ice. A fortunate coincidence helps you to bump into the person you want to see while walking to lunch or window shopping. Your tact covers all possibilities of defusing the discord that results when in-laws get together. Be a peacemaker.

14. WEDNESDAY. Manageable. Pisces have a firm grasp today on financial affairs and procedures. You can maneuver yourself into a strong negotiating position. A deal currently being worked out can be tipped in your favor if you are willing to hold out for a little more than is now being offered. Do not let anyone know what you might actually accept. Be alert for clues in the actions of other people that reveal how they are reacting to your latest ideas and proposals. If there is a lot of talking going on behind closed doors, you can be sure that you are not giving away too much. Information from a reliable source is worth acting upon quickly before a competitor seizes the opportunity.

15. THURSDAY. Good. Things are likely to work out much as you hope. Find the bright side of any situation and focus on it. Do not let anyone or anything dispel your optimism. Hopes and dreams you have been nurturing for some time are finally close to being realized. You have a powerful ally who is going to bat for you. Move forward without waiting for stragglers to catch up. Whoever arrives first to a particular goal has a significant advantage; it might as well be you. Take advantage of a course being offered by a bank or financial expert. Knowing your options puts you in a good position. Your mate or date wants to tickle your fancy tonight, and you are responsive.

16. FRIDAY. Unsettling. Step back from the action to see how things develop. You may be so close to a situation that you are failing to recognize potential pitfalls. Be an onlooker today. Making an offer now could be a premature move. A request made to a higher-up or a government official is likely to be rebuffed. It is all too easy to misjudge the prevailing mood. A strong breeze of change is beginning to blow, but it is not nearly hurricane force. Stay up with the latest developments. Do not turn down an invitation where you know co-workers and bosses will be mingling. Getting to know someone socially can be a business or financial benefit later in the year.

17. SATURDAY. Positive. Put work worries out of mind so that you can relax and enjoy the company of family members. Children have excellent insight that could come as quite a surprise. Your positive relationships are a definite plus if you decide to try something new. Although there may be some doubters at home, no one is standing in your way. It is a starred day for bargain hunting at yard sales or auctions. Poke around to find what is not obvious for all to see. You will recognize a good deal when you come across it. You may be able to add to a collection, or something you buy could be the start of a new hobby. The Moon going into your sign of Pisces today accents your creativity.

18. SUNDAY. Lucky. Lady Luck is all eyes for you. A lottery ticket or other minor form of gambling can return a dividend, but do not count on coming out on top. Luck is more likely in personal encounters with people you want to impress. You will intuitively know how to get their attention and keep it. New romance is possible; friendship is the best beginning. Be sure to include a family member if you are drawing up a guest list and have to limit it. Change can be suggested now so that people become used to it. You will get better cooperation with sweet talk than with threats or bribes. Someone at a distance is hoping you will pick up the phone and call. The Pisces Moon today sharpens your intuition.

19. MONDAY. Pleasant. Temper your Pisces idealism with a dose of harsh reality. A plan needs to be scaled down in order to win the approval that is necessary for you to undertake it. You will be disappointed if you set your sights too high. Come up with intermediate goals so that you can measure progress as you proceed. Anything too massive is likely to crumble from its own weight. Travel light so that you can move quickly. Figure out who is the most likely candidate to be your right-hand helper. A valued and trusted assistant is your best ally. Events are unlikely to proceed exactly as planned, but deviations will be a pleasant and welcome surprise.

20. TUESDAY. Difficult. There are not enough hours in the day for everything you would like to accomplish. Hone in on those that are most important not only to you but to the boss or another higher-up. Pleasing only yourself is not going to enhance your reputation. You have to pay a price to draw closer to a secret wish. And once you get near it, you might discover it is not what you want after all. Be wary of loaning or borrowing money or anything of value. A debt between friends can lead to devaluing the relationship. A family member could pour cold water on social plans for tonight or later in the week. It would not be smart to go off alone to a strange place. Ask a friend to accompany you.

21. WEDNESDAY. Outstanding. A friend will come to your aid just when you are reaching a low point and do not know how to pull yourself up. Do not hesitate today to ask for a favor. Keep alert for new opportunity. A rare chance is foreseen because you are in the right place at the right time. Someone you have been working with on an independent project is becoming more important in your life. Decide now if you have room for such a relationship. If you string someone along you may soon find yourself at the end of your rope. Business expansion offers new possibilities that can lead to a substantial raise if you are willing to relocate or commute a longer distance.

22. THURSDAY. Changeable. Financial affairs require careful monitoring as the Moon enters Taurus today. You cannot act on gut feelings alone; do some research into trends. Check out the best advice being offered by those who are trained in economics and banking. Be sure that your accounts are insured. Savings must not be risked in hopes of making a quick profit. Keep notes of any conversations regarding money transactions. Later you may need to refer to them to recall who promised what. An older person is likely to come through for you when someone else lets you down. Donate time but not money to a worthwhile charity or other cause that you want to help.

23. FRIDAY. Rewarding. Efforts that you have been exerting during the month are beginning to pay off. Continue to push for what you want without letup. Your Pisces logic helps in making a decision that is unclear based on facts alone. What has been successful in the past is a clue to the future, but with updated modifications. Do not resist the technological changes going on all around you. Jump in feet first and learn as though you were a novice. If repair work is necessary, obtain a few estimates and recommendations before selecting a contractor. Professional advice, too, should be shopped for rather than settling for the first offer you receive.

24. SATURDAY. Tedious. You cannot get out of household chores even though there is a lot you would prefer to do. A slapdash cleanup will not satisfy you. Be thorough in convincing family members to help. When they understand your reasons they are more inclined to lend a hand. Proceed in a logical, step-by-step fashion. A good how-to book can be a lifesaver if you lack experience. Later in the day you may decide to go out for a walk or a drive. Being away from the source of frustration helps give you new perspective. A loved one is not being obstinate in order to provoke you; listen and you will understand their feelings. The chance to take a short trip is an unexpected, but welcome, change.

25. SUNDAY. Profitable. This social day can turn into a profitable one as well. A new partnership is particularly promising. Someone you do not know well has an idea that is just waiting to be put into motion. Your know-how combined with their inspiration is a perfect combination. Mingle with people from all walks of life. Do not confine yourself to those who think and act as you do. Someone from a different country or culture is an ideal companion. Humanitarian pursuits are important to Pisces. Focus your effort through an established organization that has deep roots in your community. Charity begins at home but should expand from there to diverse neighborhoods in your locale.

26. MONDAY. Buoyant. Let the creative side of your nature come to the surface and have free rein. Find a new way to do what has become boringly routine. Curiosity can lead to an exciting breakthrough. Look for ways to simplify your life by reducing possessions and commitments. The less you have on your must-do list, the freer you are to experiment and branch out. You are likely to make a most favorable impression on important people. It will not take much convincing to get them to back you. A new sense of relaxation spills over into all of your relationships. Home life should be more easygoing, with younger family members benefiting the most from the experience of elders.

27. TUESDAY. Deceptive. Be wary of proceeding too far or too fast. You can bring about change through gradual modifications but not in one massive upheaval. This is a good day to take a long, hard look at yourself from all angles. If you need to diet, check into alternatives and select the one that seems right for you. Exercise can be done individually or through a group; decide which gives you more impetus. A habit that you know is unhealthy for you and those around you should be brought under control starting now. You have the willpower and only need to find the way. Plans may have to be altered because of events occurring at a distance. A quick trip could be necessary so that Pisces can personally handle an emergency situation for a relative.

28. WEDNESDAY. Harmonious. The nonaggressive nature of Pisces is in control now. Harmony with family members and co-workers make cooperative effort especially worthwhile. Give in on minor matters and you stand a better chance of getting your way when you really care. Offer praise and encouragement to those who are trying hard but not seeing immediate results. A chat with a neighbor or store clerk helps you catch up on local news and gossip. There could be good reason to buy a gift for newlyweds or a new baby as a welcome to the neighborhood. Evening favors going out for dinner with that special person in your life, then getting home for a second dessert.

29. THURSDAY. Satisfactory. Deal primarily with people you know well and respect on the basis of past working relationships. You do not have to look far to find the help you require. New horizons are opening up for Pisces. Satisfaction depends on taking advantage of opportunity when your schedule permits. Otherwise you are likely to overextend yourself and be in a mad rush. Someone from overseas may be exerting influence on your decisions. Or events occurring at a distance may force you to make some adjustments. A future pay raise or promotion hinges on how you handle pressure. A humorous remark can reduce the tension in a meeting and produce agreement.

30. FRIDAY. Excellent. Keeping a low profile is the best strategy today. Conditions are ripe for change if you can figure out when and where to start. Rely on your excellent judgment when it comes to picking and choosing among all of the available options. Do not allow anyone to rush you. Even a higher-up will respect your request for thinking time. The harder you work, the more successful you will be. Delegate only those jobs that you know another person can handle as well as you. A deadline will be extended if you make a special request and have sound reasons. You are at your persuasive best in front of a group of people. Pisces teachers and coaches can rise to the top of their profession.

OCTOBER

1. SATURDAY. Productive. You will not want to be idle today. Focus your efforts on home repair and improvements. You do not have to spend a lot in order to make your surroundings more comfortable. A thorough cleaning, especially of closets and drawers, gives you more room for organizing. Gather together a pile of throwaways that you can give to a thrift store or other charity. What you no longer want or need can be a treasure for another person. A good how-to book can give you all the information you need to build a bookshelf or install extra lighting. Pay attention to personal health. If you have been slacking off an exercise program, get back in the swing now.

2. SUNDAY. Pleasant. Pleasure is where you find it, so go looking. Family members make excellent company today. Be sure to include a youngster in your plans. You may have to slow your pace so that others can keep up, but you will not mind. Adjust to the wishes of your mate or date later in the day. What they have planned may not appeal at first, but once you become involved you will have a fine time. Someone new on the scene is likely to attract a lot of attention. If you happen to run into a famous person, be sure to get an autograph or a photograph. Pisces who must be on the job today can look forward to extra compensation for extra effort. Your organizing skills are a key to success.

3. MONDAY. Mixed. You are apt to be pulled in many directions and not know which way to turn next. Set your own agenda after considering all that is being asked of you. Priorities have to be established. You cannot do an adequate job, much less a good one, if you are only half thinking about the task at hand while worrying about what is to come next. Your Pisces abilities are bound to shine through when you proceed in an orderly, step-by-step fashion. Intuitively you can come up with a solution to a problem plaguing a friend or co-worker. You are tuned to their wavelength and understand their needs perhaps better than they do right now.

4. TUESDAY. Stimulating. Teamwork is favored in all areas. As part of a group you can gain more publicity for your efforts and demand a hearing from the person or agency in charge. It is also a positive time to write a letter to the editor if you want to voice a complaint or a proposed solution. People you have been trying to reach since the start of the month should be reachable today. Do not leave a message and expect them to call back; keep trying until you make contact. You should be equally as persuasive by phone as in a face-to-face meeting. There is some opposition to your views, but your reasons are sound and your judgment good. You can persuade the most obstinate person to come around to your way of thinking.

5. WEDNESDAY. Important. Be sure to take advantage of a lucky break that comes along early in the day. Important changes at home or at work are now falling into place, based in good part on your hard work. Help people adapt by focusing on all that is positive about the change. You are setting the pace and tone for others to follow. This is a day for speaking your mind and clearing the air. Do not sweep a problem under the rug. Hang it out for all to see and analyze. Be willing to listen to proposed solutions that differ from those you have in mind. It may be that someone younger or less experienced than you has the best suggestion; it is up to you to listen and help to implement novel ideas.

6. THURSDAY. Satisfactory.   After a good night's sleep you are alert and raring to go this morning. An early start gives you an edge. You will never obtain total agreement to your plans, but by holding steadfastly to them you are gaining admiration. You must not relax a stand based on principles. Do not hesitate to putting into action a plan that has been checked with a fine-tooth comb and come out clean and workable. Give yourself that extra push to work through roadblocks and surmount them. Let your Pisces creativity find an answer when logic alone is not sufficient. Your self-confidence is contagious, carrying along those who tend to sit on the fence and go with the leader.

7. FRIDAY. Sensitive.   Someone who seemed to be on your side may prove you wrong. Be alert for indications of double-dealing or backstabbing. Be ready to counter an argument or a refusal with irrefutable reasons. Facts and figures back up what you say, but the power of your personality is most persuasive. It is not a good day to share sensitive information or feelings except with the person closest to you. Even then you may be reminded at a later time of something you say today that you would rather forget. Business and pleasure do not mix well. Avoid having lunch or meeting after work with someone who has economic or even emotional power over you.

8. SATURDAY. Happy.   Personal relationships are the blazing stars today. You will enjoy the companionship of family and friends. This is an excellent time to begin a new partnership that is purely social or a mix of fun and work. An affair that has been stagnating can be given new life if you are able to spend some uninterrupted time together. You may want to plan a weekend getaway or a longer vacation to rekindle passion. Enjoy reminiscing with a photo album or old love letters. Your intuition is not going to steer you wrong. Good news from a relative at a distance may include an invitation. Rush out to buy a congratulatory card or a small gift.

9. SUNDAY. Variable.   Laugh at a joke made at your expense. It is not wise to take yourself too seriously, although the tendency now is to ignore the humorous side of a situation. Show that you are a good sport and can take as well as give. Arguments may arise at home, especially for the Pisces parent whose patience is wearing thin. Think back to your own childhood and draw some parallels from it. Handle loved ones with kid gloves so that serious quarrels are avoided. Any plans that you make should include family members. If you go off on your own you will leave some angry faces staring at your back. A creative hobby offers an outlet for stress if it includes the people close to you.

10. MONDAY. Quiet. Play a waiting game. Do not reveal even half of what you are planning and plotting. Your secretiveness is a great attraction to those whose help you will ultimately want. Wait for others to make the first move; then you will be ready to counterattack from a position of strength. Have facts and figures to back what you say. It is not enough to believe something is true; you have to prove it. Keep in mind that the best defense is usually a good offense. Avoid chancing your luck in any area. Gambling and all forms of speculation are unlikely to return a dividend. Invest savings with an eye to safety and a reasonable return, not a windfall.

11. TUESDAY. Enjoyable. An influential person is willing to go to bat for you. Call in a favor that you have been owed for some time. There is special opportunity now to get a higher paying job that includes new responsibility. First, however, you have to prove that you could do the work. Be prepared to present letters of recommendation from at least one previous supervisor. In an audition or interview your Pisces talent will shine through loud and clear. There is no need for pretense, but you should emphasize all that is positive by way of accomplishments. It is up to you to blow your own horn and attract attention. An intimate setting for a romantic date enables you to let go of certain inhibitions.

12. WEDNESDAY. Useful. Your energy level is high and enthusiasm is keeping pace. It should be easy to tackle more than one project simultaneously. Move swiftly throughout the day instead of sitting back and luxuriating in one accomplishment. You can trust people who work with and for you. Delegate tasks that they can handle as well as you. This leaves you free for what only you do best. Higher-ups are aware of your progress and abilities. Work performed now will have a direct impact on a future promotion or pay raise. Do not let up as you near a goal. Push to make a project a little better than even you had predicted. Pisces intuition is right on target.

13. THURSDAY. Unsettling. Competition is becoming more intense, making this a time to adopt a new strategy or at least think about one. Play up your own strengths, not the weaknesses of others. Refuse to be pressured into signing a contract or agreeing to any deal before studying all the pluses and minuses. When you find the balance in your favor, act quickly. If it does not add up to a plus for you, stall as long as possible. A colleague has a realistic plan for making money. You can benefit from joining forces if the responsibility is going to be shared. It is not smart, however, to invest money now if you will have no say-so in management decisions from the start.

14. FRIDAY. Changeable. Keep in the background of all affairs. Let others hog the limelight while you flip the switches. There is much to be gained by working behind the scenes. Matters yet to be resolved should be thrashed out in a day-long session, if necessary. You cannot afford to have them hanging fire over the weekend ahead. Wait until a contract is signed before boasting of your good financial sense. Unexpected fees may take you by surprise. Travel is not advisable today. There is too much occurring at your home base to be far removed from the action. Tonight favors a quiet dinner and a movie blazing with action. The Moon entering Pisces this evening indicates changing moods.

15. SATURDAY. Harmonious. With the Moon in your sign, Pisces sensitivity for people is keen. You will do all that you can to help a relative or friend wrestling with a tough decision. Be a willing listener; letting them talk out the problem could result in a solution without you saying a word. Someone who is down on his luck may request a loan. Before taking out your wallet, consider alternatives that might be more useful in the long run. Whatever is given is never as appreciated as something earned. At home, hint at what you want rather than making demands. Loved ones are willing to change some plans to accommodate you, but there is a limit to how agreeable your mate or family members are inclined to be. Do not push your luck.

16. SUNDAY. Rewarding. Home entertaining can be personally rewarding and might benefit business as well. Get to know a co-worker on a more personal basis. Friends make excellent company. This is a starred day for hatching a plan for a joint vacation trip before the end of the year. You may want to share the expense of renting a cabin in the woods or a villa on a tropical island. Be sure to include all family members in your planning session, although you may decide to go to your separate ways for a weekend get-away. Children will relish some of your undivided attention. And a pet needs pampering also. Today's Pisces Moon makes you extremely sensitive and sympathetic to the plight of all living creatures. Be kind to yourself, too, instead of being a martyr.

17. MONDAY. Outstanding. Steady progress gives you a renewed rush of hope and inspiration. An idea that is taking shape can be made even better with a dash of imagination. Once you determine what you want there is no holding you back. Dealings with people at a distance are apt to be particularly successful. You can break through language or other barriers and reach a meeting of the minds. Investing abroad is also favored. Special opportunity exists to hop aboard a new trend that has not yet become a boom in your area. Keep up with technological developments in your field. Taking a class or studying a manual can be rewarding. Be alert for an interesting stranger tonight.

18. TUESDAY. Buoyant. Conditions remain extremely favorable for all Pisces interests. The Moon in Aries makes this a starred day for putting a new plan into immediate operation. Do not hesitate because you have not lined up all the help you know you will need. Once your idea becomes better known there will be people beating at your door to sign on to your team. A loan can be arranged, or private financial assistance secured from a friend or relative. Everything is going your way. Relax and enjoy it; avoid thinking of potential pitfalls unless you are looking for ways to counter them. A newcomer may soon be a permanent part of your social, romantic or professional life.

19. WEDNESDAY. Profitable. You do not need luck to turn a profit today. An idea that you began experimenting with earlier in the year is showing much potential. Push ahead with it in an expanded version. You are definitely on a winning wavelength. An opinion that you stuck to despite opposition is now being accepted without question. Your reputation is growing among those who matter. There is a way to turn an enjoyable hobby into a money-maker if you are willing to streamline your techniques. Do what you can to improve conditions in your area for people less fortunate than you. Consider volunteering time or contributing money to a cause you believe in wholeheartedly.

20. THURSDAY. Tricky. You may trip and tumble today, but the accident is not so serious that you cannot pick yourself up and start again. It is fine to aim for perfection, but do not expect to achieve it overnight. Whatever is worth doing is worth doing well. Concentrate on the small details that set your project apart from similar ones. Put your Pisces creativity to work. Pace yourself throughout the day. If you become overly tired you can make foolish errors of judgment. Or someone may take advantage of you when you do not care enough to protect your interests. You may have to deny a rumor although it is not altogether untrue. Learn from the experience; you cannot trust people randomly when you are bursting to tell a secret.

21. FRIDAY. Cautious. Do not apply pressure to anyone to make a decision. If you force their hand you will not like what they have to say. Give them time and room enough to seriously consider a proposal that you have presented. Resistance is certain if you set deadlines and give ultimatums. Pisces private life could be experiencing turmoil due to the absence of a family member. A realignment of roles is foreseen, at least for a short period. Upset in one area of life should not be allowed to spill over into other areas. If you are angry at one person, come right out and say so; do not talk behind his or her back but directly face-to-face. It can be hard for you to speak the truth to vulnerable loved ones.

22. SATURDAY. Disconcerting. There is more to do than you can possibly fit into the day. Figure out what takes priority and concentrate on those matters. Family and friends may offer help, then not come through as promised. Talk is cheap now; action is at a premium. Your feelings are no more sensitive than the people around you. Give a little and you will get a little in return. If you expect something for nothing you are apt to be sorely disappointed. By evening you may be seeing a problem in a new light. In fact, it could all but disappear when you put it into the context of the entire year. Minor matters must not be blown up out of proportion. You have enough on your mind without making trouble over nothing.

23. SUNDAY. Easygoing. Let your artistic nature take over a project that you have been working on following prescribed directions. Results will be more pleasing if you use your own combination of colors and materials. Chores around the house can be put off; if they are not done this week, they can wait until next. If a family member objects, offer to allow them to handle the task personally. Pisces parents will enjoy shared activity with children, especially a sports competition. Enjoy watching a youngster's team in action, or sit together on the sidelines and root for the home team. You will be content to spend the evening at home, resting or relaxing or studying. Read aloud to the children.

24. MONDAY. Mixed. Misjudging someone's words or reaction can start you down the wrong path. Any promises made today should be in writing. Even a good friend is apt to perplex you. What is said and what is meant could be poles apart. It will be difficult to obtain the go-ahead from higher-ups. What seems obvious to you is a matter of concern for them. You may be overlooking matters that are important, but it is more likely you are willing to take a chance and they are not. Left on your own, much can be done. A plan launched today has good potential. Small investment can escalate into a pretty profit for the Pisces with inside knowledge.

25. TUESDAY. Productive. Someone who recently refused a request has had a change of heart. Ask again and you will be gratified by the response. Ambitious plans can be moved forward at a fast clip. There is no reason to dilly-dally over matters that are straightforward. Go after what you want with single-minded dedication. People are looking to you for ideas. Your enthusiasm is contagious, especially with people who are used to being led. In a tense situation you will automatically come up with the right thing to say if you follow your basic inclinations. There is such a thing as overplanning; if making a speech, have only notes before you and not the whole presentation written out.

26. WEDNESDAY. Sensitive. Your recent enthusiasm may have led to hurtling along at too fast a pace. Slow down today and take stock of where you are and where you want to go. Interview co-workers to learn their views. It is important not to move so fast that you outdistance your helpers. Also allow extra time for people to adjust to change. Some criticism is foreseen for recent work that was not quite up to your normally high standards. You know that you can do better; no one has to tell you so. There is always something to learn no matter how well trained or experienced you may be. Your mate or date has arranged a welcome surprise for you tonight, so get home early.

27. THURSDAY. Good. Morning hours are most favorable. Whatever request is made then is sure to be fulfilled. You may be seeing a co-worker in a new light that puts a special glow on joint effort. Do not dawdle over minor details. Focus on the main thrust so that you do not miss the mark. There is a strong element of luck affecting business and financial dealings. A loan application is apt to be approved. A contract signed now will be increasing in value over its life expectancy. Opt for the longest terms available. You can afford to take a calculated risk. Go all out to increase your take-home pay. When you compare your salary to what others are making, it is clear that you deserve a raise.

28. FRIDAY. Exciting. Operating from home base is favored if possible. In any event do not venture far from normal surroundings. If you must meet with someone from a distance, do so on your own home turf. Good luck continues today. A visitor or a letter contains the news you have been hoping to hear. Be quick to take advantage of it. While thinking about solutions to one problem you are likely to come up with an ingenious idea to handle another situation. Daydreaming can pay off. The unconscious is seeing especially clearly. This is a happy evening for affairs of the heart. The Pisces in love can be transported to another time and place by a lover.

29. SATURDAY. Manageable. Keep costs within budget and you have nothing to worry about today. Be on guard if attending a craft show or other tempting sale. You can easily be carried away when the artist is right in front of you. Set a good example of energy and enthusiasm for members of the family to follow. Even children can be persuaded to lend a hand with a home repair or remodeling job. Keep entertainment on the light side. An informal get-together with friends or neighbors is more enjoyable than a dress-up affair. Your intuition helps you grasp what a person wants or means with hardly a word being spoken. A ticklish situation deserves a laugh.

30. SUNDAY. Rewarding. What comes as a surprise is likely to be the most interesting part of the day. Be ready to change plans on short notice or on none at all. Dress according to the weather, not necessarily in the height of fashion. When you are comfortable there is no holding you back. But if your feet hurt or you are too hot or too cold you will be itching to flee home. Drop-in guests can be stimulating, or you may choose to let someone else play the role of host. Keep conversation as neutral as possible when you are in the company of strangers. Later you can have a heart-to-heart talk with a friend and compare your impressions. Children figure importantly now. Pisces parents and teachers will be responsive.

31. MONDAY. Variable. Take one step at a time, and make it a small forward move. It is all too easy to overlook important details. Be sure to recheck facts and figures. Do not rely on a single source. Any attempt to deal in secret is apt to explode like a time bomb. You have to follow rules and regulations that are designed for everyone; you cannot expect an exception to be made for you. Keep up self-improvement attempts through a class or independent study. Feeling better about yourself gives you a better outlook on life in general. Luck may be involved in a chance meeting, although it is more likely that you have intuitively figured out where the action will be.

NOVEMBER

1. TUESDAY. Outstanding. Pisces persuasion is reaching a peak. Turn on the charm with a co-worker or higher-up who has some control over your progress. Prove that what you want is in their best interests. A government official can be convinced to bend a rule on your behalf but not break it. Give compliments generously. You have a chance to show off your skill and creativity today. Break with tradition if you think you have come up with a better plan. What has been successful in the past is no guarantee of future usefulness. Money is foreseen from an unlikely source. You may be in line for an inheritance or lottery prize. The chance of improving your fortune through partnership or marriage is high.

2. WEDNESDAY. Fair. Stay calm and in control throughout the day. Do not allow a loudmouth to get you angry or a crybaby to make you feel guilty about not dropping what you are doing and rushing to help. Mull over possibilities before making up your mind about any matter. Nothing is certain now; choices abound. Seek advice from more experienced people, although listening to them does not mean you must accept what you are told. It is important to be open to new ideas. Recycling the old is also worthwhile. Look for ways to save small amounts here and there so that you do not have to give up a major pleasure in order to add to your bank account.

3. THURSDAY. Easygoing. A shopping excursion can turn up a special bargain, especially in clothing. Scout around out-of-the way stores instead of a major mall. Plan on having lunch with a friend. There is nothing so urgent today that you cannot put it off if you choose. Creative work is likely to appeal, particularly for the Pisces in search of part-time income. Something you invent, make or do can be turned into a source of extra money. A notice in your local newspaper may be all it takes to draw customers. The Pisces employee who keeps a low profile will not be saddled with extra work. Pretend to be busy even if you are not. Difficulties arise toward the end of the day advising against travel.

4. FRIDAY. Stressful. Some explaining may be necessary regarding recent work or a recent decision. Be prepared to justify your actions without getting angry or defensive. A discrepancy must be resolved before taking off for the weekend. Do not rely on memory alone; dig up old receipts and working papers to find out why certain things were done the way they were. Pisces with any sort of health problem must guard against added stress. Deep breathing as well as outdoor exercise can have a definite calming effect. Partnership financial affairs must be handled gingerly. Do not withdraw money without first obtaining the go-ahead from your mate or partner. You will not make much progress if one person strives to save while the other squanders.

5. SATURDAY. Useful. You will get special satisfaction from work around the house that you do yourself. Consider ways to liven up a room by adding a wallpaper border or some stenciling. Plants, too, can be effective decorating accents. Find a way to display a collection that is now put away in a closet or drawer. Discuss an idea with a friend or neighbor to get the benefit of their experience. There is no reason to reinvent the wheel when you can obtain advice. Be wary of undertaking a months-long project that may add stress to the upcoming holiday season. Although you may feel that you are in a rut, you have the willpower to change circumstances. It is a favorable time for studying.

6. SUNDAY. Unsettling. Pisces are apt to feel left out or bypassed in the swirl of today's activities. Family members have their own agenda. While they will not rebuff you, it is clear that you have not been included in their plans. Find activities that please and satisfy you. You can be together without physically being in the same room. Share the rudiments of a talent you have been developing. Do not get into it in such detail that your listeners lose their enthusiasm. Slow but steady progress is the goal if you are teaching or learning. Be wary of acting in a holier-than-thou manner when dealing with younger or less experienced people. What is obvious to you may be difficult for others to see or even envision. Avoid gambling of any kind today.

7. MONDAY. Tricky. Nothing is quite as it seems. Your intuition could play you false, especially if you are involved in negotiations or the hiring process. Separating fact from fantasy does not come easily. The person who seems to have all the answers may be the one trying to pull the wool over your eyes. Do not make any commitments that involve your family or business associates without first consulting them. Someone pressuring you for a quick reply is apt to be concealing pertinent facts. Do not believe even half of what you read, less of what you are told. Check first with independent sources for verification. Advertisers may be trying to lure customers with outrageous claims or prices.

8. TUESDAY. Confusing. Who is supposed to do what creates confusion and stress today. Extra work may be heaped on you, or a job you are enjoying could be reassigned to someone else. If no one seems to be taking charge, it is up to you to step in and make sense of the situation. There may be some bias based on sex or educational achievement that has nothing to do with being able to perform the job. Financial restrictions could force curtailment of a project that is just beginning to arouse excitement and interest. A loan that seemed assured could be withheld at the last moment. This is not the time to make any ironclad commitment because you may not be able to honor it.

9. WEDNESDAY. Mixed. Let the dust settle from yesterday's upsets before bringing up any sensitive new ideas. The boss or another higher-up is anxious to conclude outstanding projects rather than tackle anything new. You will be most productive working on your own. All forms of teamwork are potentially stressful. Getting along even with your best friend demands restraint and extra courtesy. All forms of speculation should be avoided. You could easily gamble away the rent or food money on what is touted as a sure thing. Whatever is left to chance is likely to be less than successful. Romance has reached a plateau that is comfortable but unexciting.

10. THURSDAY. Quiet. Be content to take it easy today. Sit back and let others carry the load for a while. Conditions are too slow for change to have an effect. If you try to stir things up you are likely to be rebuffed in no uncertain terms. Frustration is bound to result if you set goals that are unattainable. Take one small step at a time; leaps can send you sprawling to the ground. Be sure to weigh options against one another. Although there are many good ideas being generated, some are too expensive and others too expansive. It is a good day to enjoy a personal hobby that lets your Pisces creativity shine through. When you are familiar with tradition you can comfortably break with it.

11. FRIDAY. Changeable.   Unlike yesterday, this is a period to be on your toes. Changes are coming and you should be ready to adapt or stand your ground and fight them off. If you hear a disturbing rumor, track down the source to find out if it is true. If someone has been talking about you behind your back, confront them directly. A flash of insight or a burst of creativity can be the beginning of a profitable sideline. Do not work alone; turn to a friend or associate for ideas, support and an extra pair of willing hands. Do not overlook the possibility of patenting or copyrighting what you dream up. The success stories of other people are sure to inspire you. The Moon rising in Pisces now goads you on.

12. SATURDAY. Pleasant.   Family members are clearly behind you all the way. Joint effort with them will produce the desired results with some fun times thrown in for extra measure. A youngster is a great companion. What they say can give you special insight from a wide-eyed perspective. A brisk walk or a game of catch is sure to be pleasant. Listen more than you talk. You can understand without having to be told in precise terms. Love life is steady and easygoing. You do not have to put on any airs with your mate or date. A promise made today can be relied upon without hesitation. Good intentions are the start of a mutual effort that will make you proud.

13. SUNDAY. Uncertain.   Begin planning a trip even though it is not certain if it will get past the planning stage. Conditions are up in the air; nothing is written in permanent ink. You can only act according to the best instincts and intentions of the day. Family and friends are caught up in their own interests, forcing you to fend for yourself except at mealtime. A hobby can be good company, particularly one combining mental and physical talents. It is also a positive day to consider taking a class just for the fun of it. Star gazing, scuba diving or anything in between may appeal. Pisces pet owners should not overlook getting necessary shots for their animal. Children's activities should be monitored today.

14. MONDAY. Confusing.   Although not obvious to the casual observer, there is confusion stalling a project that seems to be moving forward. If you can get to the bottom of it much greater movement toward a goal is likely. Have a heart-to-heart talk with the boss or other higher-up who is supposed to be in charge. You may discover that they have lost interest and are only too willing to turn over the reins of day-to-day operations to you. One small error can cause long-lasting confusion. Proceed slowly and cautiously. Vital information is not flashing a red light to attract your attention; you have to dig deep in order to find it. Follow all safety precautions if you are driving or using machinery today.

15. TUESDAY. Excellent. Unexpected money is coming your way, although probably not in a spendable form. Take advantage of a special offer that you know to be legitimate. It is a starred day to apply for a loan, scholarship or fellowship. Blow your own horn loud and clear in order to impress those who are in charge. Highlight all of your accomplishments as well as your hopes and dreams for the future. Standing still is never a Pisces trait. You are ready to move onward and upward. Taking on additional responsibility, even without an immediate pay increase, helps prove what you are capable of doing when given an opportunity. Loved ones want to share your delights.

16. WEDNESDAY. Disturbing. Although there are changes you wish you could initiate, this is not the moment to propose them. Conditions are not favorable for urging or enforcing. You can expect much opposition if you even mention the idea of rearranging furniture or reassigning responsibility. Pisces who are in charge should beware of angering a person who knows how to use the system for retaliation. Steer clear of lawsuits and threats of a suit. You may have to swallow your pride and give in to avoid a protracted walkout or other separation. You have the willpower to make personal changes, however. This is a good day to give up a habit you know is unwholesome.

17. THURSDAY. Demanding. You cannot accomplish much on your own with all of the demands being made of you. Try to respond to a family member first, then to the boss or another higher-up. You are apt to be on the phone; long-distance calls are especially important. Affairs occurring at a distance have a direct impact on your options now. Travel can be a waste of time and effort. Reports from those on the scene will keep you amply informed. Guard against overoptimism. When things seem to be going well, stay alert. If you become complacent you lose the advantage. Assess your chances of success before making any commitment. There is no use plunging into a no-win situation.

18. FRIDAY. Good. Freedom from restraints that have been imposed since the start of the month gives you renewed optimism. Your powers of persuasion are back on track. Someone who has been opposing you loud and strong is now ready to make a deal that allows them to save face. Steel yourself for some continued rumormongering that puts you in an unfavorable light. Prove by actions rather than words that you are right. Someone in a position of power needs as much encouragement as a newcomer. A pat on the back can be a push into the future. Plans are beginning to jell and only need to be monitored. If you have assigned tasks, let the people in charge carry on as they see fit to do. You cannot keep your fingers in all the pies.

19. SATURDAY. Successful. Results today are determined by your individual effort and dedication. No one is going to offer much help, although you can count on occasional sporadic assistance. Neither, however, is anyone blocking your way. Independent action can help you achieve a small goal that puts you in line for greater accomplishment. Break down a major project into manageable parts. Work at home should not be all-consuming. Consider hiring a professional for at least part of home remodeling or redecorating. It is not a matter of lack talent but of time. You will grow impatient and increasingly unhappy if confined to one task. Pisces need variety.

20. SUNDAY. Difficult. Someone has to take the blame for a mistake that is beginning to be obvious. You should accept some responsibility, but only your rightful share. It is not necessary to cover for other people. A difficult decision has to be made today in consulation with family members. Work for a consensus so that no one can come back to you later and ask why you alone decided on a certain course of action. Attending a religious service or meditating in private puts you in better touch with your feelings. Emotions must be part of any intellectual decision; you cannot separate the two. Try to be more tactful with older people. Do not put them down before helping them financially or in any other way.

21. MONDAY. Variable. Possessions, or accumulating them, can take over your life if you allow it. Limit yourself to what is important to you rather than trying to keep up with friends or co-workers. You do not need the latest and the newest in order to be satisfied. Trying to hurry things along today probably will only cause extra work in the long run. Do not rush through a job or apply pressure on other people to hurry. Slow and steady wins many races. Work toward a goal in measured steps. Results may be slow coming in, but you can count on them. Careful preparation is vital. Check facts and figures so that you can vouch for them without any reservations.

22. TUESDAY. Mixed. A personal relationship is going through a period of doubts and second thoughts. Hang in until you know for sure how you and the other person feel. Do not allow temporary upsets to cut short a promising affair, Work, too, may undergo strain, especially if you are adjusting to a new boss or new assignment. No major breakthroughs are foreseen now, but you can make some progress. Avoid taking on more than you can comfortably handle. It may be best to back out of a social obligation that is worrying you. Stay out of conversations that are more gossip than information. If you would not openly express an opinion to a person directly, do not say it behind his or her back.

23. WEDNESDAY. Outstanding. Focus on improving home life, work or your community. Pitch in with a voluntary effort to make conditions better. Working with children or the elderly has special rewards. You may want to buy high-priced tickets to a charity event or give a donation. It is also a good day to sign a petition or to begin circulating one. All the indications point to extra success if you put more of yourself into everything that you are doing. Follow rules and regulations, but add a bit more that stamps the work as your special project. Pisces creativity is at an all-time high. Write down ideas that cannot be put to immediate practical use; later, in a dry period, you can refer back to them for inspiration.

24. THURSDAY. Good. Friends make the best company along with family members. You will feel safe and protected in a group of people who understand you. Some nostalgia is likely, especially if you are getting together with people you rarely see. Bring out old photograph albums as the starting point for stories of the past. Music also sets a special mood today. Try to avoid running in a hundred different directions. Focus on a few activities that you do better than most people. It may be that you can play the piano or strum a guitar while others are busy in the kitchen. Be ready to help those in charge without taking over and beginning to tell them what to do. Love life is the icing on the cake tonight.

25. FRIDAY. Changeable. People who have been thwarting your efforts or knocking down your ideas are beginning to have a change of heart. Welcome them as helpers and assistants now. You are likely to get the green light from your mate or partner for a major purchase that has been under consideration for some time. This is an excellent day to shop for state-of-the-art purchases such as a computer, kitchen appliance or sound system. Know what you want before beginning to compare prices. Service is as important as cost and should be factored in when you make a final decision.

A change of scenery would be welcome by family members. Plan on visiting friends during the weekend ahead.

26. SATURDAY. Quiet. Personal relationships are easygoing and pleasant. Activities with all family members are starred, although young children have to be monitored more carefully to be sure they do not become overly boisterous. If you treat loved ones with tact and consideration, there is nothing they will not do for you. Quiet pursuits will appeal to everyone. A first-run movie or a concert gives focus to the day. This is also a fine time to consider adding to your family circle through birth or adoption or marriage. An announcement now may start in motion plans for a ceremony in the year ahead. Real estate investigation if you plan to relocate soon could also be rewarding.

27. SUNDAY. Buoyant. An idea proposed by an older family member could be turned into a money-maker. Financial security is coming closer to being realized through your own efforts combined with your mate or another partner. You have special talents that can be marketed for a handsome profit if you are willing to give up some of your leisure time. Eventually you may be able to devote yourself to it without having to hold down a full-time job in addition. Your energy and intuition inspire other people to take an idea and build on it. Pisces writers and artists who live by their imagination should do especially well. You may not notice changes yet, but they are slowly and surely creeping into everyday life.

28. MONDAY. Difficult. Hold back an outburst of anger that stems from disappointment. Someone you admire is likely to let you down. Make the best of a difficult situation. You have to do your own share plus a good deal more in order to bring a project up to your high standards. Other signs may settle for less, but you are not comfortable if results are below your minimum requirements. There could be a negative reaction to the pressure you are applying. Someone you are counting on may turn and walk away. Frustration at having to live by the same rules that everyone else abides by is building. Do not set yourself apart in any way.

29. TUESDAY. Fortunate. There is a chance today to branch out on your own. Obtaining permission to do so gives you added legitimacy, but if you cannot get agreement proceed anyway. New responsibility should be accompanied by more income. A newly acquired skill gives you more bargaining power. Highlight all that you have done and all that you are capable of doing if given the opportunity. Juggle current tasks so that you are not stuck with those that attract the least attention. You need to publicize your efforts and accomplishments. Be a participant in all that is going on, not an onlooker. Entering a contest today can turn you into a winner sometime very soon.

30. WEDNESDAY. Unsettling. A relationship that has been dragging on may take an abrupt turn for the worse today. This is a time to break through obstacles or to retreat and start from scratch. There is no middle ground. If a person refuses to help or is actually hindering you, turn to someone else without regrets. You cannot cling to the past and expect to make inroads into the future. It is vital to display confidence even if you are not inwardly quite as self-assured as you seem. Bluffing can go a long way toward getting what you want. Negotiate from a position of strength. Know what you might be willing to settle for in the end, but keep this information to yourself.

DECEMBER

1. THURSDAY. Harmonious. You can avert a collision by stepping out of the way. Do not insist on your choices when those being proposed by other people seem to have equal merit. Harmonious relationships depend on how you handle potential upsets. Once a decision is made, go along with the majority. There is special opportunity today to get to know a working associate on a more personal level. A short trip together or a joint project breaks the ice and can be the beginning of a friendship both on and off the job. Romance, too, can be ignited in a close working arrangement. You will not lack companionship if you want to go out tonight.

2. FRIDAY. Fair. Unexpected visitors are full of imaginative ideas. Listen with an open mind but make no commitments. This is a prime day to work on a hobby that you hope to transform into a source of income. Read about the latest techniques and marketing strategies. The more you know before you begin, the greater your chance of success. Taking a course could be beneficial. You need to fortify your own self-confidence. You know you have the ability; now it is up to you to put it to the best possible use. Partnership is not advised at this point. Love life needs a shot in the arm to give it new life. A different setting arouses excitement; but glamour can be deceptive, so the impressionable Pisces should be warned.

3. SATURDAY. Good.   This should be an eventful day from a social view. People you do not often see away from work make excellent company. Keep on the move throughout the day. You can drop in on one gathering, stay awhile, then proceed to the next. Relax and have a good time. Put the desires of other people ahead of your own and everyone will admire you all the more. You can break with tradition without causing a breakup. Take along a camera if someone at a distance would like photographs of the day's events. Include children in your plans if they have been invited; otherwise it is wiser to leave them home. Be generous in giving a charitable donation.

4. SUNDAY. Mixed.   Early hours tend to be more hectic and potentially aggravating than later in the day. Stay in control when tempers begin to fray. People are looking to you for leadership; do not let them down. Volunteer for a job before being assigned one that will not appeal. Children tend to be rebellious now. Find a way to keep them occupied and out of your hair. Emotions are running higher than usual. What might be a joke to you is likely to be taken seriously by the person at whom you are poking fun. It might be a good idea to invite a neighbor over for a cup of coffee and find out what is going on in your locale. A rumor is escalating far beyond the truth; find out the facts.

5. MONDAY. Uncertain.   Assignments may not be clear, leaving you to wonder if you are doing what you should. The boss or another higher-up may not be available for consultation. Act on your best instincts until told otherwise. Jealousy may be rearing its ugly head. Someone you have been working with for a while may be getting more credit than you for a joint project. Or the opposite could be true. Be generous in recognizing and appreciating the help you receive. One bad turn does not deserve another. Loneliness is foreseen as the result of short-term separation. Call a friend and make plans for later in the week. Words by phone or letter will have to do for the hugs you crave.

6. TUESDAY. Stressful.   Steer clear of involvement between warring factions at home or on the job. Take the high road; refuse to be drawn into the battle. It is important to remain neutral even if pressed to take one side or the other. Be wary of action based on bribery of any nature. Promises made today are not at all reliable. Instructions are apt to be contradictory. It is not apparent who is in charge now. If something has to be acted upon quickly, do it your way and with a dash of Pisces style. Teaming up with an Aquarius can be fortunate if you are able to work out a mutually acceptable agreement. Play it safe by avoiding controversial topics such as politics or religion that would drive a wedge in an alliance.

7. WEDNESDAY. Variable. Others are carrying the full weight today. You lack energy and stamina, although ideas are still flowing freely. Any new start is likely to peter out before you get very far. Concentrate on finishing up outstanding work rather than beginning anything from scratch. It is vital to maintain an optimistic outlook in talking with important people. Mood swings are likely to worry them and could cause loss of a potential promotion. Avoid making work for yourself. Utilize time-saving machinery although final results may not be quite as good as what can be achieved in the old-fashioned manner. Plan on eating at a good restaurant tonight.

8. THURSDAY. Satisfactory. Secrecy can help you spring a surprise that benefits everyone involved. An off-the-record meeting promises success in arranging a loan or other financial backing. Someone who is independently wealthy may be willing to put up the cash you need or co-sign a note for you. There is good reason to be proud of a family member. Do not miss an opportunity to give well-deserved congratulations. Any health problem is likely to improve if you follow doctor's orders to the letter. Home remedies should only be tried for a short time; if they prove ineffective, get professional advice for a quick cure. Do not settle for second best in any area.

9. FRIDAY. Exciting. Travel is not only enjoyable but should be educational as well. Get away from your usual base of operations to find out firsthand what is going on at a distance. Reading and studying is second best but also valuable. Pisces dealing directly with the public should be unusually successful today. You have the insight to comprehend what is wanted without having to be told. Your efficiency and knowledge are bound to impress clients. A pleasing agreement can be reached with someone you do not know well. Give a little, get a little is the motto to live by today. Be true to your principles even though others may waver in upholding their own. The Moon now in your sign gives you courage.

10. SATURDAY. Quiet. Background investigation can help you understand what is going on. The dynamics of home life are undergoing some changes. A youngster is growing up and taking on more responsibility; you cannot stop the process even though you would prefer to remain in control. Set limits as the result of mutual agreement. A family member has worthwhile ideas to share if you ask for advice. If going out, plan a route beforehand so that you save time and energy. Creative work will be fun and can also be prized gifts for the holiday ahead. An evening get-together should be as informal as possible. You will not want to get dressed up to go out.

11. SUNDAY. Challenging. You could be put in a position you have never been in before. Be guided by your natural Pisces inclinations; they will not steer you wrong. A newcomer in the family circle is likely to be as cautious as you. Help them overcome nervousness and you will be helping yourself as well. High ideals can be translated into positive action. Consider ways to help people less fortunate than you through a donation of money, clothing or food. Do not pass by a charitable collection point without stopping to contribute. Work harder at pleasing your mate or steady date. It is all too easy to take a special person for granted.

12. MONDAY. Outstanding. What starts as a casual partnership based on mutual needs promises special rewards over a period of time. Today it is up to Pisces to maintain a cordial atmosphere despite the strain of a deadline. Make work as enjoyable as possible. Focus on positive aspects while trying to improve anything that you view as negative. A trip could be worthwhile providing you are not away from home base overnight. People at and from a distance are inclined to listen to your ideas if you present them succinctly. A long-winded presentation, however, can be a turn-off. Do not hesitate applying for a new position or a job transfer that will stretch you intellectually.

13. TUESDAY. Demanding. There is no reason to go out on a limb for anyone or anything. Stick to a conservative course of action that will not attract unwanted attention. The low-key approach is favored. If the boss gives specific instructions, you have no recourse but to follow them. Results are then not your fault if they are not satisfactory. You can make suggestions but not enforce changes that you believe are worthwhile. Working conditions may be in an uproar. A deadline puts everyone on alert and makes tempers flare. Be sure to take a break at least at lunchtime; get away from co-workers to a totally different environment. Heed warning signs that you may be catching cold; extra rest should improve your health.

14. WEDNESDAY. Tricky. Talk over a problem with someone you trust. When you explain it out loud, you may come up with a solution all on your own. If not, their fresh viewpoint can be reassuring that you are at least on the right track. You cannot take over for another person and expect to also keep up with your own responsibilities. Something has to give and it must not be you. Put aside nonessential activity until a more relaxed period. Working as part of a team is tricky. Your natural inclination is to act as though you were in charge. But you have only partial responsibility and should keep it that way. Your mate has a pleasant surprise in store but hopes you will not guess what it is.

15. THURSDAY. Important. News received early in the day gives you renewed optimism. Act at once on it; do not let anyone get the drop on you and beat you to the punch. Pare down your schedule to essentials primarily. An influential person is poised to lend a hand when you are ready to move ahead. When you know what you want, go after it with all your heart. In romance as well as business, you have the edge today. If you can resist the temptation to sit back and enjoy your good fortune, you can make significant progress. Before you get an answer you have to pose the question. The response is sure to please you and may exceed your expectations.

16. FRIDAY. Misleading. Instead of dwelling on what seems to be going wrong, come up with a new plan of action. Learn from mistakes and vow to do better in the future. You could come in for some undeserved criticism. Facts are misleading. They may have already put you on the wrong track for a while, or they could be causing negative reactions that are not justified. Someone may be attempting to make you a scapegoat for a project that is not measuring up to expectations. Accept only that portion of the blame that belongs to you. A misunderstanding with your mate or partner has to be talked out in a logical manner. Do not let emotion steer conversation.

17. SATURDAY. Easygoing. Enjoy a pleasant day in the company of friends and family members. Personal relationships are excellent. There is no need for elaborate plans. An open schedule allows you to take advantage of whatever invitation or other offer comes along. A new relationship is budding. Someone you did not even know at the start of the year is now an active part of your life outside your home; soon you may be even closer. Let other people wait on you for a change. Sit back and enjoy all the attention you are getting. An element of luck accompanies a mutual decision. A guess will prove right on target; rely on your intuition. Short trips to see nearby relatives or old family friends are indicated.

18. SUNDAY. Uncertain. Money is in short supply today. Even a relative who is usually willing to make a short-term loan may not be able to do so. If you must make some purchases, shop around for the best buys. Trim your shopping list to essentials only. You may be able to make do with supplies already on hand or barter with a friend or neighbor. Tension is likely in family relationships. Stress is building as the holiday weekend approaches. Come up with projects around the house to keep children from being underfoot. Decorating with natural items picked outdoors can be fun. You may also want to prepare some food treats for the birds.

19. MONDAY. Rewarding. Let emotions guide your actions in positive ways. Guard against being coolly intellectual when a situation tugs at your heartstrings. Give something to a needy cause even though you do not have a cash surplus. Before accepting an invitation, know what is expected of you as a guest. It may be that you cannot afford the lap of luxury because you do not have the proper attire or cannot arrive in the style that would be expected. You could be caught short of money if asked to pay your own way to lunch or dinner. Know beforehand who is being treated and who is expected to pay. Someone you have not seen in a while is coming to town; make time for a get-together with mutual friends.

20. TUESDAY. Excellent. This is a time for sharing and not holding back. Be generous in all that you do. Think of other people before yourself. If you must conceal something, come up with a reasonable story so that on one's feelings are hurt. You can make the best of a troubling situation by using your excellent sense of humor and good manners. Special favors are likely to be granted, particularly if you need time off. Do not hesitate to ask for what you want. Give priority to artistic and creative work that you hope to finish before the holiday. Try new combinations. Utilize materials already on hand so that you are not delayed by having to shop for special items.

21. WEDNESDAY. Pleasant. You are adjusting quickly to a new situation. Continue to look on the bright side. Push aside thoughts of potential problems. There is no use making trouble where none exists. Personal relationships are smooth and easygoing. This is a starred day for treating yourself and your mate or date to front-row seats to a musical or theatrical performance. Put aside the hectic pace of the past week so that you can relax in an enjoyable atmosphere. Love is high on your list of priorities. A phone call early in the day sets the agenda for the remainder of the week. Finalize plans now while there is still some opportunity to rearrange your schedule.

22. THURSDAY. Buoyant. You do not even need luck today, although it is at hand if a surprise situation arises. You are well loved and appreciated. It is difficult now for Pisces to make a wrong move. Relationships remain extremely good. You should have no trouble getting your way at home or on the job. People who wield power and influence are inclined to grant a favor, probably without having to be asked twice. A friend may reveal a secret that makes you grin from ear to ear. If you have been awaiting news of a pay raise or bonus, be ready to celebrate tonight. Take a co-worker into your confidence. Surprising benefits emerge from a new working partnership.

23. FRIDAY. Hectic. Strive to complete a project before taking a break. You may have to lower your expectations slightly, but getting the job done is more important than being perfect. Your high standards are not the expected norm. Avoid making any commitment that would involve work in the New Year. You have not heard all of the offers that are going to be made this month; wait until you have a complete list before making a decision. A family member's travel plans may be upset by weather or other conditions beyond anyone's control. You could be left waiting at a terminal or stranded between connections if you are doing the traveling. Allow ample time, and stock up on extra patience.

24. SATURDAY. Exciting. Find a way to channel the excitement that you are feeling and that family members exhibit. Work together on a special dessert or other recipe. You may want to make muffins or cupcakes and bring them around to friends as a holiday offering. Do not get too nosy when it comes to wrapped boxes that may be visible; patience pays in big surprises later. This is the most starred day of the year for the Pisces in love to ask that all-important question. If you are slow in coming to the point, the tables could be reversed and you will be giving an answer. Happiness is contagious. Share feelings with friends and strangers alike.

25. SUNDAY. MERRY CHRISTMAS! Be sure that other people have a merry day and you are guaranteed one as well. Pay special attention to an older family member who would like to reminisce. Even if you have heard the stories before, listen and enjoy as though they were brand-new. Some frustration is foreseen if you have to put together a toy requiring assembly. Gather necessary tools before you start, and be sure to read directions through at least once. You do not have to keep up any false appearances today. Relax and have a good time along with your guests. If you are not at home, take a turn in the kitchen with food preparation or cleanup. A present you receive should give you especially happy dreams.

26. MONDAY. Quiet. Take it slow and easy throughout the day. Escape for at least a short time to a quiet place where no demands are made on you. If you decide to return a gift because it does not fit or suit you, do not let the giver know. You could easily hurt a family member's feelings by not being as appreciative of their selection as they had hoped. Romance is under starred auspices. Being alone with that special person in your life can help you reach a new depth of understanding. Your happiness is contagious. A surprise announcement can be offset by equally pleasant news from a friend or relative. A ceremony is foreseen in the New Year with you in a starring role.

27. TUESDAY. Fair. It will not be easy to slide back into normal workaday routine. Get an early start so that you are not rushed. Try to allow enough time so that you can have an extra cup of coffee along with the morning newspaper. A new project is awaiting attention. Although you might prefer to start it next week, the boss has another schedule in mind. Pisces have to take more orders than they give today. Be agreeable when you have no other alternative. If you fight a direct order you could land in trouble. Utilize your skills as a mediator to settle a dispute among co-workers. You can get a bargain at a clearance sale. If you experience mood swings, some meditation will calm you down.

28. WEDNESDAY. Manageable. Do only what is necessary. Vitality is at a low ebb. Your mental powers are not as good as usual. An error that would usually attract your immediate attention may go undetected. Double-check not only the work that other people turn over to you but also your own efforts. Making up your mind about ordinary matters is going to be difficult. Choices are likely to be so close in nature that you cannot distinguish between them. Flip a coin if there is no other way to choose. Pisces may suddenly see the way clear in romantic matters. What has been holding you back now seems unimportant. Do and say what comes naturally.

29. THURSDAY. Pleasant. Work is grinding to a halt after the last few days of effort. New starts are not favored. You lack stamina and vitality to see them through to completion. Working as part of a team could help a little, but partners are inclined to slow each other down rather than speed the work. Plans for the day should be shelved if extra effort is required. People on whom you normally rely may be unavailable. Try to find subtle ways to get a message across; the direct approach is likely to be rebuffed. Avoid spending more than is in your wallet at the start of the day. Free entertainment is as enjoyable as the most costly ticket in town. If you are traveling, be alert for mishaps.

30. FRIDAY. Demanding. Work out financial figures for the coming year. Know what you hope to accomplish in broad outline. Details can be worked out later. A contract under negotiation demands careful attention to the fine print. Hold out for what you want even if doing so forces postponement of the starting date. Some physical exercise during daylight hours should help you relax and unwind. Consider joining a health club for the benefits of membership other than working out. Someone you meet in a social setting could become an important part of your life in the year ahead. Go along with plans concocted by a family member. To refuse could incur their anger.

31. SATURDAY. Exciting. You do not have to wait until dark to begin partying. Get together with friends whose company you enjoy for good conversation. Keep talk happy-go-lucky; avoid subjects that you know arouse strong feelings. It is also a fine time to get in touch personally or by phone with family members living at a distance. An overseas call could be the best present of the year. If you are making any resolutions, keep them within the realm of possibility. Setting impossible standards for yourself or for other people can lead to ignoring them right from the start. A dream is close to coming true. Act on a hunch and you will not go wrong. Pisces have cause for optimism on this New Year's Eve.

November–December 1993

NOVEMBER

1. MONDAY. Changeable. Pisces should have a good grasp of language, whether written or spoken. It is a good day for attending to correspondence but do not allow letters to pile up in the in-tray. It is good too for convincing people of the validity and viability of your ideas and projects. Unexpected complications can make journeys far more expensive than anticipated. A steady and measured approach to business affairs is advised. Sudden changes of direction or impulsive moves can be read as irresponsible by people who matter. It is best not to mix money matters and friendship. Something extremely beneficial could develop for you, but not necessarily along the lines you have been anticipating.

2. TUESDAY. Productive. Take a little time to clear the decks and tie up loose ends. With an extra push it should be possible for Pisces people to complete jobs or projects that have overrun the time they are allotted. It would certainly be a mistake to start out on fresh moves or initiatives with unfinished business still to occupy you. Keep your nose to the grindstone in routine occupational affairs. Employers will be delighted if you are able to finish assignments ahead of schedule. Bear in mind that financial bonuses can be won under such circumstances. A delicate matter can be resolved simply by listening. The individual who is the cause of the problem could provide you the solution.

3. WEDNESDAY. Encouraging. You might try drawing up plans for home improvement projects and submitting them to local authorities. Not only is construction permission likely to be granted, but government grants or subsidies may be offered to offset the costs. People you have known since childhood may now be in a position to do you a special favor on account of the authority they now wield. Do not hesitate to ask such people for a helping hand if you are in a tight corner or in need of special advice. People living under the same roof as you can finally gain recognition and even fame in their particular line of work. Goings-on behind the scenes tend to favor you, especially where your finances are concerned.

4. THURSDAY. Easygoing. Pisces should be able to take the day at a free-and-easy pace. There should be fewer pressures and demands placed upon you at work. You can afford to stick your neck out. A calculated risk can pay off handsomely. You will probably find the time to attend to personal needs or run errands. Today is also good for pursuing special interests, hobbies or recreational activities. Employers are likely to be thoroughly cheerful and sympathetic. Now is the time to arrange for extra time off from work for extended holiday breaks or a midwinter vacation. Continue to look for new channels that could provide you with a second source of income. A favorite hobby could become profitable financially and also enhance your social prestige.

5. FRIDAY. Cautious.   The more impulsive side of your nature could lead you into difficulties if you are not careful. It is vital that you look before you leap. Try to stand back and view all sides of new moves or decisions before making them. Your outlays in the next few weeks are likely to be high, so do not throw your money away now on unnecessary purchases. Neither should you be tying up your cash reserves in long-term financial agreements. On this score also, you probably need to get your spending priorities clearly sorted out. Do not underestimate the costs involved in eating out or visiting places of entertainment. You might have to make an important decision today that will have far-reaching effects involving others as well as yourself. Pisces can be easily swayed, but it is vital now that you stick to your convictions.

6. SATURDAY. Enjoyable.   The weekend gets off to an easy-going and relaxed beginning. Pisces will probably be feeling very much at peace with themselves and the world. A break from routine can prove most refreshing. Some new faces and places will renew your zest for life. You will probably be at your happiest in the midst of friends and family members. Congenial companions can help to offset any gloomy feelings that could otherwise gather on this relatively uneventful day. Youngsters should be in a cheerful and perceptive mood. Allow some quiet time together with them. What you receive from them will be more valuable than anything you give.

7. SUNDAY. Constructive.   Pisces are apt to be in an energetic and industrious mood and will probably want to apply themselves to some useful and constructive work. Overtime rates will more than compensate for any loss of free time. Moreover, the extra money can be put aside now for special Christmas presents next month. The quiet conditions surrounding occupational affairs will allow you to give complete concentration to the work at hand. Some information you receive from one party is of great value to a second party. If you bring these two divergent factions together today, everyone could profit, including yourself. An individual you found success with in the past may want to team up again.

8. MONDAY. Starred. There are likely to be some interesting and exciting developments in your love life. An attractive and compatible partner may be met under unlikely circumstances. There can be a lighter aspect to the more arduous side of occupational affairs. Restrictive habits and patterns can fall away from Pisces people now, giving them a new sense of freedom. The adventurous side of your nature will probably welcome the possibility of travel. You are likely to get a hint of the interest and excitement that is in store for you before you set out. There are indications that you may start to cultivate an extremely important business relationship. Keep all doors open and remain flexible.

9. TUESDAY. Manageable. Friends occupy your thoughts and are likely to encroach on time that should be devoted to work. Postpone personal calls until after quitting time. An office romance may be starting to attract notice from the boss. Strive to keep your love life totally separate from job-related activity. There is a good opportunity to earn extra money if you are willing to work overtime. Eagerly accept the chance to travel out of town on company business. You will be most effective dealing with people at a distance. A face-to-face meeting is likely to be more productive than conferring by phone or letter. A pending legal matter may drag on longer than anticipated. Be prepared. What has until now been a hobby could be turned into a lucrative sideline.

10. WEDNESDAY. Sensitive. Do not hesitate to lend a helping hand to someone who has suffered a setback. Favor the underdog in most situations. Translate your humanitarian ideals into practical action both on the job and in your personal life. Pisces interested in switching career fields should look into service-oriented work. You are especially effective dealing directly with the public instead of shuffling papers all day long. A persistent pain or ache that has not responded to over-the-counter remedies probably requires a doctor's expertise. Make an appointment today so that you are not forced to worry needlessly any longer.

11. THURSDAY. Uplifting. Romance makes Pisces step lively throughout the day. You must stay on your toes to keep pace with your mate or steady date. A significant age difference can be a great asset in love. Avoid putting in writing anything you do not want a family member to read. Pisces who keep a diary should keep it well hidden from prying eyes. A relative may offer advice supposedly for your own good, but you would prefer not to hear what they have to say. You may be caught in a tug-of-war between your urge for independence and the necessity to rely in some regards on family members. Do not give in to emotional blackmail. You can make it on your own if forced to do so. Give a little and you will get a lot.

12. FRIDAY. Taxing. There is no escaping the pressures of work. The boss is likely to be breathing down your neck. A report or other project that was not due until later in the month may be needed at once. Although you wish for improved conditions, changes cannot be made right now. Plug away diligently. Working with new equipment can be especially frustrating. Keep a how-to manual close at hand and you should soon catch on. Do not let the unknown paralyze you with fear. Dredge up an extra amount of self-confidence to help you overcome hurdles. Assign priorities so that you can figure out what must be done first and what can be put off. Be sure to take some time for exercise to clear your mind.

13. SATURDAY. Changeable. Trying too hard can produce the opposite results. Go with the flow today. Let other people set the tone and pace. Be a follower rather than a leader, both at home and with your friends. Straightening up your home can help reduce tension. Clear the surfaces at least. It may be hard to put names together with faces. Memory can be evasive just when you are ready to make an introduction. If you know you are going to be meeting new people, concentrate on remembering not only who they are but their line of work, also. A person you do not know now is going to influence your life in the very near future. Making a good impression can be of great benefit to you later.

14. SUNDAY. Useful. Keep things moving along at home by making a list and working steadily. It would be all too easy to fritter away the day thinking about what should be done. Enlist the help of family members. A little bribery can help get things rolling. A few well-chosen words encourage younger relatives to try even harder. If schoolwork is a problem, consider hiring a tutor. Do not drop by a friend's house and expect to be welcomed with open arms. Phone ahead to be sure it would be convenient to visit. An older relative would welcome a call from you. It is also a fine day to visit a resident in a nursing home or a patient in a hospital.

15. MONDAY. Unpredictable. Money can all too easily come between you and your mate or partner. It is likely that you enjoy spending while they are intent on building up savings. Compromise is important. A new budget could help alleviate any guilt you feel when you want to buy. Rather than charging a major purchase, open a bank account specifically for that purpose. Try to pay off any outstanding loans. Stay away from people who are holding a grudge. You could land in hot water if forced to take sides. Also be guarded about talking about a person behind his or her back. What you say supposedly in confidence could leak out, putting you in the embarrassing position of having to explain your intentions.

16. TUESDAY. Constructive. Lighten your load by getting rid of excess possessions. Plan on renting or borrowing equipment that you need for a single project rather than buying it. Money earmarked for a special purpose ought to be kept in an insured account. If you risk it in stocks or at the track you could lose a bundle. It is important for Pisces to be more introspective than usual. Figure out your strengths as well as weaknesses. Capitalize on what you can do best. Your reputation is on the upswing. Someone who hesitated joining forces with you is now ready to sign on as an equal partner. Your ideas are great but beware of with whom you share them. Be sure you can trust their confidence.

17. WEDNESDAY. Uncertain. Concentrate on ways to ensure the future security of your family members. Get in touch with an insurance agent who can explain options to you. Be sure you are covered where it counts. A new appraisal of property value can be an eye-opener. A deal involving a large amount of money is at risk because of fluctuating interest rates. Sign on the dotted line when you get a chance, otherwise opportunity could pass you by. If you must take a trip, use public transportation rather than driving. Pisces tend to be preoccupied today, which can make you careless behind the wheel. Stay in the background until it becomes clear which faction is gaining prominence. At the moment you have too many choices and no clear-cut direction to pursue.

18. THURSDAY. Promising. Disappointment first thing in the morning can be offset by your own diligent efforts. Do not take no for an answer. If you look hard enough you can find supporters as well as financial backers. Advancement depends on your willingness to make changes and accept compromises. Keep an ace in the hole while negotiating. An element of surprise can give you the upper hand. Single Pisces need to be more careful in their choice of companions. You may be deluding yourself into thinking that physical attraction is the equivalent of true love. Check out a potential partner before making any sort of commitment. A relationship that has been floundering can be put back on track.

19. FRIDAY. Successful. Someone for whom you did a favor earlier in the year is likely to come through for you today. It is important to be precise in wording a letter or report. Ambiguous statements can land you in hot water. Higher-ups are aware of your effort. A future promotion or pay raise hinges on the success of your current work. Someone you are dealing with may be holding out on you. Be ready to make some changes. Creative efforts are apt to be most rewarding. Your Pisces artistry helps you put the personal touch on all that you do. Break with tradition and try something new and somewhat daring. Evening is the time to put aside work concerns so that you can relax and enjoy yourself.

20. SATURDAY. Enjoyable. Do not burden yourself with too much work today. You will be at your best surrounded by good friends and family members. Someone with whom you argued during the past week is making a peace offering. Do not reject their apology. Children highlight your leisure pursuits. Family-oriented activity promises to be more enjoyable than anything else you might do today. The great outdoors beckons. Physical activity promises to be invigorating. A physical problem that has been a restraint should be clearing up now. Be sure to wear comfortable clothes and shoes even if your gear is not the height of fashion. When you feel good, your personality shines and people cannot help but be drawn to you.

21. SUNDAY. Outstanding. Family caring and affection make this a perfect day to spend at home. You will especially enjoy being around younger relatives and taking part in some activities with them. Their outlook can be so crystal clear that it banishes a problem you have been tossing around in your mind. Your energy level is high. You may even want to try rollerskating or skateboarding to prove that your balance is as good as those half your age. A group get-together is also favored, particularly for a charitable purpose. Go out of your way to share your good fortune with someone enduring a difficult period. Evening entertainment can center around a board game or cards instead of television.

22. MONDAY. Lackluster. Pisces must be alert throughout the day. Options have to be decided upon short notice. You will not have the luxury of discussing them with numerous people. Physical activity is also demanded, both at home and on the job. Someone who usually handles the more demanding tasks may be absent, forcing you to take on their chores as well as your own. If cleanup or repair jobs are falling behind, you may want to hire a professional. Do not read too much into what is actually an innocent request. Give others the benefit of the doubt, at least the first time. You have a way of bringing out the best in people. Even if you are disappointed, you are not apt to become cynical or jaded.

23. TUESDAY. Satisfactory. Moderation is the key to success in all matters. Avoid overdoing in a rush to reach your ultimate destination. Results are going to be much more satisfactory if you take your time and double-check all details. Traveling demands close attention to schedules, and in particular to schedule changes. If driving, stay within the speed limits even if others on the road are exceeding them. Jealousy can interrupt a relationship that was just beginning to grow from the acquaintance stage to friendship. Try hard not to allow a third person to come between you. Concentrate on everyday courtesies such as saying thank you and please. Giving curt orders, even when you feel pressured, will not help you achieve what you want. Why not ask for assistance?

24. WEDNESDAY. Manageable. Avoid going out on a limb for anyone or anything. Stick to tried-and-true methods that have served you well in the past. A superior will not be pleased if you make arrangements outside normal working parameters. You could be denied a promotion or pay raise in the future if you seem to be a loose cannon. Give some extra attention to health matters. A recurring problem should be diagnosed and treated by a doctor. Be sure to eat regular nourishing meals on a prescribed timetable. If you snack throughout the day you are likely to wind up with an upset stomach. Vitamins can also ensure that you are getting the important nutrients you need. Exercise some self-discipline.

25. THURSDAY. Excellent. Pisces will have much to be grateful for on this Thanksgiving Day. A relative you may have been estranged from for a long time could show up unexpectedly at your front door. Catch up and reminisce without dwelling on past troubles. If dining out this holiday, choose a restaurant offering good service and fine food. You are in a mood to be indulged and pampered. Show loved ones how much you appreciate all that they do for you behind the scenes. Acknowledge the encouragement you have been given by them. Do a favor for someone you care about deeply without expecting anything specific in return. Remember, what goes around, comes around. When you next need help with something important, you can count on this person coming through for you.

26. FRIDAY. Starred. Suggestions made to you will arouse your curiosity. A trip may be the natural extension of your new-found interests. Unabashedly ask questions without worrying about displaying a degree of ignorance. The more you inquire, the more information you will receive. What you learn firsthand is more reliable than anything in a book. There is also a strong possibility of new romance for Pisces yearning for love. A person you have known quite a while may suddenly be seen in a new light. Friendship can escalate into intense bonding. Beating a deadline can give you a sense of relief. You now have time to lay the foundation of future projects.

27. SATURDAY. Frustrating. Concentrate on work around the house, especially those little repair jobs. If you do not take care of them now, you might have to pay a professional for major work down the road. Pisces parents may need to lay down the law to their offspring. Chores at home should be shared, even if unwillingly. Follow through when you make a request. Make sure things are completed thoroughly. An invitation from a friend may have to be refused because of the cost involved. You cannot afford to go into more debt now. A worthwhile cause would welcome a donation of your time instead of money. Be guarded about what you say in front of younger family members. They are likely to get the wrong message.

28. SUNDAY. Stressful. There is not going to be much that goes according to plan today. An offer of help may be withdrawn at the last minute, leaving you to struggle alone. Necessary materials may be in short supply, with no chance of restocking until the new workweek. Someone who is usually quite agreeable may exhibit aggressive behavior that makes you question your own judgment. A close friend may want to talk, though what you say will not make much of an impression. What seems to you an obvious solution to their problem may not be acceptable. You could find that you require the services of an accountant or book-keeper. Sloppy record keeping over the year could be coming back to haunt you.

29. MONDAY. Cautious. Someone you have never met before may be trying to make life difficult for you. The reasons for this are so unclear that there is no chance of resolving the matter until you talk face-to-face. A mutual acquaintance or work colleague may be able to arrange a meeting on neutral territory. Guard against putting in writing any promises you might not be able to honor. Steer clear of speculative deals, especially if you would be expected to put up the lion's share of the money. There are too many uncertainties when it comes to business finance. Manipulations are going on behind the scenes that you know nothing about. Manage your funds conservatively to maintain your security.

30. TUESDAY. Mixed. Concentrate on projects that are close to being finished rather than starting anything new. Results should be good if you can avoid distractions. Take the phone off the hook for a while, or turn on the answering machine so that you are not disturbed by phone calls. Pisces can find themselves in a ticklish situation largely due to the interference of other people. Someone who had appeared to be on your side may be having second thoughts. It is up to you to turn on your persuasive charm. A person who shares your home or office is apt to be getting on your nerves. Minor mannerisms can quickly become very irritating. Since you cannot change them, it is up to you to be more tolerant.

DECEMBER

1. WEDNESDAY. Outstanding. Firm friendships can develop from rather casual beginnings. You can find you have more in common with someone than you suspected at first. Pisces business people can maneuver themselves into strong positions in negotiations and other transactions. Deals can be concluded on a highly favorable note for all. It should be worth your while to devote more care and thought than usual to publicity matters. Advertising can be crucial to the continuing or recently established success of your operations. Today is a good day for friendship activities and socializing. Pisces can be the life of the party. Do not stop to question your soaring popularity. Just relax and enjoy it.

2. THURSDAY. Promising. It should now be possible to put an end to frustrations caused by people who are hedging their bets. Pisces can corner these people and insist on getting definite answers from them. Prolonged discussions regarding money matters can finally be concluded on a satisfactory note. But arriving at such success will largely depend on your own firm handling of financial situations. People will tend to take a mile every time if they are given so much as an inch. You will probably get your best work done alone and in relatively quiet surroundings. Your efforts are likely to be rewarded in a manner entirely unexpected. The peaks and valleys of your self-confidence are in sync.

3. FRIDAY. Uneasy. You probably know exactly where you stand with new romantic partners, and are sure of your feelings for them. But there is still likely to be some pain and embarrassment in your love life. The trouble is that parents or other family members may take a dislike or disapprove of your choice of a sweetheart. So you are apt to be faced with an agonizing conflict of loyalties. Unexpected setbacks or problems can be encountered when redecorating or refurbishing homes. Minor changes can bring more serious structural problems to light. It will be easier to be dazzled by expensive and beautiful objects that you know you do not really need. An urge to be extravagant should be ignored for the time being.

4. SATURDAY. Excellent. Today will be favorable for a tour of the shops and stores. Secondhand goods can represent a high saving without any real loss of quality. It is also good for giving yourself a special treat. You can be somewhat indulgent, especially where clothes or shoes are concerned. Buying something special and different for the family to eat tonight will win you cheers. Sporting activities can provide a major focus of the day, no matter whether you are taking part or watching from the sidelines. There may be exciting new developments in your love life. Outings with a new date can come fully up to expectations. At this time of the year you should be feeling full of life and vigor.

5. SUNDAY. Constructive. Time and luck are on your side, so do not give in too easily when vital personal issues are under discussion. Pisces should now stick up for their rights. Do not let anybody push you around. Others are more likely to give way when they see how strongly you feel on key matters. Do not look for support from anyone else. It will be up to you to make a stand. You may be underusing your considerable skills and abilities. Look to see if you can find other means for putting more of your potential into practice. Your ideas and proposals are likely to be especially attractive to management. There is no need to be shy about the brainstorms that have occurred to you. Draw up a plan.

6. MONDAY. Uncertain. Haste in financial affairs can prove disastrous. Give yourself plenty of time to look at all the ins and outs where money is concerned. Other people will resent being pressured into quick decisions. Right now, just flow with the tide. Hidden problems can come to the surface during waiting periods. These can put a whole new complexion on important situations. Keep your nose to the grindstone at work. Superiors will not fail to notice your efforts and concentration. Rewards and acknowledgment can be received. But a degree of self-sacrifice may be required later on. Pleasure and entertainment plans can be displaced by other needs. With patience and determination you can reach your goals.

7. TUESDAY. Encouraging. Things should now take a distinct turn for the better. Pisces can suddenly feel that everything is back on course. People in key positions may have sensed that you were going through a difficult time, and have now probably made positive moves toward you. A new bond of friendship and support can be forged with influential people. The actions of publishers can delight authors and writers, with good news finally arriving. A most interesting and stimulating person can be added to your circle of friends. Profits may suddenly shoot up as a result of successful advertising campaigns. Let loved ones know the depth of your feelings for them. A small gift can speak volumes.

8. WEDNESDAY. Satisfactory. Pisces should now be given some respite from the usual hustle and bustle. There may be less to do both at home and at work. With more time on your hands, it may be possible to give others, and especially close friends, some active help and assistance. It is not a day for taking anything for granted, however. Do not wade in, regardless of other people's needs and feelings. Get the advice of people who have greater knowledge and experience than you. You will only manage to land yourself in deep water if you are headstrong and willful. Single Pisces may feel the pang of loneliness more acutely than ever now. This is to be expected at this time of year. Turn to your family for love and reassurance. They will receive you with open arms.

9. THURSDAY. Successful. Justice is very much on your side at present. Legal decisions are more likely to go in your favor. Other people involved will probably have to bear the costs of legal proceedings. Prospective employers can choose you for new positions from among a host of other applicants. Your self-confidence is boosted. Professionals and experts can supply the missing link or other vital information that solves long-standing problems. Access to influential people can be made easier for you through the contacts of close friends or family members. Collaborative enterprises can receive the financial boost they need at this stage.

10. FRIDAY. Unsettling. Pisces may suddenly have cause to doubt the sincerity of their romantic partner. Someone who has professed love for you may have become cold and distant. You may find that you are doing all the giving and getting little in return. Some difficult decisions may have to be made if you are fed up with being taken advantage of. Bankers and others holding the purse strings will want hard facts and well-reasoned arguments before they part with money. Mere charm and personality will not cut any ice with such people. Club and group events or activities can be spoiled by lack of order and organization. Perhaps your skills and talents could be best put to use in individual pursuits.

11. SATURDAY. Manageable. It is important to respect other people's privacy and feelings. Friends, in particular, can be especially sensitive if you pry into their affairs too deeply. Let others lead their lives in the ways they see fit. The best method to protect yourself where joint funds and savings are concerned is to keep financial partners informed of your moves and intentions. Any losses that occur without the knowledge of those who have a vested interest are certain to bring trouble and conflict. Minor disagreements can grow into major upheaval in romantic affairs. Perhaps you have temporarily forgotten that love is a matter of give-and-take. Do not be too hard-headed. You will be cutting off your nose to spite your face. Compromise is the key.

12. SUNDAY. Pleasant. Pisces will enjoy a shopping trip to a discount center or outlet mall. Bargains can be found, but you will probably have to sort through a lot of cheap imitations to find them. Less expensive, foreign-made goods may seem to be made well, but they can fall to pieces in no time. This is also a good time to visit holiday displays in public parks and at special festivals. Though your spouse's parents probably have the best intentions, they can be forgetful and unreliable. Be understanding, rather than making a scene. Close acquaintances can introduce you to interesting new people who, in turn, become firm friends of yours. Or you may meet a new romantic partner through a gathering organized by friends this evening. Expect the unexpected.

13. MONDAY. Slow. This will not be a very important period. You will be grateful that the pressure is taken off you to a certain extent. This will be a quiet and peaceful day. You will be able to take a breather before the Christmas season gets into full swing.

This would be a helpful day for tying up the loose ends of work and business. There are some especially vital matters that you do not want to have hanging over your head during the next week or so. Now is favorable for putting the finishing touches to pleasure plans that you will be involved in fairly soon. An unexpected call from an old school chum tonight will surely delight you.

14. TUESDAY. Misleading. Check up on the state of your bank account. You may find that you are not as well off as you had at first thought. People may be taking advantage of Pisces' kind-heartedness. You may want to help friends in distress, but the best way may not be with monetary handouts. You may not find the atmosphere at your place of employment to be the easiest in which to operate. Children may not be telling the truth. You will not want to be too harsh on youngsters at this time of the year. Nevertheless, it may be necessary to discipline them for their own good. There is a greater risk than ever of estrangements right now, so tread lightly.

15. WEDNESDAY. Sensitive. Turn to a trusted friend if you need advice of a personal nature. It would not be wise to discuss a home situation with work associates or the boss. Although on the job you must be unemotional and objective, when it comes to family matters you tend to lose a degree of control. Someone who is not intimately involved has better insight. Steer clear of people who have extremely rigid ideas. It is a waste of time to argue with them. Plans of a social nature need to be put into final form now. Buy supplies if you are going to be hosting the event. Be sure to have ample food and drink so that you do not run out. Make it easy on yourself by buying festive paper and plastic items instead of using your china and silver. Keep the affair informal.

16. THURSDAY. Constructive. Look into courses offered locally that can help you expand your skills and interests. Branch out in a new direction by learning something that will make use of your innate Pisces talents. Even if you do not have exceptional natural ability, you can acquire basic knowledge. Your social life can also improve if you join a group of people who share your interests. It is a good day to track down information that you need in order to make a major decision. Do not allow yourself to be brushed off by a secretary or personal assistant. Insist on speaking to the person in charge. A little flattery is sure to help.

17. FRIDAY. Fine. Catch up with letter writing and other tasks that are necessary but unappealing. Call the bank if you forgot to enter a check when you wrote it. There is danger of bouncing a check if you guess at the amount. Money may be the best gift you can give a family member who has very definite tastes. Even if you devote a lot of time to shopping for a present for them, it is apt to be unsuitable and have to be returned. Most Pisces people appreciate the thought more than any gift they receive. But if you have some specific items you would like to get, be sure to tell the Santa in your life. It may not be easy to console a friend whose expectations were way too high. Temper your response with humor.

18. SATURDAY. Enjoyable. You need some time alone to sort and wrap and get ready for the fast-approaching holiday. If there are youngsters in the house it might be a good idea to find a new hiding place for their presents. Cultivate a much lighter touch in dealing with boisterous children. Find outlets for their boundless energy instead of letting them get on your nerves. You will be more comfortable if you act naturally rather than putting on airs in a crowd. Although you may be less sophisticated than some of your friends, you come across as interested and enthused about life. This trait is especially appealing to the opposite sex. What has been a budding friendship may be turning into love.

19. SUNDAY. Starred. An event that unfolds today may be just as you had dreamed it. You have exceptional insight into what people are thinking and what they want. Do not put off saying what has been on your mind for some time. Let your heart have the upper hand. Go out of your way to get to know an older person who could ultimately cast a deciding vote. New doors are opening for you. In a group you will quickly become the center of attention. A last-minute invitation can bring you into contact with influential people. Avoid letting their power or position overwhelm you. If you treat everyone as a respected equal your popularity will soar. A phone call later this evening makes you smile from ear to ear. Pisces will be keeping a secret for a while.

20. MONDAY. Stressful. There is much to be done, but you may not feel up to it. Minor aches, pains or other complaints should respond to home remedies. If they persist, however, make an appointment with the doctor or dentist. Avoid setting too lofty goals for yourself. You need to see some immediate results. You will feel all the better for sharing your possessions with others. A favor done for you should be returned at the appropriate time. Bring a meal to a friend who is going through a difficult period. Just knowing you care will be a lift. It is not the best day to sign a contract or any legally binding document. You could miss the importance of fine print. Stay home tonight and try to retire early.

21. TUESDAY. Uncertain. Forces beyond your control may keep you from traveling or meeting people from a distance. There may be a strike or delay on the highway. Or your car may need some repairs. Changes forced on you at the last minute are sure to be frustrating. Seek an outlet to vent your feelings. A co-worker or friend understands you well enough to offer the sympathy you want. By the time you finish talking, you will probably be laughing at the situation. It is unwise to let curiosity get the better of you. In time you will be let in on a secret that is now only conjecture. Pisces must respect the privacy of family members as well as associates in the workplace. Do not say something to a lover or even a best friend you might regret later.

22. WEDNESDAY. Sensitive. If you lose your temper you could lose an ally. Stay in control. Arguing is apt to be a waste of time. Although there is general agreement, details need to be worked out. Be sensitive to the needs of others. However, realize that you cannot solve all the problems of the world. If you let them get you down, you will only be adding to the difficulties. Good news can come by letter. Affairs at a distance are moving in your favor. New government regulations can put more money in your pocket. Read the business section of your newspaper. People in authority may be offering words that sound sincere, but their actions are apt to contradict what they say. Remain open-minded.

23. THURSDAY. Rewarding. Share an idea with a friend or work colleague. Their reaction should delight you and give you new direction. Stay on your toes for opportunity. Step in when you know you are needed without waiting to be formally asked. A pay raise will accompany added responsibility, but it may not be immediate. Take some time to write a letter to an out-of-town friend who will be spending this holiday period alone. Your thoughtfulness can ease their loneliness and brighten their outlook. A major decision is yours to make now. People on whom you normally rely for advice may be unavailable when you need them. Delay could mean lost time if not money. It is up to you to take the initiative.

24. FRIDAY. Challenging. Although you have been generous during this Christmas season, today's request is worthy and warrants digging deep into your pockets for a donation. Do not ignore those who are less fortunate than you. Plans made earlier in the month may have to be altered at the last minute. A rendezvous could be delayed due to weather conditions or traffic problems. It is up to you to suggest alternative arrangements, which may include housing guests because hotels are overbooked. If you are going to be traveling, be sure to allow extra time to make connections. Take along as little luggage as possible. If you do not have to check baggage, you will get to your destination with much fewer hassles. You will delight in the spirit of Christmas Eve wherever you are.

25. SATURDAY. MERRY CHRISTMAS! Pisces people have a lot of hard work to do today to make it a success, but that is no reason not to enjoy yourself also. Be especially attentive to the needs of children. Have tools ready to put together the toys they receive that require assembly. Play games with them even though you might prefer to take a nap or read a book you received as a gift. Be sure to keep a camera close at hand to record memorable expressions of love. It would be best not to spring any surprises on your loved one. Express gratitude for all the gifts you receive, even if some are totally opposite to what you like. Anything that has been handcrafted should be admired and lavished with praise.

26. SUNDAY. Relaxing. The good feelings remain but the pressure is off. Enjoy a quiet day with the person you love best. Words may be unnecessary as you have a meeting and melding of the mind and spirit. Inveterate Pisces shoppers could enjoy a day at the mall, returning presents or looking for special bargain merchandise. You could even be thinking about picking up some reduced-price items for next year's gift giving. Particularly creative Pisces may want to begin a new project utilizing materials already at hand. Color and texture are especially important to you. Traditional patterns can be a stepping-stone to new arrangements. Some reminiscing tonight can put you in the mood for romance.

27. MONDAY. Uneasy. Getting back into the flow of work takes some time today. If you plunge in too quickly you are apt to make false starts or some serious errors. Proceed slowly and deliberately. What seemed settled at the end of last week may now have to be reviewed and changed. Conditions are in a state of constant flux. A person you were relying on may have an announcement to make that does not please you. But if their mind is made up, you must make other arrangements without counting on them. Closer liaison with business colleagues should be a goal for the coming year. Look for ways to improve communications, perhaps by starting a newsletter or scheduling regular weekly meetings.

28. TUESDAY. Buoyant. Social relationships are going well. Plan a party for this weekend. Invite a mix of people with varying backgrounds to keep the conversation flowing. You could be the guiding force behind a romance or other partnership. Utilize your knack for blending people of different backgrounds and interests. A private conversation with the boss lets you know what your job prospects are for the future. You will want to work harder to live up to expectations. You can count on a future pay raise. Linger over a long lunch, or enjoy a meal with friends tonight. Be open with your feelings and aspirations.

29. WEDNESDAY. Constructive. Changes can be made at home or at work. People are surprisingly agreeable. Start in a small way. Emphasize the benefits to be derived. There is good opportunity to begin something new, but eventual success depends on whether others encourage you along the way. It is all too easy to lose interest halfway through a project. Aims and dreams you have been working toward for some time are coming closer to fruition. Given a little extra attention and concentration, you can achieve a lifelong aspiration. Do not allow an emotional reaction to take away from your success.

30. THURSDAY. Manageable. Handle necessary jobs before doing what appeals to you personally. Be sure current bills have been paid. Balance your checkbook carefully. If there are any omissions, call the bank to find out if the check has cleared. You could overdraw your account if you do not write down every single check. Also keep receipts when shopping, and count your change if paying by cash. A friend would be hurt if you revealed what you recently heard. Keep quiet. The gossip mill is churning along, but there is no reason you should participate. Someone is taking slight advantage of you. Your instincts are excellent when it comes to helping people who cannot speak up and ask for help.

31. FRIDAY. Sparkling. Get out and mix with all sorts of people. You need their encouragement and enthusiasm to keep you going. Tackle a problem one step at a time. Overcoming the first hurdle makes all the rest seem easier. It is a fine day for any group activity, whether or not you are in charge. There is power in numbers. Contacts at a distance, perhaps overseas, are influencing you and providing new opportunity. Do not draw back from unconventional methods. Pisces should be paying extra attention to financial matters. An investment that has turned a small profit for you this year is likely to take off and become a real windfall in 1994. Celebrate these promising prospects this New Year's Eve.

NOTES

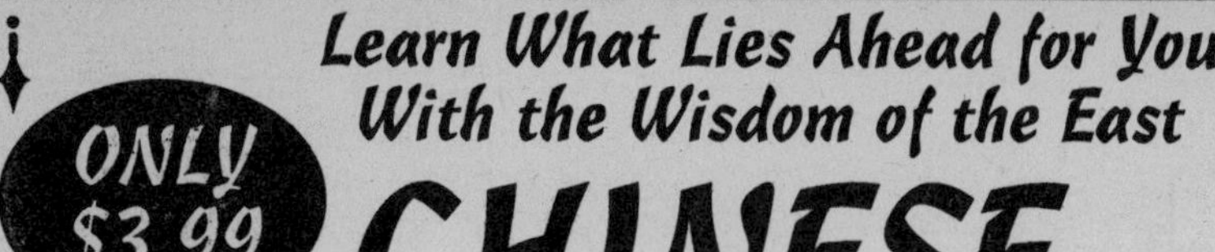

Are you a Tiger with power and passion, but who is rebellious and unpredictable? Are you a Cat who is independent and sensitive, but sometimes moody and detached? Or perhaps you were born under the sign of the Horse — cheerful, popular, often exuding raw sex appeal, but rash and headstrong at times?

The animal ruling the year in which you were born has a profound influence on your life. As the Chinese say, "This is the animal that hides in your heart."

Originating in 2637 B.C., Chinese astrology is the oldest method of forecasting the future and is completely different from Western Astrology. Whereas astrology in the Western world is based on the solar calendar, Chinese horoscopes are based on the lunar(moon) calendar, which is more accurate.

If you have never had a Chinese horoscope, you are in for the surprise of your life.

> **YOU WILL RECEIVE AN EXCITING FORECAST REVEALING HOW YOUR ANIMAL SIGN AFFECTS YOUR LOVE LIFE, RELATIONSHIPS, LUCK, FINANCES, CAREER AND YOUR FUTURE.**

Once you understand the animal "that hides in your heart," only then may you realize your full potential. And you should find it easier to understand the demanding nature of your Dog supervisor, the stubbornness of your Rooster friend, and the charm and manipulations of your Dragon lover.

Learn what lies ahead for you according to the wisdom of the East. Send $3.99 +$1.00 shipping for your Chinese horoscope to: CALIFORNIA ASTROLOGY ASSOC., DEPT. SH-1, P.O. BOX 8005, CANOGA PARK, CA 91309 (Please include your birth date, place of birth and time, if known.)

IS LOVE IN THE CARDS?
Authentic, Gifted Psychics Can Forecast Your Future! IT'S LIVE!
Speak LIVE with a compassionate counselor. You'll feel like you've gained a new friend.
Ask about love, marriage, career or money. The answers will change your life!
CALL NOW! 1-900-860-1115
$2.95 Per Minute
Sponsored by Telecom USA, P.O. Box 487, Wallingford, PA 19086

AMAZING PSYCHIC PREDICTIONS
Now you too can experience the Astonishing Accuracy of the world's most gifted psychics!
Discover YOUR Destiny! Ask About
LOVE • SUCCESS • MONEY
LIVE ANSWERS TO ALL YOUR QUESTIONS!
1-900-420-2696
CALL ANYTIME! OPEN 24 HOURS A DAY. $3.49 per minute. Callers must be 18.
© PHONE VISION, INC. P.O. Box 307, Mill Valley, CA 94942

Wash Away Your Worries

Flush bad luck out of your life! *Drink in good fortune, health, happiness, and limitless abundance!*

REVEALED IN NEW BOOK 'WATER MAGIC' WHICH SHOWS HOW TO USE THE SPIRITUAL POWER OF WATER IN YOUR OWN HOME OR PLACE OF WORK TO BRING WHAT YOU SEEK IN LIFE. No complicated rituals. No mumbo jumbo. All you need is a cup or jug – and water!

Water Magic can:

* **BRING BADLY NEEDED CASH – WITHIN HOURS!**
* **BRING RELIEF FROM PAIN – WITHIN MINUTES!**
* **BRING SOMEONE TO LOVE YOU!**
* **BRING PROTECTION OF HOME & POSSESSIONS!**
* **BRING REJUVENATION OF BODY!**
* **BRING WINS AT BINGO & RACE TRACK!**
* **BRING PROTECTION FROM EVIL!**
* **BRING BACK A DISENCHANTED LOVER!**
* **BRING LUCK OVER AND OVER AGAIN!**

All Martha had to do was sprinkle her purse with water when she recited the special words in this book.

That very day Martha returned home with *three times as much in her purse as* when she left!

Jenny, cursed by chronic pain in her hip *experienced immediate relief after she performed the jug and water rite in this book!*

Sue, broken-hearted by her fiance's calling off their engagement, turned to the magic power of water, and that *very same day* he called begging her forgiveness! She performed the water rite again, and a month later they were married!

But why should so seemingly a foolish and superstitious faith in the power of water make such an impact?

Simply because *water is imbued with a spiritual and magical power which no other substance possesses.*

In drought people will kill each other for water. We cannot live without it. Two thirds of the human body is made up of it and almost three quarters of the earth's surface is under water.

Both religion and science – which can hardly agree on anything else – concede that life originated in water.

In the religious rites of every faith water is used as a purifier and as an agent for blessing and protection.

In the most ancient times people the world over believed in a Mother Goddess who came forth from the waters and created everything out of water.

In our mother's womb we are immersed in her protective fluid.

Small wonder that subconsciously we hold water with such regard!

RESULTS WITHIN HOURS

Now both women and men can begin experiencing the *material benefits* of Water, Magic, thanks to this amazing new book!

You could find your most pressing problem washed away within hours.

Jim from Atlanta was miraculously helped by Water Magic. He was only one hour away from eviction from his home. With nothing left to lose he believed in the God-given power of water as he spoke the special words you will find in this book.

He was not turned out of his home.

Fortunately Mae from Tacoma didn't face anything so serious. She enjoyed life's creature comforts, a nice home, and financial security. But she had no-one to share it with.

She performed the water rite on Monday. On Saturday the person of her dreams entered her life.

WHY THESE WATER RITES MUST WORK FOR YOU

Because water is so potent as a spiritual and magical metaphor it becomes irresistible. Mind power adepts speak of an '*Ocean* of mind'; the invisible universe is conceived in terms of fluid movement. We speak of the *thirst* for knowledge or power as if somehow those things that cannot be felt physically must therefore be liquid, that is – water.

We instinctively know its not nonsence to say 'bathed in luxury' or 'flooded with work'. An abundance of water suggests *an abundance of everything else.* Earth – physical density – is barren without rain.

You can now *receive and enjoy all the things you desire* by using the power that brings them – physical and metaphoric water!

You only need a jug or cup – and water! – to make this magic happen!

NOTHING COULD BE MORE NATURAL – OR POWERFUL!

SHE CAME TO ME

'I sought the company of the most beautiful woman in our corporation. So incredible were her looks that she seemed like Venus incarnate to me. But I honestly felt I didn't stand a chance with her.

'She knew me, but it was obvious that I was about as important to her as a fly on the wall. I couldn't even begin to summon the courage to ask her out. But I was crazy about her and I felt miserable.

'Then I learnt about the power of water and how it can affect women.

'It seemed as if I was dreaming when the very day after using the water rite *she asked me* for a date!

'It was then I became a believer.

'That happened just a few months ago and the lady in question is now my steady date!'

This extract from a testimonial from a Montreal man is strong proof of the power of water in matters of the heart!

WATER WORKS WONDERS!

Nothing could be easier than the water rites in this book.

You don't need paraphanalia of any kind. No withcraft or mumbo jumbo.

Even a child can perform the rites in this book!

They can be performed almost anywhere without attracting the undesirable attention of others. And there is absolutely nothing in Water Magic that will compromise your religious beliefs.

You will be amazed at the results – results which can sometimes manifest within a few hours!

The uses of Water Magic are without end. Think of what you want, adapt the appropriate rite to your needs, and then wait for the result! Water Magic can bring you:

* WINS IN GAMES OF CHANCE, LOTTERIES, AND POOLS!
* THE LOVE AND ADMIRATION OF ANOTHER PERSON!
* RELIEF FROM HEALTH PROBLEMS! (Even cures have been reported!)
* A FLOOD OF ENDLESS RICHES INTO YOUR LIFE! (Perform Water Magic regularly to achieve this)
* STREAMS OF GOOD LUCK! (For making events *flow* to your advantage; let the tide of good fortune always be in your favour!)

Yes! Through the inexhaustable renewing power of *the very source of life itself* you can enjoy an ENDLESS FLOW OF GOOD FORTUNE!

Perform the water rites as often as you like to receive everything you desire!

Persons from all walks of life are benefitting from the life-enriching powers of Water Magic! Read how:

WATER RITES HELP ANIMAL! – Pat C. was distressed by her cat's suffering. She sprinkled water on the painful area and the cat was immediately relieved!

WATER RITE BRINGS LOTTERY WIN – Kay W. won $10,000 after she slightly moistened her entry coupon with blessed water!

COLD LOVER PROPOSES SEX! Always indifferent to her sexual needs, June A. tried the power of water. She was astonished at the result!

KEEPS UNWANTED RELATIVES AWAY! – Ted G.'s relatives forever sponged on his good will. He had had enough of them so he sprinkled water outside his doorway making his wish – they never returned!

WATER RITE PREVENTS COLLISION! – A careful driver, Sally B. was always worried about the recklessness of other drivers. She 'blessed' her car with mystically charged water. When her car was completely untouched by two cars colliding only inches away from hers' she was convinced it was thanks to Water Magic!

WATER RITE MADE WEDDING BELLS RING! – Ann W. couldn't get her boyfriend to agree a wedding date. She believed in the power of water, and the *very next day* he said he wanted marriage at the *earliest possible date!*

Now you can 'wash away your worries' and 'drink in' life's riches. With this book and nature's most precious commodity you cannot fail!

To order your copy simply quote 'Water Magic' with payment of **$14.95.**

FUTURE
Love
Success
Money
Use the Ancient Science of Astrology to guide you through a New Age
1-900-226-6758
Talk directly to Professional Astrologers
49¢ the first minute. $2.95 per each additional minute.
Average length of call 4 minutes $11.80
1-900-329-8726
Find out what's in the stars for you!
Only $1.50 per minute.
Average length of call 4 minutes. $6.00
Must be 18. Entertainment only.
ASTRAL RESEARCH
P.O. Box 804, Rockport, MA 01966
TO ORDER CATALOG, CHARTS OR SOFTWARE CALL
1-800-533-4676   508-546-9361   FAX 508-546-2151